Debt and Delusion

PETER WARBURTON

Debt and Delusion

CENTRAL BANK FOLLIES THAT THREATEN
ECONOMIC DISASTER

ALLEN LANE
THE PENGUIN PRESS

ALLEN LANE
THE PENGUIN PRESS

Published by the Penguin Group
Penguin Books Ltd, 27 Wrights Lane, London w8 5tz, England
Penguin Putnam Inc., 375 Hudson Street, New York, New York 10014, USA
Penguin Books Australia Ltd, Ringwood, Victoria, Australia
Penguin Books Canada Ltd, 10 Alcorn Avenue, Toronto, Ontario, Canada m4v 3b2
Penguin Books (NZ) Ltd, Private Bag 102902, NSMC, Auckland, New Zealand

Penguin Books Ltd, Registered Offices: Harmondsworth, Middlesex, England

First published by Allen Lane The Penguin Press 1999
3 5 7 9 10 8 6 4 2

Copyright © Peter Warburton, 1999

Set in 11/14 pt PostScript Monotype Sabon
Typeset by Rowland Phototypesetting Ltd, Bury St Edmunds, Suffolk
Printed in Great Britain by The Bath Press, Bath

A CIP catalogue record for this book is available from the British Library

ISBN 0-713-99272-7

To the memory of my parents,
Jim and Claire

Contents

List of Figures

Preface

One of the hazards of business and economic forecasting is that, occasionally, an amazingly accurate prediction will result. I shared in this happy experience in the spring 1988, and again in 1990, in the context of the UK economy. Golfers will recognize such an occurrence as a hole-in-one. There is a great temptation at these moments to believe that a breakthrough has occurred in one's understanding of the underlying process, be it the economy or the aerodynamics of a golf ball. Out of the forecasting successes of the early 1990s, I drove straight into the bunker of over-confidence and my forecasts were well wide of the pin for three consecutive years. However, failure often proves much more educational than success. Although the learning process was painfully slow, I began to reinterpret the workings of the US and UK economies in the light of changes in their financial structures. After some initial attempts to set these thoughts down in research bulletins for Robert Fleming Securities, it became clear that the ideas needed the structure and length of explanation that only a book could offer.

This book is a personal interpretation of the evolving relationship between financial markets and institutions and some imprecise notion of economic wellbeing. An extraordinary reversal of roles is taking shape, whereby the large developed economies of the west (not to mention the emerging market economies) are becoming the servants of global financial activity rather than its masters. An important by-product is the diminishing economic significance of the individual. The promise of economic freedom held out by the dismantling of state ownership and control has been subverted by a personal and collective enslavement to debt. The parallel accumulation of financial wealth since the early 1980s has obscured this painful reality, but history warns that this situation is unsustainable. When stripped of their capital gains in equities and bonds, today's rising generations will appear overburdened by interest payments and debt repayment schedules. Far from commencing a golden era of economic liberty and individual choice, millions are teetering on the edge of debt default and misery.

The danger in writing about contemporary events is to become over-influenced by the fads and fashions of current opinion. For those of us born after the Second World War and its privations, it is all too easy to take peace, prosperity and economic stability to be the normal state of human affairs. This book attempts to bring the twin perspectives of economic history and reason to bear upon the particular circumstances of the end of the twentieth century.

In preparing this indictment of the economic and financial achievements of the western world, many diverse lines of argument are presented and a wide range of specialist subject areas are addressed. Experts in these fields will appreciate that this book is a demonstration of the limits of the author's comprehension, rather than its extent. Nevertheless, to wait for a complete understanding of the complex processes at work in our financial and economic systems would be to abandon any hope of sounding a warning of the perils that lie ahead. Post mortems, while rigorous and clinically correct, are less satisfying than broadly accurate diagnoses of live patients.

This book holds central banks largely responsible for the deterioration in economic and financial management since the early 1980s. The criticisms of unaccountability, negligence and inconsistency are directed at the institutions rather than the individuals working in them. Central banks have presided over a drastic reorientation of the financial system with only a belated regard for global stability. These untamed intellectual powerhouses have not demonstrated their readiness to be trusted with such a large measure of economic power. The role of central banks in both developed and emerging countries is ripe for urgent reappraisal.

Apart from financial mismanagement, the only other essential ingredient of the west's predicament is the personal and collective addiction to debt. Indeed, the most significant aspect of financial mismanagement is the failure to confront debt addiction and warn of its consequences. A secondary charge is that central banks have reduced the transparency and stability of the financial system through the promotion of complex innovations which encourage the assumption of risk without responsibility. It is unnecessary to appeal to conspiracy theory in any shape or form to explain the fragility of modern financial structures and institutions.

Physicians cannot walk away from their patients after tendering their diagnosis; the job is not complete without a prognosis and a prescription. The last two chapters of the book move from analysis to tentative prediction, including a brief agenda for financial reform. For good measure, there is also some advice for households, businesses and governments in preparation for a disastrous outcome to debt and delusion.

Most of the book was completed by July 1998. Much has already occurred that is worthy of additional comment, but such is the topicality of the book that this is inevitable. The reader may be surprised that all references to financial amounts in the book are expressed in terms of US dollars. The reason for this is quite simple: the pound sterling, as well as most other European currencies, may well have ceased to exist by the middle of the year 2002.

Finally, on a personal note, when the opportunity arose to become free of debt in 1995, I took it and have not regretted it for one moment. I urge the readers of this book to take or make the opportunity to do likewise.

Peter Warburton

Acknowledgements

In the age of personal computers, integrated software, image scanners and laser printers, it is possible to imagine a book that is entirely a solo effort. Yet, rather like a yachtsman attempting to circumnavigate the globe without a back-up team, the enterprise would be doomed to failure. I have been blessed by an understanding family – my wife Anne and our sons, James and Matthew – who have left me in peace for long hours and have endured my absentmindedness at other times. Additionally, James acted as my technical adviser, rebuilding my computer system on several occasions and keeping copies of my work on his own machine, knowing that I would be bound to forget. I am most grateful to them for their encouragement and patience.

Over the course of the project I have benefited from the pastoral advice of Reverend Graham Cray, Principal of Ridley Hall, Cambridge, and of Reverend Peter Law. I have also enjoyed the valuable support and encouragement of our friends, Malcolm and Heather Harrison. I am very grateful to Tony Dye, Andrew Hunt, Professor Geoffrey Wood and Malcolm Foster for undertaking to read the whole text and for giving me their reactions and comments. Alastair Rolfe and his colleagues at Penguin Books have served me admirably in the publication of this book.

I would like to thank Tom Hughes-Hallett at the investment bank, Robert Fleming, for the opportunity to work as a part-time consultant while this book was in preparation. The flexibility of this arrangement enabled me to stay in touch with market developments and to sharpen the arguments of the book. I am grateful also to my colleagues at Robert Fleming who have tolerated my less frequent appearances with good humour. Nigel Sedgley and Gillian Lummis have given me valuable assistance. I should stress, however, that the opinions expressed in the book are personal and are not to be attributed to Robert Fleming.

The ideas, arguments and illustrations in the text have been culled from many sources. While I have tried to acknowledge as many as possible in the bibliography, I apologize in advance for any omissions. I am particularly indebted to the many provocative and contrarian writers – too numerous to mention – whose articles and newsletters have challenged and altered my perceptions and beliefs over the years. Thanks to Martin Wolf for writing a feature article in the *Financial Times* entitled 'How to learn from the debt delusion' on 6 January 1992. This was the inspiration for my title.

Among the very many people who have enabled this book to appear, I gratefully acknowledge three fundamental contributions. My father was a constant source of encouragement and inspiration, spurring me on to set new goals and achieve them. I have been emboldened to the task of writing this book by his confidence in me. Second, while working at L. Messel & Co. (latterly the investment bank, Lehmans), Tim Congdon urged me to write intelligibly, and to length, for the first time, and I owe him a special debt of thanks. Finally, thanks to Arthur Goodhart, my literary agent, whose frankness and persistence have greatly improved the coherence of the finished product. Any errors or omissions remain my sole responsibility.

I

A Clearing of the Mist

'Then lots of food was brought in to them – milk and pancakes with sugar, apples and nuts. Afterwards two beautiful little beds were made up with white sheets, and Hansel and Gretel climbed in and thought they were in Heaven.'

The Brothers Grimm, *Hansel and Gretel*

INTRODUCTION

In the early days of maritime navigation, sailors relied upon the stars to fix their night-time course. If mist or cloud obscured the stars and the sea was rough, it was not uncommon for a vessel to veer some way off course before the error could be rectified. This deviation would carry with it the danger of running aground or becoming shipwrecked. The crew would wait anxiously for the dawn and the opportunity to correct their course. However, those who had fallen asleep belowdecks before the mist or cloud appeared were none the wiser; they had slept soundly in the belief that their course was true.

This book is intended as a wake-up call for those sound sleepers who have found no cause to question the authenticity of the economic and financial achievements of North America and Western Europe since the mid-1980s. Far from continuing on a steady course, the western world has embarked on a speculative journey for which all the historical precedents are ominous. This book is also written for those whose perspective on economic and financial matters is closer to that of the anxious crew: they are aware that the ship is some way off course but feel powerless to do anything about it. They long for the dawn, hoping that disaster can be averted.

Whether the reader identifies more readily with the sleeping crew belowdecks or the anxious ones above, the priority is to recognize that an appalling navigational error has occurred. This false course has been influential in some diabolical risk-taking and decision-making. Billions of savings dollars have been entrusted to countries and to companies which lack the ability to deliver modest returns, let alone the rich ones that have been promised. Governments have forfeited effective control over interest rates in return for a few years' postponement of financial discipline. Individuals have been lured into extremely tentative investments with little or no insurance against adversity. Worst of all, the impressive performance of global equity markets in recent years has been constructed on the shaky platform of unlimited credit. Rather than wait for a shipwreck, it is surely preferable to embrace reality. It may still be possible to change course before disaster strikes.

In daring to suggest that the recent progress of the large developed western economies may be flawed, it is plain that the burden of proof rests with the author. On the surface, these economies seem to be performing reasonably well. The early-1990s recession is well past, yet there has been no recurrence of inflationary trouble. Asset values, particularly shares, have risen strongly giving the impression of unprecedented national prosperity. The multimedia age provides a constant source of amazement and entertainment. Surely, only the pathologically gloomy could raise an economic critique of the western world at the end of the twentieth century?

In fact, the perilous financial and economic condition of the west is remarkably well concealed. Periodic bouts of price inflation, the tell-tale signs of a long-standing debt addiction, have all but vanished. The central banks, as financial physicians, seem to have effected a cure. While there is still plenty of suspicion that inflation will return, each year that passes brings a growing conviction that the patient is genuinely healed. Few have bothered to ask how the central banks have accomplished this feat, one which has proved elusive for more than 20 years. Those who have asked searching questions have usually been discouraged by the answers, unable to grasp the intricacies of global capital markets and the role of information technology. The dominant mentality, both inside and outside government, is that these matters are extremely technical and best left to experts. As long as inflation is absent, who really cares exactly what the central banks have been up to?

EXCURSION INTO FANTASY

The excursion into the realm of financial fantasy has taken place gradually since the mid-1980s. The pace and variety of innovations in the global financial system have been so remarkable that there has scarcely been time enough to catalogue them, let alone analyse them. Figure 1.1 provides some basic definitions of the terms 'capital markets', 'money markets', 'financial markets' and 'securities markets' for the uninitiated. Access to personal and business credit has burgeoned, financial activities have been de-regulated and a host of new financial instruments have been developed. At the centre of this revolution is the world bond market. Both governments and companies issue bonds as a substitute for borrowing from the banking system. The world bond market has grown from less than $1 trillion ($1,000,000,000,000) in 1970 to more than $23 trillion in 1997. It has tripled in size since 1986 and its staggering rise to prominence is worthy of a furious debate. The development of the world bond market has been closely linked to the financing of government budget deficits in almost all western countries since the mid-1980s, including the cost of German unification since 1990.

Whereas almost everyone in the western hemisphere has a good idea of what money is, it seems that very few people understand about bonds. Bonds belong to the invisible world of high finance; they change hands between governments, companies and investment funds without, apparently, touching the lives of ordinary folks. When the treasury (or finance) departments of governments or large companies decide to borrow in the form of a bond, they will typically look to raise hundreds of millions of dollars. One issue in 1998 raised $5 billion ($5,000,000,000). Only a small proportion of these bonds is held directly by individuals and most of these by wealthy and experienced

Figure 1.1 A glossary of capital markets

	Examples
1. The money and foreign exchange markets	Currency (notes and coins)
	Deposits with banks and other financial institutions
	Loans from banks and other financial institutions
2. The securities markets	Certificates of Deposit (CDs)
	Commercial bills
	Government debt (e.g. Treasury bills) maturing within one year
	Bonds issued by governments and their agencies
	Bonds issued by industrial, commercial and financial corporations
	Bonds issued by banks
	Bonds issued by supra-national organizations (e.g. the World Bank, the European Investment Bank)
	Equities issued by industrial, commerical and financial corporations
	Equities issued by banks
	Equities issued in the context of the privatization of state-owned assets
	Loans which have been 'securitized' (that is, repackaged as bonds)
	Derivatives (forwards, futures, options and swaps)
	Interest rate (money market) derivatives
	Bond derivatives
	Equity derivatives
	Credit derivatives
	Commodity derivatives
3. The financial markets	All of the above
4. The capital markets	All of the above, plus the markets in residential, industrial and commercial property

---

investors. To the vast majority, even the workings of a straightforward bond are a mystery. However, today's bond markets are complicated by the extensive use of financial derivatives – futures, options and swaps – and a host of other innovations. The use of higher mathematics and powerful computers has virtually guaranteed that this branch of financial activity will remain beyond the reach of most citizens. Yet, no matter how remote transactions in these complex instruments may appear, they have the capacity to transmit violent financial disturbances to communities, regions and entire nations.

An example may prove helpful. Proctor & Gamble (P&G) is a huge US conglomerate which manufactures soap, among many other things. In the early 1990s, P&G's treasury department successfully used financial derivatives to boost group profits by reducing the company's funding costs. In November 1993, P&G was persuaded to enter into a deal which would potentially reduce the interest costs on $200 million ($200,000,000) of borrowings by $7.5 million over five years, if all went to plan. Under the terms of the deal, P&G's interest rate on the loan would vary according to a complex formula that involved the yields on five-year and 30-year US Treasury bonds. By mid-January, P&G was losing around $17 million on the deal, because US interest rates rose instead of falling as the architects of the deal had supposed. Worse was to follow. At the beginning of March, these notional losses had swelled to $120 million. By the time P&G's patience was exhausted and it sought to extricate itself from the deal, the cost was an estimated $157 million. For such a large profitable company, this loss was manageable; in other circumstances a loss of this size would prompt the loss of thousands of jobs or even the closure of the business.

The treasury department officials at P&G were not novices with regard to sophisticated financial products. They had the full authority of the company's management to enter into this type of transaction. At the outset, they had the confidence to embark on this extremely risky and ultimately disastrous deal. But how was it possible to lose $157 million on a deal involving $200 million of borrowing? The answer lies in the complexities of derivatives and in the effects of financial gearing. Just as the different gears of a car are used to alter the ratio between the speed of the engine and that of the vehicle on the road, so financial derivatives are used to change the ratio between the amount invested (or borrowed) and the resulting profit or loss. The nominal value of the contracts that P&G had entered into was not $200 million but $3,800 million! An error of judgement about the future course of US bond yields which might have cost $10 million in additional interest payments over five years ended up as a $157 million loss within six months.

The development of derivatives markets since the mid-1980s has been even more spectacular than that of the bond markets. In combination, these developments constitute a radical rearrangement of the balance of power in the financial system. The global capital markets of the late 1990s hold the potential for greater economic efficiency and stability on one hand, but also for greater inequality and volatility on the other. Depending on the size and the objectives of the participants, the power of these markets can be harnessed for the benefit of the many or of the few. What is beyond dispute is that the complexities of financial markets have invaded the national, corporate and personal lives of all the large western economies.

As the western world has wandered deeper and deeper into the enchanted forest of financial sophistication, the capacity of individuals to discern the absurd and the grotesque has become greatly impaired. The incongruity of the massive accumulation of government and corporate debt with a low inflation environment no longer provokes much curiosity, even among professionals. A stratospheric stock market has become accepted as the normal state of affairs, requiring no special explanation. The abandonment of cash and of assets readily convertible into cash is likewise regarded as perfectly rational behaviour. Queues form to subscribe to investments in politically fragile nation states with unpronounceable names whose very identities have been established only a few years previously. The unfamiliarity of the financial landscape is tempered only by the reassurance that this epic journey has been marked out by an expert guide, the noble central banker.

The various elements of this collective departure from economic reason are a little harder to disentangle. The closest that most media commentators and analysts come to casting doubt on the achievements of the late 1980s and the 1990s is to worry about the emergence of a stock market bubble. The likening of a speculation in financial assets to a bubble is an appealing and often appropriate metaphor, as in the contemporaneous and related South Sea and Mississippi bubbles of 1719–20. At that time, one new issue prospectus read: 'A company for carrying on an undertaking of great advantage, but nobody is to know what it is.' Similar examples of naïvety in financial matters can be observed today.

When a bubble bursts, only a damp patch on the ground marks its place. Shortly afterwards, nothing remains; the pretence is over. However, the heady stock markets of the late 1990s do not conform to the typology of the bubble. In the most obvious example of the US equity market, its valuation has climbed successively higher between 1982 and 1998, interrupted only briefly by the crash of 1987 and the hiccup of 1990. Indeed, the dominant view of western stock markets is that of a sustainable process. A host of arguments have been deployed to justify current market values, of which the most pervasive is the transition from the industrial age to the information, or cybernetic, age. It is argued that its fixed assets alone can no longer describe the value of a modern company; intellectual capital, research and development expenditures, customer loyalty and brands must also be included.

For this reason, it may be that a mist offers a better metaphor for the late 1990s. It is a mist that breeds confusion, illusion and delusion. It renders intelligent market practitioners incapable of drawing proper conclusions from the evidence all around them; the mist parts for a short while, enabling a few brief insights, and then closes in again, smothering them. Repeated attempts have been made to pin down the logical flaw in the financial markets process, and yet none has been entirely successful. No sooner does some well-respected commentator deliver a prediction of impending financial doom, than the stock market catapults even further into the stratosphere, spurring economic growth into the bargain. No wonder that most commentators and analysts have preferred to rationalize the exuberance of the financial markets rather than risk their reputations by warning of a collapse.

HOW DID WE COME TO LEAVE THE PATH
OF ECONOMIC REALITY?

For most western countries, between 1945 and 1985, economic reality
has been described by a succession of boom–bust or stop–go cycles.
These interludes of faster and slower growth, higher and lower
inflation and interest rates have not always been pretty to watch but
they have been authentic. Whether induced by the animal spirits
of private enterprise or the errors of judgement of governments,
alternating phases of boom and bust have become familiar patterns
of behaviour. Every few years the western economies would boom,
providing millions of extra jobs, and shortly afterwards they would
succumb to a downturn when many jobs would be lost. France is
probably the best example of a country in which these oscillations
were muted, and New Zealand is a good illustration of a country in
which they were amplified. French economic reality was a good deal
more palatable than the New Zealand version, but both expressions
were honest.

While it would be difficult, if not impossible, to trace the precise
origins of our departure from economic reality, the loss of control of
bank credit systems in Anglo-Saxon countries during the mid-1980s
presents itself as a strong candidate for blame. What distinguishes
this period from other episodes of irresponsible lending by commercial
and savings banks is the degree of debt delinquency among businesses
and individuals that followed in its wake. The high incidence of debt
delinquency, encompassing loan arrears, defaults, bankruptcies and
insolvencies, weakened the commercial banking systems of the USA,
the UK, Canada, Australia, Sweden and Finland, to name but a few.
The urgent desire to restore banks' profitability and allow them to
rebuild their capital reserves led central banks to adopt excessively
liberal credit policies. These, in turn, played a key role in the rapid
development of the capital markets in the early 1990s and in the
transformation of the financial intermediation process.

A financial intermediary is simply a middleman or agent who deals
with the general public on one side and with the capital markets on
the other. Commercial and savings banks are the principal intermedi-

aries in the money market; investment funds, comprising pension funds, insurance funds, mutual funds and unit trusts, are the main intermediaries in the bond and equity markets. Banks and funds compete with each other for individuals' savings and borrowings. A remarkable change in the relative shares of these intermediaries has occurred.

In 1980, banks handled 58 per cent of these savings and investment transactions in the US economy, and institutional investors (mainly pension and insurance funds) held a 31 per cent market share. By 1994, the banks' proportion had fallen to 33 per cent and that of the institutions had jumped to 44 per cent. The pace of transformation has been similar in France, the UK and Canada, but rather slower in Germany and Italy. The loss of the banks' influence and status in the financial system at the hands of investment funds has been matched by a shift in the centre of gravity from money markets to financial markets, and to bond markets in particular. The fortunes of the money and bond markets diverged sharply at the beginning of the 1990s. While commercial and savings banks added little to their stock of loans as a reaction to the unprofitable lending of the late 1980s, government and corporate bond issues abounded. Many countries adopted the German model, which combined tight credit policy (short-term interest rates high in relation to the inflation rate) with a more permissive fiscal policy (a large public sector budget deficit).

A flood of government bond issues since 1985 has fuelled the growth of the global capital markets. Whereas the life span of a bond can extend to 50 or 100 years (or even in perpetuity), the most popular and heavily traded bond maturity is ten years. Ten-year government bonds have become known as the benchmark bond; the natural focus of the market and an obvious choice for international comparison. Corporate bond issues are priced against the comparable government bond. Large companies, which previously borrowed from the banks, raise finance directly and more cheaply from the capital markets using their own financial subsidiaries. As companies began to use the capital markets more intensively, so the infrastructures of these markets developed. The widespread use of hedging strategies, derivative instruments, stock lending and many other technical devices has added many layers of complexity to the operation of money, debt and equity markets. Greater financial sophistication has also amplified the opportunities for highly geared investment, undermining the transparency of bond ownership which once existed and reducing the average holding period of a ten-year bond to a few days and even, sometimes, a few hours.

The great majority of citizens are oblivious to the significance of these developments, being content to leave this subject-matter to the experts. Yet this undeserved respect provides an ample cloak for the systematic under-pricing of investment risk, not to mention the more sinister manipulation of asset prices which occurs from time to time. The two main types of investment risk are capital risk and credit risk. Capital risk arises from the uncertainty of capital returns associated with any investment project or business venture. Credit risk refers to the possibility that a borrower will default on loan interest or repayments. The lack of risk awareness among ordinary citizens sits uneasily alongside the increasing sophistication of the savings, investment and borrowing products they have bought. It is high time that this gulf of understanding was bridged.

In summary, there have been some profound changes in the structure of financial intermediation in mature western economies within a very short time. These have begun to affect the scope of governments to direct economic policy. Some policies may no longer work, because the financial markets will frustrate the intended outcome. Others may work differently or unpredictably. Large interest-rate changes might have no apparent effect in some circumstances while, at other times, small interest-rate changes may send massive shock waves via the financial system to the economy, affecting output and employment. The large western economies might sustain, for a while longer, the pretence that steady growth and moderate inflation will continue for many years; but the reality is very different. The loss of predictable financial responses to interest-rate changes opens up, not only the flattering possibility of an inflation-free boom – the proverbial 'new paradigm' – but also the alarming possibility of a sudden and enduring recession, induced by violent movements in bond and share prices. No better recent example of this can be found than Japan.

JAPAN: A CASE STUDY IN CREDIT EXCESSES

The behaviour of western governments and their central banks with respect to financial innovation and liberal credit policies is all the more surprising given what has happened in Japan during the 1990s. If ever there was an object lesson in the dangers of credit over-extension, it is modern Japan. A rapid, credit-induced inflation in property and financial asset prices in the late 1980s exploded in January 1990, leaving behind massive personal and corporate debts, a prolonged economic slump and deflation of consumer prices (that is, falling prices). Japan experienced a phenomenal upsurge in the demand for bank borrowing between 1983 and 1989 that fanned the flames of speculation in residential and commercial property and financial assets. Companies borrowed cheaply from the capital markets, using a variety of instruments, including equity warrants and convertibles, and from tax-efficient tokkin funds. Figure 1.2 gives a graphic illustration of the expansion of the Japanese credit system in relation to the size of its economy since 1967.

In 1998, eight years after the credit bubble burst, land was worth less than half as much as at its peak and the Nikkei stock market index had fared no better. Banks and credit companies were nursing loan books in which non-performing assets (those on which little or no interest is received) represented anything from 10 per cent to 30 per cent of the total. Late in 1998, the Ministry of Finance was still deliberating over its plans to rescue the banking system and revive the economy. Meanwhile, bankruptcies in Japan had soared to record levels and company profitability remained inadequate. After three successive years of 0.5 per cent official interest rates, domestic personal and corporate sector demand for new loans was still very subdued. Japanese debtors longed for the return of inflation, but to no avail.

In 1990, it was possible to derive some comfort from the fact that Japan's credit expansion was more reckless than anywhere else in the world, that its banks were under-capitalized and that its stock market was preoccupied with capital gains at the expense of dividends. But, since 1990, the USA and several other western countries have gone a long way towards emulating Japan's reckless credit expansion. As in

Figure 1.2 Japanese credit expansion in relation to its economic size

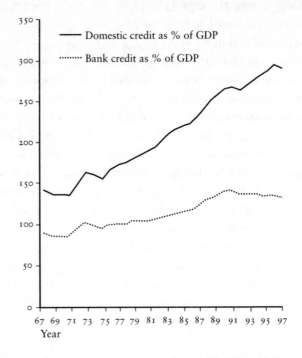

Japan, much of this new borrowing has taken the form of bond issues rather than bank loans. Unlike Japan, the rapid pace of western financial innovation has opened up many new channels of credit creation.

WHAT IF THE CAPITAL MARKETS REVOLUTION HAD NOT HAPPENED?

The capital markets revolution of the late 1980s and the 1990s was facilitated by several parallel developments, of which five stand out. First, the incapacity of the banks, due to non-performing loans; second, the adoption of liberal credit policies by governments; third, the displacement of discretionary consumer borrowing by obligatory government borrowing (to finance budget deficits); fourth, the concentration of the management of private wealth in the hands of large funds;

and fifth, the increased use and acceptance of financial derivatives. In order to appreciate the significance of this revolution for western economic development, it may be helpful to consider how events might have unfolded in its absence.

If this powerful shift from traditional bank borrowing towards the capital markets in North America and Western Europe had not taken place, it is most probable that there would have been a much longer period of economic recession and consolidation in the aftermath of the late-1980s property bust. Governments would not have been able to offset the weakness of personal and corporate spending by running large budget deficits to the same extent. If the tide of government bond issues had met an indifferent demand from the institutional funds sector, then these deficits would have been funded only at unattractively high bond yields.

Deprived of the easy option of selling bonds to investment funds and individuals, the government would probably have resorted to greater monetization of their borrowing. Monetization refers to the act of adding to the stock of liquid assets (cash and bank deposits) in the hands of the private sector, that is, individuals and companies. In effect, the government covers its budget deficit by levying a tax on existing money holdings; this is sometimes referred to as an inflation tax. The principle is not dissimilar to that of a rights issue by a company wishing to raise additional capital. Shareholders who do not take up their rights to buy the shares (which are offered in proportion to existing holdings) suffer erosion in the value of their shares. In practice, monetization occurs when the central bank expands the issue of notes and coins in general circulation or when it persuades the banking system to hold more government securities and the private sector fewer. The net result is an expansion of the private sector's holdings of bank deposits, which constitute the money supply.

If this traditional course of action had been followed, then there is little doubt that the inflationary fires would have been rekindled in the western economies during the early 1990s. By pressing additional liquidity (cash and bank deposits) into the hands of consumers and firms, the demand for goods, services and assets would have increased relative to their available supplies. After a couple of years or so, the outcome of excessive money creation would have been a resurgence of consumer price inflation, following the pattern of the 1970s and early 1980s. This inflation would have alleviated the debt burdens accumulated during the late-1980s property boom and would have lowered the real cost of borrowing. In time, a steep rise in interest rates, deemed necessary to address the inflationary problem, would have stifled any revival in private sector loan demand.

If the post-war inflationary history of the large western nations had repeated itself in the 1990s, then the progress of western stock markets would most probably have been stopped in its tracks long ago. Bond yields would have risen in anticipation of higher inflation rates. Financial asset prices would have followed a weaker trend as higher bond yields weighed on the equity market, and households would not have committed such a high proportion of their savings as investments in equities and bonds. In the context of much less impressive financial market returns, there would have been less incentive to shun bank deposits and Certificates of Deposit (CDs) in favour of stock market investments.

In summary, sometime around 1985, the western economies were diverted from the inflationary path along which they had travelled for the previous 20 years. Instead of repeating the inflationary cycle described above, these countries embarked on a capital markets adventure holiday.

THE CRITICAL ROLE OF THE CENTRAL BANKS

Every adventure holiday needs a tour guide, and for this one who better than a central banker to lead the way? Central banks, such as the US Federal Reserve Board, the German Bundesbank and the Bank of England, play a key role in the formulation of monetary policy and have particular responsibility for their country's internal payments system. Often, they are also charged with the supervision and regulation of financial markets and institutions. As the guardians of the financial system and professional advisers to their governments, it is unthinkable that major financial reforms could ever have been implemented without the support and encouragement of the central banks. While some of them have a long history, central banks came to prominence in most developed countries during the 1970s and 1980s in the context of the fight against inflation.

Inflation reared its ugly head in the aftermath of the OPEC oil price shock of November 1973. On this occasion, western governments validated the price shock by expanding the money supply, thus enabling consumers and businesses to afford the higher fuel and heating costs. When the second oil price shock arrived in 1978, many countries repeated their mistakes, leaving behind rapid consumer price inflation in 1980–81. The inflation peaks in the USA (15 per cent), Canada (12 per cent), Sweden (15 per cent) and Norway (15 per cent) were actually worse in 1980–81 than those which followed the first OPEC price shock. Even countries with good inflation records, like Germany, the Netherlands and Switzerland, suffered inflation rates of around 7 per cent. Those with poor reputations for price control fared much worse, including the UK and Italy, whose inflation rates soared above 20 per cent, and France with a 14 per cent peak.

Stung by a second serious inflation within seven years of the first, governments turned to their central banks for advice. The thrust of this advice was given in three parts: to raise short-term interest rates in order to restrain bank borrowing by individuals and businesses, to cut government borrowing and to finance the budget deficit by selling debt instruments (mainly bonds) to domestic and overseas investors. As a reward for adopting this three-pronged attack on inflation, the politicians were tempted to believe that they would step through a golden gateway of prosperity. The orthodoxy preached by central banks in the 1980s was that low inflation was a precondition for strong and sustainable economic growth. Furthermore, the lowering of inflationary expectations would reduce the cost of servicing public sector debt. As the burden of debt interest fell, the budget deficit would close more rapidly. Thus persuaded, senior finance ministry officials throughout the western world urged upon their governments a tough anti-inflation stance.

There should be no doubt, therefore, that the US Federal Reserve Board (commonly known as the Fed), the Bundesbank, the Bank of England and, indeed, the Bank for International Settlements in Basle, have played a pivotal role in manoeuvring the global financial system away from conventional banking arrangements towards capital market finance. Through their support for the strengthening of capital adequacy regulations on commercial banks, for the de-regulation of domestic financial systems, for financial innovation and for the adoption of light or self-regulation of capital markets activities, the central banks have waved a green flag to almost every development which would secure this cultural transformation.

Conspicuous financial failures, such as the bankruptcy of Orange County in California, the Mexican peso crisis in late 1994 and the collapse of Barings Bank in 1995 have not dented the central banks' confidence in their judgement. The financial community treats each new disaster as an unfortunate special case of incompetence or fraud. These disasters soon become 'ring-fenced' by their particular circumstances so that the collective complacency of the financial markets is preserved. In some ways, the financial markets (and the central banks) appear to become even more persuaded of their invincibility after such crises.

Amidst their vigorous promotion of the global capital markets, central banks seem not to have appreciated how the cultural shift from the money markets to the bond and equity markets would undermine their own authority. Gone are the days when the central banks could announce a new interest rate and validate it indefinitely through their operations in the money markets. Nowadays, the most important source of information about future interest rates is to be found in government bond markets, not in the minds of central bank policy committees.

FINANCIAL DE-REGULATION HAS LEFT BEHIND AMBIGUITY

One of the by-products of financial de-regulation has been to diminish the distinctive characteristics of banks. While banks have retained some of their special features, the responsibility of the central bank to act as lender of last resort only to the banking system is difficult to justify in a world in which many other financial institutions are large enough, should they fail, to corrupt the whole financial system. A striking manifestation of this difficulty was the rescue of Long Term

Capital Management (LTCM), a highly leveraged hedge fund, in September 1998. The Federal Reserve Bank of New York, acting with the full support of the US Fed, facilitated an orderly bail-out of the fund using a consortium of fourteen banks. The injection of capital was $3.6 billion.

The role of lender of last resort implies that the central bank accepts ultimate responsibility for the integrity of the payments system. This pledge has been highly effective in deterring bank 'runs' this century. But as banks themselves have engaged more fully in the bond, equity and derivatives markets, there is an increasing possibility that a central bank could be called upon to assist a bank that has suffered financial losses in these securities markets. Financial de-regulation poses the dilemma of whether to withdraw the lender of last resort privilege from the banks, thus reviving the general public's ancient fear of bank failure, or to extend it to a wider universe of financial institutions.

Implicitly, central banks have embraced the latter option. Apart from the sighs of relief from grateful citizens, some serious questions are raised by this choice. Will individuals come to expect financial compensation, if not deposit or investment protection, in the event of the failure of *any* financial institution? Who will pay the premiums for this insurance? What is to stop the lower quality tier of financial companies from deliberately increasing their risk profiles (as did the Savings and Loan institutions in the USA) with a view to offering higher returns to investors? This is an example of moral hazard, where higher risks are accepted only because of the perceived protection from bankruptcy in the event of a collapse. A dangerous ambiguity has arisen in several countries as a consequence of financial liberalization, whereby financial institutions and subsidiaries are not only permitted to enter unfamiliar areas of business but are also emboldened to take risks.

The possibility of financial failure used to play a critical role in educating both individuals and banks in the importance of diligent risk assessment. Anyone who has lost significant amounts of his or her own money in a financial venture will exercise great caution in future. It is becoming increasingly obvious that central banks are less tolerant of financial failure in the 1990s than they were in the 1970s. The interrelationships of institutions engaged in the sale and repurchase (repo) markets, for example, presume that no financial institution can be allowed to default. This insurance does not come free: either the taxpayers, the investors or the consumers of financial services must pay for it. Yet, in the absence of serious failures, the illusion of costless insurance can be sustained.

ONE DAY THE MIST WILL CLEAR

In an age of unprecedented sophistication the need for level-headed supervision of the financial system is paramount. Whatever freedoms an open society affords, access to unlimited credit facilities cannot be counted among them. In the same way that currency counterfeiting undermines the value of money, reckless offers of credit alongside phoney promises of wealth precipitate financial ruin and the misery of large-scale bankruptcy, as the poor Albanians discovered when their pyramid investment schemes collapsed in 1997. In their extreme forms, both counterfeit currency and reckless credit expansion pose a direct threat to the authority of government and the rule of law. Without a legal system and a law enforcement agency, no one would be truly free to pursue his or her own affairs. It is no less true that a centralized authority with powers to sanction and regulate the total supply of credit must circumscribe the financial freedom of individuals. The alternative in both cases is anarchy: the denial of property rights, of access to compensation or redress and a rejection of social responsibility.

For the moment, anarchy in the global financial markets masquerades as an agent of national prosperity and personal freedom. It is a compelling disguise, underpinned by many clever arguments and supported by many persuasive advocates. There are some falsehoods that are easily exposed and thwarted, while others are so subtle and complex that they can remain undetected for long periods. The longer they last, the greater the collective delusion and the greater the subsequent disappointment. But one day the mist will clear, exposing the true extent of past follies.

The argument of this book is that the leading economies of North America and Western Europe have fallen victim to a dangerous illusion, related to the anarchic development of global capital and credit markets. On one level, the thesis is very straightforward: that both citizens and governments have become heavily addicted to borrowing and no longer care about the consequences. But to understand how this parlous state of affairs has arisen, it is necessary to examine the context, the ingredients and the anatomy of this act of collective folly. Only then can the falsehood be exposed and some remedies prescribed.

2

Inflation: Public Enemy
Number One

'There was a great famine in the city; the siege lasted so long that a donkey's head sold for eighty shekels of silver and a quarter of a cab of dove's dung for five shekels.' 2 Kings 6: 25

'Inflation is like a drug in more ways than one. It is fatal in the end, but it gets its votaries over many difficult moments.'
Viscount D'Abernon, British Ambassador to Berlin, 1920–26

Price inflation has been around for a very long time; it is probably as old as human society itself. Like toothache, warts and lousy weather, inflation has connotations of inconvenience, injustice and trouble. Yet, in common with dentists and the manufacturers of wart cream and umbrellas, inflation has always spelt good news for someone. For governments, inflation is a hidden form of taxation; for working households with large mortgages, a bout of inflation is a godsend; for companies with large unsold stocks of finished goods, inflation represents an instant accounting profit. It's an ill wind that blows nobody any good.

A BROAD SWEEP OF THE HISTORY
OF INFLATION

Inflation is defined as a persistent increase in the average prices of domestic goods and services. For as long as there have been wars, sieges, floods, famines and droughts, there have been periodic bouts of inflation. It is possible to identify inflationary episodes even in barter economies, since there is generally at least one non-perishable commodity whose principal function is to act as a store of value. More often than not, this commodity is a precious metal. Harking back to the biblical quotation above, for the besieged Samarians of around 900 BC the standard trading unit was the silver shekel. Valued at the April 1998 silver price, the donkey's head would have cost about $200! One of the earliest documented inflations in the ancient world occurred after Alexander the Great's conquest of the Persian kingdom in 330 BC. The Roman empire also suffered rapid inflation under Diocletian at the end of the third century AD.

One of the obvious problems in attempting to measure price inflation across centuries is the instability of the underlying basket of goods or services in common use. As economic life becomes more complex and consumer appetites become more diverse, the composition of the 'cost of living' basket needs to move with the times. The longest continuous study of the price level was carried out by Henry Phelps-Brown and Sheila Hopkins, spanning almost 700 years of UK history. Using the meticulous records of provisions purchased by stately homes, they were able to establish that the average price of consumables was almost unchanged between the early fourteenth and the early sixteenth centuries. A Bank of England study established that the index of average prices in Britain merely tripled between 1694 and 1948 (an average annual inflation rate of only 0.4 per cent), but rose almost 20-fold between 1948 and 1994 (an average rate of 6.7 per cent per year). US and French data tell a similar story.

In the developed western world, almost every generation for at least 300 years has witnessed episodes when annual inflation rates soared above 10 per cent. In this sense, the experience of the second half of the twentieth century is nothing unusual. What distinguishes the post-war years is the absence of intervening episodes of deflation, that is, periods of falling average prices. Between 1825 and 1913, there were seven deflationary periods in Germany, mostly of three or four years in length, but one which was much longer. The price level fell between 1874 and 1887, spanning the years of the first Great Depression. Yet, during the past 50 years, price inflation, measured by consumer price indices, has hardly ever ranged beneath zero in any of the major western economies, nor, indeed, in Japan. In fact, less than 5 per cent of the present population of these countries has any first-hand experience of living in a deflationary climate, and most of these people are now retired and very old. For the vast majority of us, it is as natural for prices to rise as for the leaves to fall from the trees; we do not know any different. Our ignorance of deflation is akin to the Algerians' ignorance of snow and the Egyptians' ignorance of rain.

POST-WAR INFLATIONARY HISTORY

A series of charts (Figures 2.1–2.5) document the consistency of the post-war inflationary experience in ten OECD countries. The similarities are the greatest for the years between 1948 and 1971, when the Bretton Woods agreement held most world currencies together in a fixed exchange-rate system. As the US dollar was the dominant reserve currency and the anchor of the system, the USA was the only country free to determine its own inflation rate during this time. All other nations imported the US inflation rate via their fixed exchange rates with the US dollar. For most of this period, the annual inflation rate was maintained at 1 per cent or 2 per cent, but US involvement in the Korean war, the Suez Canal crisis and the Vietnam war spilled over into monetary policy on each occasion. The US authorities loosened policy in order to ease the financial burden of military expenditure, allowing prices to rise more rapidly for a time.

We can look back on the inflationary record of the 1950s and 1960s with a mixture of pride and nostalgia; pride, because we know now how disruptive an influence inflation can be; nostalgia, because we sometimes long for the irretrievable simplicity of national economic life in those days. Yet there were crises even then. France, Italy, Spain and the UK were among those forced to devalue their currencies relative to the US dollar, in order to stabilize their balance of payments positions. Currency devaluation carried with it the stigma of failure and the inevitability of a jump in the price level, as rising prices of imported goods and services provoked demands for higher wages. All too often, the one-off adjustment of prices after devaluation set in motion an expectation that higher rates of inflation would persist into the future.

The periodic devaluation of individual currencies against the US dollar was a convenient means of resolving tensions in the fixed exchange-rate system, but there was one kind of tension that could not be accommodated by the Bretton Woods agreement, namely a need for the US currency to devalue. The long-running and inconclusive deployment of US military forces in Vietnam contributed to the circumstances in which a devaluation of the dollar became imperative. Late in December 1971, the Smithsonian agreement brought to an end the formal structure of fixed exchange rates. Some countries, including Canada, elected to maintain a US dollar link, but most opted to let their currencies float.

Under floating, or flexible, exchange rates, each country has responsibility for running its own monetary policy. Its success in restraining the expansion of bank borrowing by individuals, companies and government and in attracting and retaining foreign capital, among other things, will determine its own inflation rate and the external value of its currency. Apart from the USA, only Germany and Switzerland appear to have had the slightest idea how to operate a domestic monetary policy in the early 1970s. While other western countries were still coming to terms with the task, the world suffered a double shock in the shape of soaring dollar commodity prices, in 1972, and a quadrupling of crude oil prices towards the end of 1973.

The policy choice was straightforward: either to expand the stock of domestic money (known as the money supply) so that companies and consumers could afford to pay the higher food and fuel prices, or to keep monetary conditions tight, forcing the private sector to economize on all other categories of spending. In the first case, there would be a jump in the overall price level and a steep increase in the prices of oil and commodities relative to other goods and services. If the latter course is chosen, the same relative price changes would occur but the overall price level would hold to its previous trend. A glance at Figures 2.1 (the USA and Canada), 2.2 (the UK and Australia), 2.3 (Germany and France), 2.4 (Italy and Spain) and 2.5 (Japan and Sweden) should be sufficient to determine which choice most countries made.

Figure 2.1 Annual inflation in the USA and Canada (% p.a.)

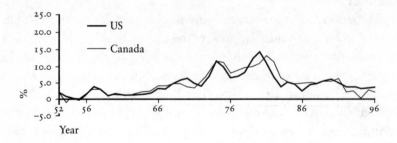

Figure 2.2 Annual inflation in the UK and Australia (% p.a.)

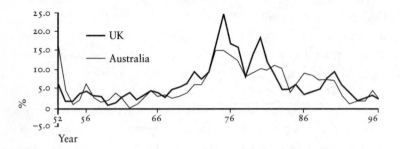

Figure 2.3 Annual inflation in Germany and France (% p.a.)

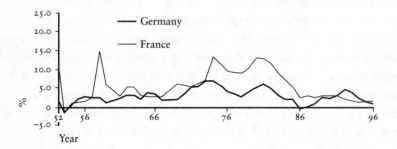

Figure 2.4 Annual inflation in Italy and Spain (% p.a.)

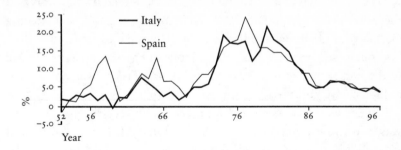

Figure 2.5 Annual inflation in Japan and Sweden (% p.a.)

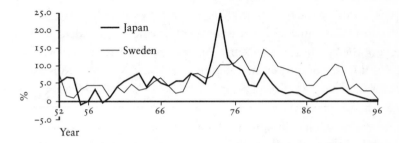

Annual inflation rates approaching 25 per cent in the UK and Japan, around 18 per cent in Italy and 15 per cent in Spain and France exposed the inadequacies of domestic policy-making in a world of flexible exchange rates and the vulnerability of certain sections of the population to radical increases in the cost of living. In seeking to avoid the severe social and political repercussions of the sudden leap in inflation, governments allowed their budgets to deteriorate and their currencies to depreciate. It was only after a second oil price shock (following the Iran–Iraq conflict of 1978–9) and almost a decade after the breakdown of the Bretton Woods agreement that many countries next regained monetary control. Only (West) Germany could claim that its monetary policy had been successful throughout the various crises of the 1970s.

Ever since the mid-1970s, Germany has asserted its credentials as the linchpin of a new fixed exchange-rate system, confined to Europe.

The other original members of the European Economic Community were France, Belgium, Luxembourg, the Netherlands and Italy. Of these, only the Netherlands seemed remotely capable of matching Germany's tight monetary discipline. France and Italy remained wildly off-course, requiring frequent devaluations of their currencies relative to the Deutschmark. It is easy to forget that France was not able to hold a steady parity with Germany until 1986.

Nevertheless, the deep and long economic recession of 1980–82 was a turning point in post-war inflationary history. It fractured strongholds of pricing power in heavy industries and labour unions, it ushered out the era of economic planning that had taken hold of Western Europe in the 1960s, and it paved the way for central banks to play a much more significant advisory and executive role in economic policy. During the recession, there was a cumulative loss of 4 per cent of national income and a rise in unemployment equivalent to 3 per cent of the labour force in North America and Western Europe. These painful losses of output and employment were sufficient to persuade governments of almost all political flavours that anti-inflation policy was the top priority.

By 1984, a clear majority of large western economies had been purged of the high inflation virus and were returning to good health at varying speeds. France and the UK took two years longer to establish sub-5 per cent consumer price inflation, while Italy and Spain were content with their moderately higher inflation rates. Alas, the return to good health was celebrated too boisterously in the Anglo-Saxon countries; urgent and well-intentioned moves to liberalize and de-regulate these economies confused the operation of monetary policy once more. As a result, a sub-group of developed economies, including the USA, the UK, Canada, Sweden and Australia, indulged in another damaging bout of monetary excess and subsequent inflation in the second half of the 1980s. Japan participated in the folly, both dom-estically and through the overseas activities of its banks, insurance and credit companies, with disastrous effects.

Inflation peaks of 5.4 per cent in the USA, 5.6 per cent in Canada, 9.5 per cent in the UK and 10.4 per cent in Sweden in 1990 or 1991 were an embarrassing reminder of the frailty of our understanding of the inflationary process and the inadequacy of our policy structures.

That the USA and Canada escaped so lightly from the escapade is a tribute only to their willingness to tolerate huge deficits in foreign trade. Perennial trade deficits are a substitute for higher rates of domestic inflation. In essence, an abundant foreign supply of goods and services weakens the domestic pricing power of producers and suppliers. This device can work only if foreigners are prepared to accept claims on assets in exchange for their goods and services.

The interest rate increases that terminated the inflationary boom of the late 1980s carried the UK, the USA, Canada, Australia, New Zealand and Scandinavia into another costly recession, whose nadir was in 1991. Uncharacteristic errors of monetary judgement tempted Germany into a post-unification boom and delayed the knock-on effects of Anglo-Saxon recession in continental Europe until 1993. It is by this circuitous route that the large western economies have seemingly arrived at their inflation paradise.

WHAT'S SO BAD ABOUT INFLATION?

At the start of this chapter it was acknowledged that inflation has connotations of injustice, inconvenience and trouble. There are several substantial reasons why inflation is regarded as an economic evil. Under the heading of injustice, the criticism of general price inflation is that it confers arbitrary gains and losses on different groups of people, depending on their particular circumstances. As a generalization, the indebted young gain from an increase in inflation while the older savers and pensioners lose out. There are three main types of transfer which occur when a significant inflationary process (i.e. an annual inflation rate of more than 5 per cent) is in force.

First, there is a transfer between prime age workers (typically, those aged between 20 and 44) and those dependent on benefits and retirement pensions. Prime age workers tend to be more than fully protected against general inflation because their skill levels are still increasing and their career opportunities are still expanding; this enables them to move into new jobs with relative ease if they are dissatisfied with pay or conditions in their existing employment. Benefit and pension recipients may appear to be protected against consumer price inflation through an annual up-rating exercise, but there are often reasons why this does not work out in practice. The government may be struggling to reduce its expenditures and may decide to cut back on additional pensioner privileges such as subsidized travel, healthcare or housing allowances. Occupational pensions may be only partially indexed, for example, compensating for annual inflation up to 3 per cent, but not above. In this way, inflation transfers economic resources away from the retired population and from benefit claimants towards younger working households.

A second type of transfer is between net borrowers and net savers in the economy. In most developed countries, the interest paid by a household in respect of a home loan qualifies for tax relief up to an arbitrary nominal limit, and some countries give relief for other types of personal loan as well. The higher the inflation rate, the higher the average nominal interest rate is likely to be, and therefore the higher the implied level of tax relief on interest payments. Quite apart from the interest subsidy, inflation erodes the real value of borrowers' debts over time. Because the money value of a debt is usually fixed at its inception, all subsequent rises in the average price level reduce the effective burden of debt repayments. Net savers, whose heads of household tend to be aged over 45, also qualify for tax exemption on some types of interest received, but most of their investment income is liable to be taxed. In addition, the real value of their accumulated wealth is worn away by progressive price increases. For some assets, the total return (in the form of capital gain or investment income) may compensate for the current rate of inflation, but for others it will not. Hence, inflation typically transfers control over real resources from net savers to net borrowers.

A third transfer mechanism is the progressive personal income tax system used in most western countries, whereby the marginal rate of tax rises with the level of pre-tax income. The faster the pace of wage and price inflation, the greater is the tendency for individuals' income to cross higher tax rate thresholds. This phenomenon is variously described as fiscal drag or bracket creep. In between successive revisions of the nominal tax thresholds and allowances, the government collects additional taxation from the personal sector. Infrequent indexation of the tax system can be used as a covert method of raising the effective personal tax burden. It is also important to appreciate that inflation is inherently a form of taxation in that notes and coins (and some types of bank deposit) bear no interest.

INFLATION AS A NUISANCE

In addition to the charge of economic injustice, inflation is also condemned as an inconvenience. At its most basic, there is the nuisance of continually revising price lists and product labels. The faster the pace of inflation, the more frequently prices, wages, rents and so forth need to be updated. In low inflation countries, it may be possible for companies to make a single annual adjustment to prices or occasionally, none at all. Where the annual inflation rate is between, say, 10 per cent and 25 per cent, quarterly price adjustments may be needed. In extreme situations, where the annual inflation rate is more than 50 per cent, it is not uncommon for prices, wages and rents to be adjusted every month. Provided the inflation rate is reasonably stable, even above 50 per cent per annum, the experience of various Latin American and East European countries is that the people learn to live with it. Nevertheless, the burden of price updating represents a waste of time and resources.

However, it is far more likely that the crisis of monetary control which allows the annual inflation rate to climb to 50 per cent will not be arrested before progressively faster paces of price escalation result. Hyperinflation, usually defined as an inflation rate of 50 per cent or more per month, has the effect of rendering the domestic currency virtually worthless. The misery of life during a hyperinflation is well documented in the circumstances of Germany, Austria, Hungary, Poland and Russia in the early 1920s, of Germany, Hungary, China and Greece after the Second World War, and of mainly Latin American countries in the post-war years. Brazil had an annual price inflation rate of over 2,000 per cent as recently as 1994; and in 1990, Argentina, Brazil, Nicaragua and Peru all had inflation rates which exceeded 2,000 per cent, requiring prices and incomes to be increased almost continuously. Mourning the doubling or tripling of prices over the New Year holiday in 1990, a shopkeeper in Buenos Aires was quoted in *The Times* as follows: 'We lost money on everything we sold on Saturday because prices have risen between 100 per cent and 200 per cent. Some of us prefer to wait until the dust settles instead of losing more money.'

Under the extreme conditions of hyperinflation, the inconvenience of inflation boils over into trouble and turmoil. The costs of inflation described above are serious enough when the rate of inflation is between 5 per cent and 15 per cent, but if an inflationary process is not checked in its early stages, then the results can be devastating. As a general rule, annual inflation rates of more than 50 per cent will provoke social unrest and even civil war if wages and prices are not fully indexed. At more than 100 per cent per annum inflation, confidence in the local currency is likely to evaporate, leading to parallel markets which will only accept a hard foreign currency, e.g. US dollars or German marks, and a marked increase in criminal activity. Capital flight, meaning the expatriation of private wealth to other countries by legitimate or other means, is also likely when inflation becomes so rapid. Economies suffering from hyperinflation generally require a strong military presence to discourage riotous behaviour, illegal trading and capital flight. Not much remains of a free society when inflation is tolerated at more than 100 per cent per year.

A more complicated criticism relates to the uncertainty surrounding the future inflation rate. If inflation were steady at 3 per cent or 5 per cent, then businesses could plan accordingly; but if inflation rises or falls suddenly, then costly mistakes can result. For example, when a company experiences an upturn in demand for its products, its natural reaction is to order more raw materials and take on extra staff. But if the company has merely misjudged the inflation rate and sold its goods too cheaply, then the profitability of these sales will be inadequate. When it readjusts its prices, demand for its goods will fall back again and there will be no justification for buying in more materials or hiring more staff. A volatile inflation rate induces businesses to hold larger inventories in order to cope with unexpected surges in demand. These additional inventories absorb working capital that would otherwise be deployed in more profitable parts of the business. In this way, inflation uncertainty raises business costs and reduces economic efficiency.

In case the foregoing paragraphs may have left the reader in any doubt, this book is not proposing a revisionist thesis about price inflation. Inflation has many undesirable features and it would be folly to pretend otherwise. There is no denying the damage that has been caused through the misguided tolerance of double-digit annual inflation rates in Europe alone. However, when it comes to evaluating the relative merits of stable zero inflation and stable 3 per cent, or even 5 per cent, inflation, the author must part company from the zero inflation zealots. Despite the frequent assertions by finance ministers, there is little evidence to suggest that targeting a zero inflation rate confers an additional benefit to long-term economic growth as compared to targeting 5 per cent per year. Before the 1970s, many empirical studies disputed even whether inflation had a significant detrimental effect on economic growth. Judging only from the low inflation episodes of the 1950s and 1960s, it was impossible to determine a negative statistical relationship between inflation and growth. Only with the added insights obtained in the 1970s and 1980s has this result become established.

An obscure working paper written in 1995 by Michael Sarel, a researcher at the International Monetary Fund in Washington, DC, produced a striking result. Pooling information from 87 countries for the years 1970 to 1990, Sarel discovered a structural break in the relationship between rates of economic growth and inflation. The break is estimated to occur when the annual inflation rate is 8 per cent. Between zero and 8 per cent, he found that the inflation rate either has no effect or even has a slight positive effect on economic growth; above 8 per cent per annum, the estimated negative effect of inflation on growth rates is significant, robust and extremely powerful. This result simultaneously endorses the economic wisdom of eliminating double-digit inflation while spurning the idea that the inflation target should be zero. If there is no appreciable loss of economic efficiency attached to low inflation rates, then why bother with a zero target?

DANGERS OF ZERO INFLATION ZEALOTRY

Quite apart from Sarel's findings, there are several good technical arguments for targeting low rather than zero inflation. First of all, the measures of consumer price inflation that are in common use are themselves subject to error. Price indices require that appropriate items be included with weights that accurately reflect patterns of consumer spending. The sampling frame used to collect data on all the constituent items is also vulnerable to innovations in consumer purchasing. New types of stores, such as large discount warehouses, may be under-represented in the sampling frame, leading to an implicit upward bias to the price index. Secondly, cost of living and price indices have limited scope to capture quality changes in goods and services. If quality improvements are scored as effective price reductions, then again conventional price indices will over-state the average inflation rate. A third argument concerns the degree of flexibility in the economy. In an economy dominated by private enterprise and lightly regulated markets for goods and labour, resources flow freely from region to region and from sector to sector to meet new opportunities and to obtain better rewards. In a zero inflation world, a significant proportion of disadvantaged regions and sectors would suffer extended periods in which their nominal incomes, including wages and salaries, would fall. In a low inflation economy, the same relative transfers can occur without the widespread stigma of wage cuts.

To the zealot, the slightest tolerance of inflation is tantamount to heresy. He would argue that, if rapid inflation is very bad and moderate inflation is quite bad, then surely it is best to have no inflation at all. This simple logic is impeccable when applied to crime, disease and waste, but it does not work for inflation. One of the many misconceptions about inflation is to think of it as a killer disease, like bubonic plague or smallpox. For these, there can be no worthwhile objective other than eradication. But whereas there is an effective vaccination against smallpox, such that the risk of a fresh outbreak has been reduced to negligible proportions, inflation can disappear and reappear effortlessly. Moreover, smallpox has no antithesis, but inflation has a mirror image called deflation that has demons of its own.

PRIDE COMES BEFORE A FALL

At the end of the twentieth century, the dominant perspective on inflation in the western hemisphere is an intolerant and moralistic one: that we would all be better off if prices had no particular tendency to rise or to fall. This is a creed that all central bankers must repeat before breakfast, lest they forget. It is a creed that all political parties must include in their manifestos. But saying and doing are not the same thing; the political administrations with the strictest codes of practice have been responsible for some of the biggest inflation blunders. It was Edward Heath, the British Prime Minister, who in 1973 coined the phrase that forms the title of this chapter. The abhorrence of inflation has not led to a common understanding of the inflationary process, nor to an agreed method of inflation control.

The gulf between the high moral tone and the permissive reality forms one of the central themes of this book. For the past 20 years a hate campaign has been growing against the bitter injustices that inflation brings. This consensus has shaped government priorities; it has led to the formation of new institutions and to the amendment of national constitutions. The common fight against inflation has united political enemies within countries and has promoted a high degree of economic co-operation among the large developed nations of North America and Western Europe. Plans for Economic and Monetary Union (EMU) in Europe could never have come to fruition were it not for the commitment of member nations to the strict control of inflation. Germany's insistence that this should be so derives from its own searing experiences of hyperinflation. The war waged against inflation is, arguably, the dominant economic story of the second half of the twentieth century.

HAS THE WAR TRULY BEEN WON?

Reams of statistics, some of them used to generate the charts and tables in this book, provide a powerful argument that the war against inflation has been won. Between 1990 and 1998, more of the OECD countries have enjoyed a low inflation rate (under 5 per cent per year) than at any time since the 1960s. For most adults in the west, the rapid inflation rates of the mid-1970s are a faded memory. However, the perception of inflation as an undesirable trait of economic life has been steadily reinforced through the media. Rising inflation is portrayed as a national disgrace. Whenever it threatens to recur, financial commentators and political adversaries demand prompt remedial action, usually in the form of higher interest rates. Such levels of public awareness and intolerance towards inflation have developed in most western countries only in the past 20 years. Moreover, each of these countries has a central bank whose governor or policy committee has a powerful position in public debate. The issue of central bank independence from the day-to-day whims of politicians has become a celebrated cause.

While there are still many poorer countries of the world where conditions of rapid inflation and even hyperinflation prevail, the dominant mood in the west is one of confidence that the war against inflation is being won and will remain won. The struggle to bring down annual inflation rates from 20 per cent to 10 per cent, from 10 per cent to 5 per cent, and from 5 per cent to 2.5 per cent, has often been very costly in terms of lost output and higher unemployment. The victory over inflation is precious and is still being savoured. Moreover, the institutional framework for keeping inflation under control is still under construction. Any suggestion that these arrangements may be preventing an effective response to a much more serious threat is destined to fall on deaf ears. Indeed, the achievement of a European single currency, the euro, is seen as a culmination of the anti-inflationary battle; the irrevocable locking of once-inflationary economies into a single currency union, whose central bank (the ECB) is constitutionally committed to virtual price stability.

CONCLUSION

However commendable the desire to eradicate inflation and its litany of injustices may be, the fact remains that inflation is not the sole economic evil; it never has been and never will be. Whenever a

34

country or a group of countries has targeted one economic objective exclusively, problems have invariably arisen in other spheres of social, economic or political life. The narrower the policy focus and the more obsessively it has been pursued, the greater the likelihood of an ensuing crisis. This book argues that the policy obsession with inflation is paving the way for a crisis of immense proportions. In a cruel but familiar twist of logic, the only antidote to this forthcoming crisis will be a deliberate and co-ordinated reflation of the large developed economies. This crisis is destined to replace the inflation of the 1970s as the defining economic event of today's adult generations, just as the second Great Depression of 1929–39 became the dominant experience of the generations recently deceased.

The compression of inflation rates cannot be used to justify the means by which it has been achieved. Later chapters will describe how a diversification of the credit process has shifted the centre of gravity away from conventional bank lending. The ascendancy of financial markets and the proliferation of domestic credit channels *outside* the monetary system have greatly diminished the linkages between credit expansion and the money supply and between credit expansion and price inflation in the large western economies. The impressive reduction of inflation is a dangerous illusion; it has been obtained largely by substituting one set of serious problems for another.

In order to convince the reader of this thesis, a great many strands of argument and evidence must be assembled. This chapter has sought to explain why inflation has become public enemy number one. Without a reasonably thorough grasp of the history of inflation during the past 50 years and some background knowledge of inflation in much earlier times, it is difficult to appreciate why the commitment to anti-inflation policy in the final quarter of the twentieth century has become so strong or so pervasive.

Throughout the western world, our institutions, our shops and our personal financial decisions have been moulded by the experience of continuously rising prices. Contracts such as rent agreements, mortgages, leases and pension arrangements have all been structured on the presumption that the average price level for goods and services will not fall, except possibly over very short intervals. While stable prices have an intuitive appeal, the problem is that post-war western civilization has absorbed the reality of inflation into its structure; it is much more vulnerable to the unknown threat of deflation than to the well-understood threat of higher inflation. In the over-zealous pursuit of low inflation, there is the considerable risk of tipping some of the largest economies in the world into outright deflation.

This risk would be important under any circumstances, bearing in mind the unpleasant experiences of deflation in the two Great Depressions, but it is of overwhelming importance today. Behind the mechanistic anti-inflation rhetoric of the politicians and the central bankers (whose role in this sorry tale will be elaborated in the next chapter) lies the stark reality of the unfettered expansion of financial market borrowing. Like the householder whose property is spotlessly clean and tidy, but who has merely shifted all the mess to the attic, the borrower has much to fear on the day when the ceiling falls.

3

The Pied Pipers of Zurich

All the little boys and girls,
With rosy cheeks and flaxen curls,
And sparkling eyes and teeth like pearls,
Tripping and skipping,
Ran merrily after
The wonderful music
With shouting and laughter.

Robert Browning,
The Pied Piper of Hamelin

'By and large, if the overriding objective is price stability, we did better with the nineteenth-century gold standard and passive central banks, with currency boards, or even with "free banking". The truly unique power of a central bank, after all, is the power to create money, and ultimately the power to create is the power to destroy.' Paul Volcker, Chairman (1979–87),
US Federal Reserve Board

At the end of the twentieth century, the existence and importance of central banks is one of the unquestioned facts of western economic life. The merits of having a centralized banking system, with a nationalized bank in sole control of issuing currency and holding reserves, have long been taken for granted. According to the banking historian, Vera Smith, most of the serious discussion on this topic took place in Western Europe and America between 1830 and 1875. There are a number of alternative banking models to a centralized system, including the currency board, the monetary institute and the ultimate competitive system in which privately owned banks issue their own notes and coin, make loans, take deposits and hold reserves. While 'free banking' still has its advocates today, most people take fright at the thought of a return to the days when banks went bust, leaving depositors high and dry. On a practical level, a return to free banking might be impossible, given the sophistication of modern counterfeiting. Forgery of bank notes was a headache in the early nineteenth century; how much more so would it be today?

CENTRAL BANKS: THE HALLMARK OF A CIVILIZED SOCIETY

It is as well to begin with an explanation of what a central bank is and does. It is a monetary authority, normally wholly owned by government, but separated in law from the ministry of finance or treasury. Typically, the central bank has discretionary monopoly control over high-powered money, that is, the notes and coin in circulation with the public plus bankers' obligatory deposits at the central bank. As such it has the discretion to pursue an independent monetary policy without reference to a formal set of rules or the requirement to make profits from its operations. The wide range of discretionary control is the defining characteristic of central banking, distinguishing it from other models such as currency boards and monetary institutes. Even so, few central banks are politically isolated. In most cases, they are obliged to defend their actions before government committees from time to time.

It is not strictly necessary for the central bank to act as lender of last resort (LLR) to the private sector banking system, but in practice there are no exceptions. In essence, the central bank acts as LLR in order to prevent a collapse of the money supply in times of general panic over the health of the banking system. Henry Thornton and Walter Bagehot expressed the rationale for the LLR as a set of rules for stopping bank crises and panics, which were a common occurrence in the eighteenth century. These rules stressed the responsibility of the LLR to protect the integrity of the money supply, to support central bank objectives, to allow insolvent institutions to fail, to accommodate only creditworthy institutions, to charge penal rates to other borrowers, to require good collateral and to pre-announce its policy in order to forestall crises of confidence. Nowadays, open market operations render it unnecessary for the LLR to channel aid to creditworthy borrowers.

At the end of the twentieth century there is no serious challenge to the centralized banking system. Central banks are widely respected by the general public as one of the hallmarks of a civilized society. While central banks are not above reproach, they are deemed essential to the smooth running of the financial system that underpins industry and commerce. Political interference in the setting of interest rates, for example, is widely condemned; the moral outrage it provokes is proof of a groundswell of support for central bank independence in monetary matters. In western democracies, the bank's status as a national champion of the cause of sound money and a repository of wise counsel in financial affairs has become well established. Even the architecture of central bank buildings exudes austerity, prudence and longevity – if also grandiosity.

The ascendancy of the central banking movement has taken some curious turns. After Sweden (1668) and the UK (1694) established national banks, there was a long gap before the Banque de France arrived on the scene in 1800. Next came the other Scandinavians, Belgium, the Netherlands, Spain, Portugal and Indonesia in the first half of the nineteenth century. The forerunner of the German Bundesbank, Bulgaria, Romania, Japan, Serbia and Italy joined the central banking list between 1875 and 1893. The Swiss National Bank in Zurich, the home of the proverbial gnomes, did not arrive until 1907, and the US Federal Reserve system not until the 1913 Act. Clearly, since the ending of the gold standard, central banks have been called upon to fulfil a dramatically more significant role than in earlier centuries. In all there were 17 central banks at the turn of the twentieth century, 22 by 1920, 42 by 1940, 76 by 1960, 110 by 1970, 136 by 1980 and over 170 in the mid-1990s, employing 240,000 people around the world.

Representatives of most of these banks gathered in London in February 1994 for the tercentenary of the Bank of England. As a mark of respect, the governors of the US Federal Reserve Board delayed their regular monetary policy meeting in order to attend. However, with their resolve reinforced by keeping each other's company, no doubt, the Fed members returned to Washington with the immediate intention of raising US interest rates, with some considerable effect on world bond markets. Perhaps this act, a meagre quarter-point percentage increase in the Federal funds rate, was the clearest indication that the large central banks had finally achieved the status of the supreme executives of economic policy. The European Central Bank (ECB), which came into being in the middle of 1998, subsumes the monetary policy functions of the Bundesbank, the Banque de France and nine other central banks, and represents a further concentration of policy control.

THE ROAD TO STARDOM

The popularity of central banks can be explained by three key factors. First, the huge priority accorded to the control and ultimate defeat of inflation after the upheavals of the 1970s has raised the profile of credit and monetary policy, and hence the power of its executive agency. In particular, there has been a determined effort in many countries to distance the operation of policy from the political process. Second, for developing countries, the creation of a central bank is regarded as a necessary step along the road to acceptance by the wider business and financial community, the IMF and the World Bank; it is seen as part of the successful model of development. Third, as the international financial system has become more liberal and more complex, even small countries have found it necessary to build defences against the disruptive economic influence of massive inflows or outflows of capital. A central bank is well placed to collect market intelligence and to design suitable policy responses.

However, in the case of developing countries, none of the above may provide a decisive argument for having a central bank. A study by Dr Kurt Schuler, an academic at Johns Hopkins University, Baltimore, USA, takes a critical look at the relationship between currency quality and monetary systems in 155 countries. He argues that monetary disasters in Argentina, Brazil, Cambodia, Guinea, Jamaica, Mexico,

Nigeria, the Philippines, Russia, Tanzania and Zaire would all have been avoided if these countries had adopted the US dollar as their currency instead of operating their own monetary policy through their own central bank. In developing countries with central banking, despite legal barriers to holding foreign currency, many people and businesses still prefer high-quality foreign currencies to the local ones. It is estimated that 50 per cent to 70 per cent of all US dollar notes and 20 per cent to 30 per cent of all German mark notes, by value, circulate outside their countries of origin. Schuler's study concluded that, for the years 1983–93 in particular, developing countries with their own central banks had much poorer inflation performance than those which did not.

CENTRAL BANKS: THE VANQUISHERS OF INFLATION?

The last chapter discussed the inflationary experiences of the largest western economies and the key role in the reduction of inflation played by central banks in the 1980s. The story of this period is all too easily characterized as a struggle between wicked, profligate governments which overspent their budgets and noble, upright central banks which, at the cost of unpopularity, raised interest rates to correct the politicians' excesses. However, this neat subdivision of honour and blame does not bear serious examination. It presupposes that the central banks' sole means of exerting influence on the economy is through their money market operations and through changes in policy interest rates. This is very far from the case. Central banks carry out many other functions, apart from initiating or implementing interest rate changes, managing the gold and foreign currency reserves and the note and coin issue. Most controversially, in many countries they have a significant role in supervising or regulating the domestic financial sector and in vetting proposals for structural innovation.

During the past 20 years, central banks have played a key role in implementing and supervising the liberalization of financial markets and institutions in a large number of western countries. The positive aspects of financial de-regulation are the abolition of restrictive commercial practices, the elimination of the excess profits earned by a few favoured institutions, and the increasing variety of choice offered to companies and individuals by new providers. The negative aspects include the commitment of extra financial capital to lending activities (which presumes a rapid expansion in personal and corporate borrowing), and the likelihood that bank and non-bank diversification into unfamiliar business areas will bring an increased incidence of failure. While central banks cannot be held responsible for the enthusiasm with which western governments have embraced financial de-regulation, they must surely have recognized that the task of monitoring a de-regulated credit system would become far more difficult.

Successful financial de-regulation transfers risk, responsibility and reward from government and its agencies to companies and individuals. It is vital that this package – risk, responsibility and reward – remains intact. Providers of financial services have the opportunity to expand their empires and earn higher profits, but they must accept the risk that some of their new ventures will be loss-making. Consumers gain access to a greater variety of products, many of which are cheaper than before, but they must take full responsibility for the consequences of choosing badly. However, this recent wave of de-regulation has not dispelled the notion that government will step in to safeguard any institution, whether or not its failure would threaten the stability of the financial system. Central banks' unquestioned roles as LLRs to the commercial banks and guardians of the financial system maintain an ambiguity over the ultimate responsibility for catastrophic loss, however and wherever it occurs. This ambiguity has promoted excessive risk-taking in the private sector and has fostered the very circumstances in which financial disasters have occurred before.

Indeed, the Fed has already deviated significantly from the classical LLR model described earlier. In general the Fed lends only to commercial banks rather than to all sound borrowers. It charges subsidy rates rather than penalty rates; it values collateral at current market price rather than at book value. It lends in the strictest confidence, not openly and publicly, and occasionally it has lent to banks of doubtful soundness, particularly when banks were judged 'too big to fail'. Since the equity market crash of 1987, the Fed has become increasingly alert to the danger of a collapse of the financial system. Several times since 1994 it has failed to tighten monetary conditions, or has loosened them, despite clear signals from the domestic economy of escalating inflationary risks. The pursuit of some wider objective, presumably relating to global financial stability, appears to have overridden normal policy-making on these occasions.

While the idea of the national central bank as the embodiment of monetary virtue and archaic traditions may remain firmly entrenched in the public psyche, the reality is otherwise. Central banks have been caught up in every stage of financial innovation and de-regulation of credit markets; they have ushered in an era of unprecedented financial sophistication and complexity, in which few politicians have the slightest interest or comprehension. Armed with the knowledge that earlier phases of financial de-regulation (e.g. Competition and Credit Control in the UK in 1971) had been accompanied by excessive credit growth, the central banks should have been wise to the risk of repetition. They alone could have insisted on tighter capital require-ments and stricter reporting procedures. In fact, there are three serious charges to be laid at the doors of the west's great central banks: the charges of unaccountability, of negligence and of inconsistency.

THE CHARGE OF UNACCOUNTABILITY

An inherent weakness common to most central banking systems is that their officials (and most notably their senior officials) are appointed, not elected. While central banks have a formal or an informal relationship with the elected government, the price of allowing the bank executive independence is a partial separation of power from responsibility. Governments bear ultimate responsibility for actual or perceived economic failure. If they delegate certain powers to the central bank, then they must own its mistakes as well as its triumphs. Having delegated economic power, there will always be the temptation for the government to meddle in the bank's decisions. Knowing this, central bankers learn to be quick to denounce interference from any quarter. All too easily, the jealousy with which a bank guards its constitutional powers promotes an unhealthy isolation from government and from the wider economic context. This may not be the fault of the central banks; their policy mandate may have been articulated too narrowly. Nevertheless, central bank officials frequently stand accused, with good reason, of using their influence to meet these narrowly defined inflation objectives, without regard for the economic and social consequences.

The tendency for central bank presidents and governors to be accorded celebrity status by the financial media can exacerbate the problem of unaccountability. A new central bank chief may decide to act with excessive caution until his reputation is established; but this initial period of office may coincide with an economic crisis in which leniency and flexibility of policy application are called for. This is especially true of the conduct of anti-inflation policy, where it is the politicians who must take the flak from the electorate for over-zealous policy moves. Central banks, acting individually and collectively, must bear a large slice of blame for the deflationary climate that prevails in most developed countries in the late 1990s. Like the pied piper of Hamelin, the central banks may have discovered a way to get rid of the rats (inflation), but they're quite capable of killing the children (economic growth) as well.

THE CHARGE OF NEGLIGENCE

The second charge to be laid at the door of the US Fed, the Bundesbank and the Bank of England is that of negligence in the matter of financial credit. If the obsession of governments over the past 20 years has been the defeat of inflation, the obsession of central banks has been the control of the money supply. Despite perennial disagreements over the most useful definition of the money supply, the appropriate methods for controlling the money supply, and the strength of the relationship between the money supply and other important economic variables, most central bankers recognize a distinctive role for commercial banks in the economic process. The rapid expansion of banks' balance sheets, for whatever reason, still arouses suspicion in the world of central banking, but unfortunately this usually happens after the event.

This exclusive preoccupation with the commercial banking system has resulted in a significant tightening of the regulation of banks' traditional business activities throughout the western world, a topic that will receive further attention in the next chapter. Central banks' obsession with money supply control is in stark contrast to their lax and indifferent attitude to the supply of financial credit. Yet, as John Stuart Mill remarked: 'The purchasing power of an individual at any moment is not measured by the money actually in his pocket, whether we mean by money the metals, or include bank notes. It consists, first, of the money in his possession; secondly, of the money at his bankers, and all other money due him and payable on demand; thirdly of whatever credit he happens to possess' (*Westminster Papers*, 1844).

The issue of bonds by governments and companies, business and trade credit, consumer credit, leasing credit, financial market credit (e.g. sale and repurchase facilities, stock lending) and derivative market credit are all examples of activities through which additional purchasing power can be released into the economy or the asset markets. Commercial banks have become heavily involved in some of these activities, mostly through subsidiary companies, but non-banks carry out most of this credit business. While there may be rules governing the operation of these activities and supervisory bodies that are intended to enforce them, the aggregate supply of credit is effectively unregulated. New channels of credit supply are being invented at regular intervals, and new credit providers proliferate. Central banks have turned a blind eye to the dangers of excessive credit creation.

THE CHARGE OF INCONSISTENCY

Modern central banks pride themselves on the attention that they give to financial stability, that is, the integrity of the credit and payments systems. With the operation of monetary policy and the defeat of inflation safely under lock and key, financial stability considerations have moved centre stage. The collapse of Bank of Credit and Commerce International (BCCI) and of Baring Brothers has added a particular urgency to the agenda in the UK. However, if financial stability means anything it must surely include the ongoing surveillance of the credit quality of all financial institutions. For banks' loan books, there are independent examiners who carry out inspections of the quality of these assets. Where are the inspectors for credit card companies, leasing companies, corporate bonds, and so on? Consider the following three examples of inconsistent treatment of financial transactions by the central banks.

If a government runs a budget deficit, this can be financed through a monetary transaction or through the issue of a bond. In the former case, the government expands the stock of money in the hands of the public, and in the latter it does not; instead, it offers bonds at a competitive price and exchanges them for part of the *existing* stock of money. This money is used to cover the budget deficit and is thereby returned to general circulation. A fully funded budget deficit has no direct implications for the money supply, and the central bank is unperturbed.

Similarly, a corporate borrower of good standing in the financial community may elect to issue an international bond through an investment bank, rather than borrow the funds from a commercial bank. In the latter case, both sides of the lending bank's balance sheet swell and the additional bank deposits are counted into the money supply. In the former case, the investment bank offers or places the bond with its customers in return for cash. This cash, after deduction of fees, is passed on to the issuing company. The financial institutions taking up the bonds have reduced their cash holdings and the company has increased its cash holdings. The money supply is unchanged and the central bank is happy.

Let us consider a third example. If a financial institution wishes to take deposits from the public, it needs a licence from its national central bank. These licences are granted only after a great deal of information and assurances are provided. But if the same institution, or a company, wishes to lend money or some other financial asset, then the central bank appears willing to register it without much fuss. In the UK, a potential lender is required to obtain a licence from the Office of Fair Trading, costing about $100. No professional qualifications or relevant experience are called for. The logic appears to be that the central bank has a duty to protect depositors from charlatans and fraudsters, to the extent that it will typically step in and rescue

46

even a small bank to prevent default; but it is content for suppliers of credit to make bad loans and suffer painful or even catastrophic losses to their hearts' content. If this credit supplier happens to be the subsidiary of a foreign bank, so much the better.

These three examples should suffice to show that modern central banks view the act of credit creation with near-total indifference. Provided that for every willing borrower there is a willing lender, they would argue that the impact of burgeoning credit growth is at worst neutral and at best confers a benefit to market efficiency. But there is a colossal flaw in the argument: what if the proportion of inadvisable borrowing rises as credit proliferates? What if these borrowers have misled their lenders or investors as to the riskiness of their business and cannot repay their debts when they fall due? Worse still, what if these feckless commercial and individual borrowers keep managing to exploit new sources of finance as a means of propping up their business or personal affairs? The result is a credit pyramid which is effectively unsecured against property or other income-earning economic assets and which will ultimately collapse. At this point, the central banks can be expected to become terribly interested again in the act of credit creation and in the quality of all loans, not merely bank loans.

WHY ALL CREDIT IS IMPORTANT

Almost all credit arrangements hold two properties in common: they involve fixed money values and they are legally binding agreements. It is necessary to consider the implications of these properties, beginning with the fixed money value characteristic of all ordinary debts and bonds. As observed in the last chapter, a continuous rise in average prices will wear away the purchasing power of a $1 million lump sum and the real burden of a $1 million debt, simultaneously. Conversely, a downward tendency in average prices will raise both the purchasing power of the asset and the real burden of the debt. The defeat, or at least the suppression, of price inflation during the 1980s and 1990s has significantly weakened the pace of natural attrition of debt. Liberal and confident attitudes to the assumption of huge debts by young people and unproven companies in the 1970s and early 1980s were predicated on the expectation that a fairly rapid rate of inflation, particularly of property assets, would persist. In breaking the inflationary cycle, the monetary authorities of western countries have denied the borrowers their traditional release. Indeed, such is the central banks' fear of a resurgence of inflation that real interest rates are likely to remain uncomfortably high until a new crisis arrives.

For the millions of companies and households caught up in this debt trap, the proliferation of new credit providers has appeared to offer an acceptable means of escape. Rather than confront the problems that past debts have brought, and inflation has not removed, beleaguered borrowers have been able to find additional credit on competitive terms from new lenders. These borrowers also have yet to realize that inflation is not coming back for a long time. Depending on the amount of information the new entrant to the credit market is able to discover about the borrower's existing commitments, this loan may be granted only on condition that the repayments are insured with a third party. Yet the ease with which both individuals and small companies can amass huge debts before encountering the collective disapproval of the credit industry is a wonder to behold. As long as there are new entrants to the credit industry who are desperate to build a loan book of, say, $10 million, there will always be somewhere for the insolvent household or business to turn. Eagerness to find credit customers typically exceeds diligence in assessing credit quality.

Regardless of the identity of the lender or issuer, the terms and conditions governing the payment of interest and the schedule for repayment constitute a legally binding agreement. Frequently, it is not the borrower's largest creditor who commences legal proceedings against him, but one of the smallest. The proprietors of mail order catalogues and store cards tend to be among the most litigious, despite the fact that the amounts owing are usually quite small. The initiation of legal proceedings over small debts may well trigger much bigger problems, such as the cancellation of credit lines or the foreclosure of a property loan. A deterioration in any aspect of the credit system, whether it directly involves commercial banks or not, poses a threat to the whole system. As the practices of late payment, the accumulation of interest arrears, the frequent refinancing or rescheduling of debts, and of outright default become more common and socially more acceptable, the greater the resources that must be deployed in providing for, or insuring against, such losses. Faced with such an obvious source of market inefficiency, central banks should surely have concerned themselves as to the integrity of the entire credit system, not just the traditional activities of a limited range of institutions.

GIVING IN TO 'MONEY MAGIC'

During the past 10–15 years, our venerable central banks have manifestly failed to acknowledge the threat that financial innovation and sophistication pose to economic and financial stability. For whatever reasons, they have presided over an unprecedented explosion of financial credit. With a complacency found only in those who inhabit a dream-world of analytical purity, central bank officials have applauded financial innovation as the harbinger of greater economic efficiency. They seem not to have considered the possibility that unfettered credit and capital markets might have damaging side-effects. That the quantity and the quality of credit supply should be inversely related is surely a surprise to no one; as the quantity of credit expands, access to credit is ultimately extended to those with not the slightest intention or ability to repay. Perversely, and in gross dereliction of duty, these huge central banks have retained their monopoly in money creation but have sanctioned a free-for-all in credit creation. Vera Smith expressed the dangers as follows: 'Such pleas as are occasionally made in our day for free trade in banking come from sources which do not commend them. They are the product of theories of "money magic". Their demand for free banking is based on the notion that it would provide practically unlimited supplies of credit and they ascribe all industrial and social evils to deficiencies of banking caused by bank monopoly' (*The Rationale of Central Banking*, 1935).

The charge to be answered by the central banks of the late 1990s is whether the financial sophistication that they have embraced so readily over the past two decades is none other than the 'money magic' identified by Vera Smith. The bank monopoly over the issue of notes and coin and over the granting of commercial banking licences is intact, but largely irrelevant. In all other respects they have allowed 'practically unlimited supplies of credit' to permeate our modern western economies.

SPECIALISTS IN CRISIS MANAGEMENT

One of the decisive arguments in favour of a centralized banking system over the 'free banking' alternative in the nineteenth century was the superior ability of a central bank to mitigate the difficulties of a banking or financial crisis. On the premiss that financial crises will occur periodically under any system, a central bank is uniquely placed to devise a strategy aimed at minimizing disruption and panic. In a competitive banking system with no dominant bank, all banks are forced to scale back their lending in a crisis as depositors seek to convert their deposits into gold; no bank would dare expand its note issue under these circumstances. However, a central bank which enjoys a high degree of public confidence can act as the LLR to all the private banks, averting a general collapse and quickly restoring confidence. A central bank can increase its note issue in circulation at a time of crisis, since citizens are willing to accept its currency; this would hardly be the case in a situation where there were many different bank notes in issue, some of which may have been rendered worthless by the crisis. The existence of many different types of small-denomination notes, some valuable and some not, was a frequent cause of panic among the less-educated members of society in the days before centralized banking.

Charles Kindleberger, in his classic book *Manias, Panics and Crashes*, describes the financial crisis as a hardy perennial. Rejecting the notion that modern economic man has outgrown the irrational behaviour that precipitated past crises, Kindleberger's encyclopaedic historical study supplies a powerful warning against complacency. While today's central banks may be trusted to deal with an old-fashioned banking failure or even to cope with the demands of fighting an expensive war, how prepared are they for a deflation of prices or a stock market meltdown? One of the popular fallacies in circulation is that greater financial sophistication has lowered the risks of investing for individuals. Why should this be so? Because the west's powerful central banks are presumed to be able to step in to prevent a crisis.

This is a bold assumption and, most probably, a foolhardy one. Today's central banks have more experience in dealing with emergencies and much greater technical expertise than 50 years ago; but the sheer variety of shocks that could instigate a stock market crash would probably deny any hope of forestalling a crisis. The innovations and complexities of financial market instruments, the interconnections between key financial markets and the banking system, and the lightning speed with which shocks are transmitted may prevent any pre-emptive action by the central banks. In all probability, the best they could manage would be a structured and co-ordinated post-crisis response.

CONCLUSION

Today's fairy tale is that of the big friendly giant, Roald Dahl's BFG, who watches over the financial system with a benevolent eye, a long arm and a deep pocket. No central bank can fulfil this role with competence or consistency. During the past 20 years the reputation of central banks has expanded far beyond their true stature and accomplishments. The heads of the most prestigious banks have been placed on lofty pedestals, from which descent can only be abrupt and painful. Paul Volcker, a worthy candidate for the epithet of giant, left while the going was good. Alan Greenspan, while highly regarded in financial circles in 1998, must live in daily dread of the global financial catastrophe that will shatter his reputation.

Contrast two quotes from the current chairman of the Federal Reserve Board:

The excess credit which the Fed pumped into the economy spilled over into the stock market – triggering a fantastic speculative boom. Belatedly, Federal Reserve officials attempted to sop up the excess reserves and finally succeeded in braking the boom. But it was too late: by 1929, the speculative imbalances had become so overwhelming that the attempt precipitated a sharp retrenching and consequent demoralizing of business confidence (A. Greenspan, *The Objectivist*, 1966).

Why should the central bank be concerned about the possibility that financial markets may be over-estimating returns or mis-pricing risk? It is not that we have a firm view that equity prices are necessarily excessive right now or risk spreads patently too low ... Rather, the FOMC [Federal Open Market Committee] has to be sensitive to indications of even slowly building imbalances, whatever their source, that, by fostering the emergence of inflationary pressures, would ultimately threaten healthy economic expansion (A. Greenspan, *Testimony to US Congress*, 26 February 1997).

The later chapters of this book consider the circumstances in which the world's central banks will become fully occupied by crisis management. There is little doubt that they will respond magnificently to the challenge, drawing widespread admiration and relief from the general public; but their failure to alert their respective governments to the dangers of excessive credit creation is an overwhelming indictment of central bank complacency.

4

Banks Reproved and Re-invented

'A "sound" banker, alas!, is not one who foresees danger and avoids it, but one who, when he is ruined, is ruined in a conventional way along with his fellows, so that no one can really blame him.'
John Maynard Keynes, *Consequences to the Banks of a Collapse in Money Values*, 1931

'For a given banking system at a given time, monetary means of payment may be expanded not only within the existing system of banks, but also by the formation of new banks, the development of new credit instruments, and the expansion of personal credit outside of banks.'
Charles P. Kindleberger, *Manias, Panics and Crashes*, 1978

For long intervals of time since the seventeenth century, commercial banks have operated simply, effectively and prudently. They have offered loans to individuals and businesses at affordable rates of interest, safeguarded their depositors, borne the occasional burden of fraud and unavoidable disaster with patience and understanding, and enabled access to the most basic of financial services to the adult population of most of the developed world. Commercial banks have enjoyed a privileged relationship with their national central banks, and this has enabled them to maintain competitive advantages over other financial institutions. Above all, banks are still the foremost repositories of trust in financial matters for the majority of citizens. In the eyes of the general public, the safety and respectability of the remote central bank is readily imputed to the local commercial banks.

THE HERITAGE OF COMMERCIAL BANKS

Privately owned and operated commercial banks comfortably pre-date the central banks. Deposit banking existed in ancient times, as evidenced by the reference in St Matthew's gospel (25: 27). The issue of circulating notes, otherwise known as fiat or paper money, by banks began around the year AD 1000 in China and in the seventeenth century in Europe and Japan. The attractions of banks to their earliest customers were, first and foremost, the security of their deposits and, secondly, the opportunity to earn interest without effort. Banks discovered that only a fraction of the deposits entrusted to them were withdrawn on any given day, allowing a large proportion to be lent out to various individuals deemed to be creditworthy. In the early days of banking, it would have been unthinkable for a bank's management to lend to someone whom they did not know at first hand.

The vulnerability of individual banks finds its origin in the primary function of commercial banking, that is, to accept deposits and to issue promises to repay that circulate as substitutes for notes and coin. As long as depositors are confident that their deposits could be redeemed if they so desired, the bank is free to hold reserves of notes and coin which represent only a fraction of their total liabilities. Fractional reserve banking enables banks to collect a rent, known as seigniorage, which arises from the privilege of creating liabilities (e.g. loans) which are accepted by the general public as money. Banks have the distinctive ability to issue money.

The fundamental weakness in this arrangement lies in two necessary risks that banks must take. One is to borrow from depositors who want the facility to take their money back at short notice, while lending to businessmen and others who are engaged in longer-term ventures. In other words, the maturity of banks' assets (loans) is likely to be much longer than their liabilities (deposits). The second risk is that the bank commits too large a proportion of its assets to investments that cannot be sold at a moment's notice or to loans that cannot be readily recalled. If depositors suddenly want to redeem a large quantity of deposits for cash, then the bank could find its reserves exhausted. This is known as a liquidity problem; its assets are too illiquid in relation to its liabilities. John Presley and Paul Mills have summarized the classic predicament of a bank as follows: 'Hence, the combination of fractional reserves, illiquid assets and nominally-guaranteed deposits makes any bank vulnerable to collapse, no matter how prudent. Its continued operation depends upon depositor confidence. It is difficult to conceive of a less logical basis on which to run an economy's transaction system' (*Islamic Banking: Theory and Practice*, forthcoming).

The traditional image of commercial banking in society is necessarily unexciting and conservative. Banks suffer the perennial criticisms of being stuffy and hierarchical, and of charging excessively for their services. Yet these rebukes are mild in comparison with the ferocious attacks which are made when banks venture into the unknown or the should-know-better, suffering heavy losses in the process. Banks' shareholders tire of the regular issues of share capital required to replace that which has been lost, and their solvent borrowers resent paying higher interest rates because of others' failures.

For most of the era following the Second World War, private commercial banks in North America and Western Europe were either discouraged by practical obstacles or forbidden in law from undertaking certain kinds of business, specifically trading in securities. In return, banks enjoyed privileged status within the financial systems of these regions. The central bank stood ready to act as an emergency source of funds in the event of a bank crisis; it insured the deposits of the banking system (up to some limit), and this allowed the banks, in turn, to offer deposit insurance to their customers. Banks enjoyed exclusive use of the interbank markets, which offer daily clearing facilities between banks and the freedom to borrow or lend reserve balances held at the central bank. Non-banks were precluded from the interbank markets and prohibited from taking deposits from the public. During the 1980s and 1990s, a wave of financial de-regulation has widened the scope of banks' activities at the expense of some of their privileges. In many countries, the cosy relationships that existed between a handful of large banks have been replaced by a more competitive arrangement.

As their traditional activities have been opened up to greater competition, commercial banks in North America and Europe have been coerced and tempted away from their areas of proven expertise and strength to an unprecedented degree, risking their capital and their reputations. While their mainstream domestic activities are now more tightly regulated, under standards agreed by national central banks in co-operation with the Bank for International Settlements in Basle, banks' financial subsidiaries are relatively free from regulation. The de-regulation or liberalization of Anglo-Saxon banking systems has paved the way for commercial banks to spread their wings into insurance, real estate, collective investment funds and securities; for mutual insurance companies and savings banks to convert to private banks; for non-banks to open banking subsidiaries and execute banking and insurance business and many other freedoms. The character of the typical commercial bank has been transformed within a generation.

A by-product of financial de-regulation has been the proliferation of companies granting trade and consumer credit and of the available forms of credit offered to the public, such as leasing, part-ownership, mail order, unsolicited encashable loan cheques and so on. Anglo-Saxon banks suffered painful losses on credit card and consumer loan business in the late 1980s and early 1990s, leading them to tighten up on creditworthiness criteria. However, after watching the arrival of non-banks (most with no experience of non-performing debt) promoting their own credit cards, the banks were soon back in the fray, seeking to restore their market share. Increasing competition from non-banks in their core markets has encouraged the banks to embrace opportunities for financial innovation and to expand their unregulated or self-regulated off-balance sheet activities. Activities which are transferred off the balance sheet have the merit of falling outside the scope of the capital adequacy requirements by which all commercial banks are bound. Keener competition has also spawned a rash of mega-mergers in the US banking industry, most notably that of Citicorp and Travelers Group in April 1998.

BANKS REPROVED

American, British and some other European banks suffered heavy capital losses in the first half of the 1980s as a result of their exposure to sovereign lending in developing countries, especially Latin America. In theory, these loans were secured against the export earnings and foreign exchange reserves of the various nations, such as Brazil, Argentina, Mexico, Chile, Venezuela and Peru. Moreover, the principle of providing populous areas of Latin America with development capital, in the expectation that new industrial and commercial activities would ultimately yield a stream of profits, was a sound one. Unfortunately, vast commitments of foreign bank lending arrived long before these countries had taken action to stabilize their own banking systems. Instead of promoting development, a large fraction of the borrowed funds was swallowed up by higher oil prices, squandered in irrelevant government schemes or expropriated by corrupt officials. Even today, much of this sovereign debt stands at a substantial discount to its issued value in the secondary debt market, or it has been converted into Brady bonds (see page 165). If there was a consolation for the western banks, it was the commonality of their misfortune, echoing Keynes's observation many years earlier. At least, their competitors were hurting just as much as themselves.

Stung by the capital losses from inadvisable sovereign lending to unfamiliar countries, western commercial banks were keen to find new sources of profitable revenues with which to hide their embarrassment. They were particularly attracted by the comparative safety of their domestic personal loan markets and the opportunities to develop access to loans among a larger percentage of adults. However, forgetting the lessons of the 1970s, the banks also lent aggressively to small businesses and for commercial property development. Over the five years of rehabilitation, 1990–94 inclusive, Norwegian banks were forced to make loan loss provisions equivalent to 11.0 per cent of their average balance sheet value. The commercial banks of Iceland (9.5 per cent), Denmark (7.2 per cent) and Sweden (6.7 per cent) completed the unhappy quartet in Scandinavia, while those of the UK (4.7 per cent), Switzerland (4.6 per cent), Spain (4.4 per cent), Australia

(4.0 per cent), the USA (3.5 per cent) and Italy (3.4 per cent) also sustained moderately heavy damage. The banking systems least affected were in the Netherlands, where only 1.2 per cent of the balance sheet was set aside as provisions against loan losses, France (2.2 per cent) and Germany (2.9 per cent).

To have maintained an accurate case-by-case approach to the assessment of creditworthiness during this phenomenal phase of loan demand would have required the employment of thousands of extra bank staff, and would have slowed down the development of the business. Fearful of losing customers to rival banks, a critical assessment of an individual's ability to service a loan was quickly replaced by an emphasis on the value of the security against which a loan was made. The universal dependence on domestic and commercial property as loan collateral led to an exaggeration of the demand for property itself, a demand which could not readily be met through new house and commercial property construction. Demand outstripped supply as speculators, builders and others registered their interest in making a quick profit from property dealing. Without exception, in countries which allowed banks and saving institutions to expand their balance sheets on the strength of rising property prices, there followed a spectacular boom.

ANATOMY OF A PROPERTY SPECULATION

Fire prevention officers often refer to the fire triangle, fuel, oxygen and heat, which are the essential ingredients of every fire. The 'fire triangle' for property speculation consists of access to bank credit, optimism regarding future property prices and rapid market turnover. If bank credit is restricted by a lack of qualified applicants or its demand is stifled by high interest rates, then property prices will remain subdued. If business proprietors and potential homeowners lack confidence for any reason (e.g. the level of taxation, fear of political change, etc.), then they will spurn property as an investment. If the fixed costs of purchasing, selling and property removal are discouragingly high, or if there is a large gulf between sellers' expectations and buyers' purchasing power, then market turnover will be weak. Weak turnover dissuades speculative activity and restrains property prices. Only if all three elements are present will the scope for property speculation arise.

The most effective way to stop a fire is usually to deprive it of oxygen; removing the fuel source and/or lowering the temperature are normally more difficult options. In extreme cases, such as fires on oil wells, explosives are used to cut off the oxygen supply. This metaphor holds good for property booms as well. Like explosives, a sudden hike in interest rates can snuff out market optimism and price hysteria in an instant. One of the main channels through which speculation is brought to an end is through the damage inflicted on banks' profits. It is important to realize that *gradual* rises in interest rates during a property speculation are frequently ineffective. As long as property is appreciating in value at a faster annual pace than the interest rate paid by the borrower, the fire will keep burning. Only sudden rate increases inject sufficient fear into the market to challenge the predominance of greed.

Traders in property are the first to react to a rate hike, because they tend to be highly geared. Even a small increase in interest rates may be sufficient to jeopardize their hopes of a reasonable dealing profit. In their haste to beat a retreat from the market, they help to establish lower price benchmarks for property. As word spreads through the media, further waves of selling occur and the process of unwinding property speculation has begun. Once the blaze has been extinguished, the temperature drops; in the case of property, it is the pace of transactions which slackens. In some instances, the pace of transactions falls dramatically such that most of the remaining deals are forced by the particular circumstances of the seller. Property prices may then stabilize close to their peak, but with little market activity. This phase gives way to a more substantial fall in prices, to a level where realistic transactions can take place. The ashes of one speculation must be raked off before a new one can begin.

By the time property prices have retraced a substantial portion of their earlier ascent, the lenders will have become aware of their folly. A rising proportion of their loans will turn bad, with borrowers falling into arrears or outright default. Lenders are faced with the difficult decision of when to foreclose the loan and take possession of the property. Ultimately, banks are forced to commit considerable resources to a case-by-case examination of their non-performing loans. In stark contrast to the emphasis on loan collateral which prevailed during the speculative phase, lenders are obliged to re-focus on the individual circumstances of the borrower.

The Anglo-Saxon property boom of 1985–9, and its subsequent bust, had immense significance for commercial and savings banks. While the banks were writing off debt, making provisions for bad loans and generally sorting out the mess, they were unable to prevent companies turning to the capital markets for a better deal. In the low interest rate environment of the early 1990s, banks would normally have been growing strongly; instead, they were licking their wounds, widening their profit margins and rebuilding their capital. Moreover, the lack of demand for domestic housing loans meant that low interest rates failed to revive consumer demand to the usual degree. Governments compensated for weakness in consumer spending by increased expenditure on transfer payments (benefits and pensions) which was not matched by increased taxation. In essence, government borrowing in the bond market replaced consumer borrowing from the banks. During the space of only seven or eight years, banks lost their dominant position as the providers of finance both to businesses and to households.

BANKS RE-INVENTED

The closing years of the twentieth century have witnessed a rearguard action by the commercial banks. Having rebuilt their capital reserves and greatly reduced their expense ratios in the early 1990s, banks have also altered their corporate focus. Through mergers and acquisitions, and through the commitment of huge internal funds to technology and communications, banks have established themselves as key players in the global capital and instalment credit markets of North America and Western Europe. Retail banking operations are no longer the kernel of the commercial banks, but merely one division among several. In practical terms, the financial structure of today's banks is little different from many non-bank corporations. In turn, large firms such as General Electric of the USA and Great Universal Stores in the UK have come to resemble banks through the development of their financial operations.

The critical insight into today's banks is that they no longer have time for relationships with the majority of their customers. A two-tier system is developing in which most retail banking transactions have been reduced to commodity status. A residual human presence is maintained in bank branches, but banks would much prefer that customers transacted their business over the telephone, via a computer or using an automatic telling machine (ATM). On the whole, bank staff are no more interested in the details of your standing orders than is a greengrocer in your selection of vegetables. However, alongside commodity banking (which is now subject to increasing competition) there is bespoke banking, in which the customer needs advice. Anything that is likely to lead to the generation of new business, the payment of a fee or a commission commands a superior level of service.

Remote banking, whether carried out over the telephone or using a computer link, represents a welcome facility for busy people who find it inconvenient to visit a bank during the business day. But it is inevitable that the growth of remote banking will prompt many thousands of local branch closures in the years ahead. The USA with 9,000 commercial banks and 67,000 branches (excluding ATMs) at the end of 1997 is ripe for this particular revolution. The loss of direct contact between banks and their loan customers, except after a problem has already occurred, is not without significance. As the assessment of creditworthiness becomes more and more automated, using standard credit-scoring schemes and cross-referencing databases of loan delinquents and court judgements for non-payment of debts, the credit system assumes a life of its own. Opportunities to exercise professional judgement and to have eye-to-eye contact are lost. Prospective loan applicants soon learn to conceal information that will count against them in a credit-scoring exercise; how much harder it is to dissemble, face to face.

In a business context, there is no substitute for the local and industrial knowledge held by the banks in that region. On the basis of sensible assumptions about revenues and costs, ten loan applications by different people could all merit acceptance on an abstract credit assessment system; but what if all ten intend to exploit the same, limited, business opportunity in the same locality? Such anomalies often go unspotted by computers, but a network of individuals with expertise and experience can cross-reference information more flexibly. A bank that is hell-bent on credit expansion will always find willing customers; however, it is a great shame that the massed ranks of loan officers who made the collective blunders of the 1980s are not still at their posts, vowing never to let it happen again.

THE CRITICAL IMPORTANCE OF BANKS TO THE MODERN INFLATIONARY PROCESS

In Chapter 2 it was noted that the war waged against inflation by western governments has not led to a common understanding of the inflationary process, nor to an agreed method of inflation control. The world of economics remains divided into two broad schools of thought as far as inflation is concerned. One gives prominence, even primacy, to the role of prior growth in some definition of the money supply; the other ascribes the leading role to the conflicting claims of distinct groups within the economy over real resources. These may be conflicts between the public and private sectors, between shareholders and employees, or between other sectarian interests. In the deterministic models of inflation, there is a clear supposition that if monetary aggregates had risen more or less rapidly, then the inflationary outcomes would have been predictably different. The logical policy prescription which flows from this is the importance of control over the growth of the money supply. By contrast, the behavioural school of thought is concerned to build economic and social structures and institutions which will defuse the conflicts that are believed to precipitate bouts of inflation. Adherents to this school generally view money supply growth as a safety valve which permits the temporary resolution of conflict, for example, by funding an expansion of public sector employment. As such, they see no purpose in targeting the growth of the money supply, since they would deny that the government is in any position to secure an appropriate degree of monetary restraint.

Roger Bootle has sought to combine a deterministic view of very high inflation rates with a more eclectic and behavioural view of the lower range of inflation rates commonly experienced in mature developed economies: 'There is, however, one very general, all-embracing framework which has some appeal – inflation is caused by the struggle between different groups within society over their share of national income' (*The Death of Inflation*, 1996). Bootle's thesis interprets inflation in a historical and institutional context, arguing that a combination of weak government and bad times invariably produces inflation, through the abandonment of self-restraint. That this was true long before the commercial banks were born or paper money played a significant role does not necessarily contradict the monetary explanation of the modern inflation process. However, Bootle's thesis would appear to rule out the possibility that a burst of monetary growth with technical or political origins could independently raise the inflation rate, in the absence of a struggle between wages and profits or between the public and private sectors. This is a notion contrary to the author's convictions and is seemingly disproved by many recent examples of UK monetary errors, from Lord Barber in the early 1970s to Lord Lawson in the mid-1980s. Furthermore, there was no shortage of industrial conflict in 1984, the year of the last coal miners' strike, and yet inflation remained steady for the following three years.

In low-inflation Germany, where pay bargaining is still highly centralized and government decision-making relies on cross-party consensus, there may appear to be better support for behavioural models of the inflationary process, but this is not how the Bundesbank sees it. Among the few politically independent central banks, the Bundesbank has one of most rigid, formulaic understandings of the relationship between the pace of monetary growth and subsequent inflationary pressure. Moreover, the increase in consumer price inflation to 4.7 per cent in 1992 is more readily explained by the monetary shock associated with German unification in the previous year than by an appeal to militant wage demands from the east.

THE IMPORTANCE OF HAVING A
MONETARY FRAMEWORK

While accepting many of Roger Bootle's warnings against adopting a dogmatic and mechanistic approach to the causes of inflation, it is important to establish a clear framework in which to interpret events, otherwise the temptation is to seek a new explanation or excuse for every unexpected inflationary outcome. The deterministic monetary model of inflation suffers from many conceptual difficulties, but it does offer a coherent framework. If we are ever to find our way through the mist, then we must identify some landmarks and make some critical distinctions.

'In order to avoid confusion, it should be emphasized that inflation is a monetary, not a credit phenomenon. If there is a boom in bank lending, the important feature is not the provision of credit but the consequence for the money supply of credit being provided in a particular way' (Gordon Pepper, *Money, Credit and Inflation*, 1991). To explore the monetary explanation of inflation, it is necessary to define what is meant by the money supply. By definition, the money supply (on its broad measure) is made up of private sector bank deposits plus notes and coin in general circulation. The largest element of the stock of bank deposits is held by households, trusts and small businesses, which are sometimes grouped together as the personal sector. Bank deposits by companies and other domestic financial institutions are also counted in to the money supply. Private sector deposits in local currency represent the lion's share of the liabilities of the commercial banking sector. Their other liabilities are the deposits of the public and overseas sectors in sterling, all foreign currency deposits, liabilities in connection with their shareholders and any other capital market borrowings. For most practical purposes, the rapid growth of banks' balance sheets is synonymous with the rapid growth of the money supply.

THE PRACTICAL DIFFICULTIES OF
CONTROLLING THE MONEY SUPPLY

Despite a wealth of empirical evidence published by Milton Friedman and Anna Schwartz, among others, not everyone accepts that there need be any connection between the growth of the broad money supply and subsequent price inflation (either of assets or of goods, or both). If you happen to hold this opinion, please bear with the author for the time being. For those who do accept the desirability of money supply control as a means of pursuing an inflation objective, there are two alternative approaches to the task. In the first approach, control is attempted through variations in the price of money; in the second, through variations in its quantity.

The first approach is to control the growth of the money stock by influencing indirectly the demand for deposits and cash by the private sector. This is achieved by varying interest rates so as to keep the demand for bank deposits in line with the central bank's target growth rate for the money stock. When the growth of demand is too rapid, then interest rates need to be raised, and vice versa. While this approach sounds straightforward, the many governments that have adopted it have encountered serious problems, to which we shall shortly return.

The second approach, the quantitative approach, is to control the supply of reserves available to the banking system. The stock of banking reserves, or the monetary base, is made up of notes and coin in general circulation plus commercial banks' deposits with the central bank. The central bank controls the issue of currency and has the right to penalize banks which exceed their permitted loan growth by requiring them to deposit additional balances at the central bank, on which they receive no interest. Banks' permitted loan growth is restrained by the stipulation of a maximum ratio between bank reserves and the total amount of bank lending. Because each bank loan is the counterpart to a bank deposit of equivalent amount, the growth of the money supply is regulated by the growth of the monetary base. Under this approach, the central bank sets the example by restricting the growth of its own balance sheet. This approach also has its drawbacks, however.

Suppose that the replacement cycle for cars and consumer durables is reaching a crescendo at exactly the same time that corporations are eager to finance additional investment and stockbuilding; they all come to their banks looking for loans. Even though these companies and consumers are all creditworthy or have good collateral for borrowing, the banks have to turn many of them away because they have a loan limit. The rationing of loans may take the form of a queue, on a first come–first served or a priority basis, or it may occur through the price mechanism. The US experiment with monetary base control in the early 1980s allowed the excess demand for loans to be rationed by price, with the result that interest rates exploded in 1981. Certificates of Deposit (CDs) offered almost 16 per cent at the peak, persuading savers to switch their wealth out of bonds and stock market investments, in the process creating all kinds of distortions in the financial system. For policy-makers, the dilemma was to reconcile the normal and justifiable expectations of access to bank finance at prevailing rates of interest with the strict control of the money supply. Needless to say, the policy of monetary base control was abandoned in the USA soon afterwards.

This salutary experience has led most western governments to adopt the alternative regime of monetary control. Unfortunately, the interest rate approach to monetary control has at least as many practical difficulties, though here we mention only two. First, there is an ambiguity of response between the demand for money for use in transactions and the demand for savings; a higher interest rate depresses transactions demand but raises savings demand. Furthermore, a rise in interest rates makes the return on deposits relatively attractive in comparison to the return on other financial assets. Depending on the relative strength of the transactions and savings effects, the total demand for money by the private sector may rise or fall. This is obviously unsatisfactory for control purposes.

Second, if the central bank makes no attempt to control the supply of reserves available to the banking system, then there is a danger that there will be no effective restraint on bank lending. In theory, bank lending is restrained by higher interest rates, by a shortage of bank capital and by the creditworthiness of borrowers. The experience of the 1980s has shown all three of these mechanisms to be deficient;

if commercial banks take a decision to expand their balance sheets aggressively, then nothing will stand in their way except some form of disaster. The availability of floating rate finance allows banks to pass on higher interest rates to their customers; if a bank is short of capital, it can borrow more from the eurobond market; and the painstaking business of determining the creditworthiness of the borrower can be circumvented by asking the borrower to provide collateral, usually in the form of a property asset. There can be little doubt that the combination of financial innovation and de-regulation has facilitated the banks' escape from any effective means of monetary control.

THE MONETARY POLICY DILEMMA

The foregoing paragraphs can be summarized quite simply. There is compelling empirical and anecdotal support for the hypothesis that monetary shocks are transmitted to the markets for goods and services primarily as price disturbances. Across many countries and many years, there is powerful evidence of a long-term relationship between changes in broad money aggregates and changes in whole economy price measures. In principle, there is a strong case for quantitative money supply control. The problem is that control has become both practically impossible and politically unacceptable. Whether using quantitative controls or pre-announced money supply targets, the commercial banks have plenty of scope to frustrate policy objectives. There is no guarantee that the desired degree of monetary restraint will be achieved. In addition, the volatility of short-term interest rates which accompanied experiments in monetary control undertaken by various governments in the 1980s would be politically unacceptable today.

Control of monetary aggregates via changes in interest rates is unsatisfactory because of the confused and contradictory response of money demands arising from varying motivations. In any case, the proprietors of monetary policy, mostly committees organized and controlled by the central banks, have far less latitude to determine short-term interest rates than is widely imagined. In practice, the financial markets' expectations embodied in the yield curve (that is, the spectrum of interest rates running from overnight credit through to 20- or 30-year bonds) set strict limits on the feasible range of policy options. The only effective constraints on the growth of the broad money aggregates are the extent to which borrowers are worried by the burden of servicing existing debts and the degree to which banks' managements are concerned about the prospective profitability of their lending. At critical junctures, changes in interest rates set by central bank policy committees can have dramatic effects on monetary behaviour, but at other times and for long intervals they may have little impact.

CONCLUSION

This chapter has sought to convey two strong messages. The first is that the hugely profitable Anglo-Saxon commercial banks which adorn the global stage today are very different in style and content from those which fell off the stage in the late 1980s, ravaged by property-related loan losses. After a rigorous process of rehabilitation, diversification and amalgamation, lasting several years, the surviving banks have emerged larger and fitter than ever in terms of traditional measures of capital strength. Today's successful banks are multi-national financial corporations with far-reaching influence and diverse interests. Their risk profiles are unrecognizable from those of the 1980s generation of domestic banks, let alone the traditional regional banks of the nineteenth century or earlier. Fees and commissions form a much bigger share of revenues than before, while traditional bank spreads are under increasing competitive pressure. Meanwhile, revenues from proprietary trading in securities and derivatives have soared into prominence.

The second message relates to the special role that bank deposits play in the financial system, regardless of all the innovations and close substitutes. Bank deposits form the bulk of the broader money supply definitions and banks still carry the day-to-day responsibility of ensuring that there is adequate liquidity circulating in the payments system. Banks still hold the potential for another bout of excessive credit creation, whether backed by the collateral of rising property values or portfolios of financial assets. In the absence of any viable system of policy control over money supply growth, banks are constrained only by their internal management objectives. Acting within the frame-work of their traditional balance sheets, banks have the latent potential to trigger a brand-new inflationary binge. Acting off-balance sheet, they have the potential to over-trade their assets and to squander shareholders' capital on an unprecedented scale. How safe are bank deposits, let alone bank shares, in this brave new world?

5

The Rise and Rise of the Financial Markets

'If one were to lead a stranger through the streets of Amsterdam and ask him where he was, he would answer, "Among speculators", for there is no corner [in the city] where one does not talk shares.'
Joseph de la Vega,
Confusión de Confusiones, 1688

During the 1980s, the bond, equity and derivatives markets of western OECD countries exploded into life. In terms of the volumes of new issues of securities, the turnover of existing bond and equity securities and the total value of bond and equity markets, the pace of expansion was breathtakingly rapid. Structural, cultural and technological transformations aided and abetted the meteoric growth of the financial markets. There was a fundamental change in the nature of securities business, from a highly regulated, tradition-bound activity at the fringes of most financial systems to one which radically altered the financial landscape. The most obvious structural changes were the abandonment of foreign exchange controls, permitting capital to flow freely across national boundaries, the de-regulation of domestic financial markets, leading to an intensification of competition, and the privatization of public enterprises. The use of sophisticated financial techniques, supported by significant changes in information technology, interacted with liberal attitudes towards the financial markets and their innovations.

In parallel with the rapid development of the bond, equity and derivatives markets, there has been the increasing involvement of professional investment institutions in the management of the developed world's private sector savings, including pension funds, insurance companies, collective investment schemes and other savings institutions. This centralization of the pool of savings has greatly increased the maximum feasible size of capital issues. Corporate borrowers can tap a global capital market for funds via an equity issue, a bond or a loan which is syndicated among many banks. Prior to the launch of a particularly large (e.g. above $500 million) issue of securities, the investment bank appointed to manage the issue will often 'build a book' in order to gauge the potential demand from investment funds at different hypothetical issue prices. Literally, this involves collecting provisional orders for stock from dozens of fund managers around the world. Armed with this information, the book-builder can reduce significantly the risk of an issue being mis-priced. Modern book-building and syndication techniques would be unworkable if these massive institutional funds did not exist. These themes are developed further in Chapter 11.

Many factors have contributed to the prodigious development of the global financial markets, but their cause has been advanced particularly by the consistent upward march of world bond and equity prices since 1982. Large new issues of bonds or shares are much easier to launch into a rising than into a falling market. By the time of the October 1987 stock market crash, international financial markets had gathered sufficient momentum for this to prove no more than a temporary setback; the abrupt losses could be understood as merely the cancellation of the previous nine months' spectacular gains. By the end of the 1980s, much of the structural transformation in the western OECD securities markets had been accomplished; but it was at just this time that a strategic opportunity for further rapid growth presented itself.

SEIZING THE MOMENT

In the early 1980s, conventional bank credit to firms and households was still the dominant form of finance in most large western economies. The majority of these loans were secured against the (rising) value of residential or commercial property, a practice which had much to commend it in more inflationary times. As discussed in the last chapter, bad debts and loan provisions ate into commercial bank profits, causing an erosion of the banks' capital reserves. Indeed, the Swedish banking system was on the brink of collapse before it was rescued by the government in 1992. Whereas the banks' fortunes were inextricably linked to those of the residential and commercial property markets, links between real estate and the financial markets were tenuous. The banks' ability and willingness to lend were compromised at precisely the moment when many large borrowers in the public and private sectors were eager to take advantage of falling interest rates. Within a short period beginning in the late 1980s, multinational companies gained equivalent credit quality rankings to the ailing commercial and savings banks, thus enabling them to borrow as cheaply on their own account in the capital markets as from the banks.

In the USA, the problems of the large banks in the wake of the property market bust were compounded by the failure of so many Savings and Loans institutions in the mid-1980s. These developments proved influential in setting the USA on the road to easy credit and cheap money. The discount rate halved from 7 per cent at the end of 1989 to 3.5 per cent two years later. It did not take long for falling American interest rates to usher in a regime of low short-term rates in a number of other large countries. If ever an adolescent market needed a strategic opportunity to reach maturity, this was it. Under ideal conditions, the bond and equity markets flourished, while traditional bank loan business languished. As Figure 5.1 demonstrates, capital markets quickly replaced conventional bank lending as the main source of new finance for US firms, while banks also lost the initiative to finance companies and credit card companies in the lucrative personal lending market. These habits were quickly copied throughout the Anglo-Saxon world.

National and international financial markets came of age in the 1990s. Figure 5.2 gives a summary of the composition of the world's major financial markets at the end of 1995. Equity market capitalization of $13 trillion represented just under 40 per cent of a $33.5 trillion aggregate. The global bond market swelled in size, from $2 trillion in 1980 to $12 trillion in 1990, to over $20 trillion in 1995 and around $25 trillion in 1998. At end-1995, roughly two-fifths of these

Figure 5.1 Proportion of corporate credit supplied by US commercial banks (%)

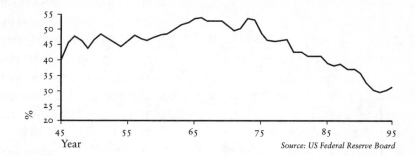

Source: US Federal Reserve Board

bonds had originally been issued to cover government budget deficits in developed countries. Other public sector bond issues account for another fifth of the total. The remainder is made up of domestic corporate and financial issues and by international issuers in a foreign currency. Capital issues by developing countries on the international markets amounted to an estimated 2 per cent of the bond market total.

CAPITAL AND SAVINGS MARKETS

In the developed countries of Western Europe and North America, almost every household is engaged in two activities: saving and borrowing. There are many different ways to save and to borrow, but somehow these two activities must be reconciled. In a simple example, this reconciliation could occur within a closed community with its own savings bank. On a larger scale, it could occur within a national economy with strict laws prohibiting capital from flowing in or out of the country. Finally, this matching of the sources (savings) and uses (borrowing) of funds can occur within a system of freely flowing international capital. Clearly, when we speak of the capital market, or even of the global capital market, we are not referring to a physical location but to a complex network of invisible electronic transfers.

The capital market is where the financial savings of millions of

Figure 5.2 Structure of world financial markets at end-1995 values and exchange rates

	Bonds ($ billions)							Equities	Total bonds & equities	
	Central government	Government agency or guarantee	State & local government	Corporate (inc. convertibles)	Other domestic	International	Total	Total ($ billions)	$ billions	% share
USA	2546	2406	1030	1742	283	830	8837	5367	14204	42.5
Japan	2003	210	99	405	745	346	3808	3472	7280	21.8
Germany	727	67	85	2	1121	281	2283	465	2748	8.2
UK	361	0	0	30	0	150	541	1292	1833	5.5
France	490	235	3	154	0	142	1024	433	1457	4.4
Italy	859	19	0	4	143	59	1084	197	1281	3.8
Canada	183	0	108	54	1	78	424	307	731	2.2
Netherlands	194	0	3	91	0	65	353	317	670	2.0
Switzerland	29	0	23	37	77	114	280	382	662	2.0
Belgium	226	7	0	18	125	36	412	92	504	1.5
Sweden	112	0	1	9	128	4	254	143	397	1.2
Spain	161	0	12	19	15	12	219	144	363	1.1
Denmark	107	0	0	0	179	6	292	48	340	1.0
Australia	68	25	0	10	0	30	133	201	334	1.0
Austria	54	2	0	5	68	3	132	26	158	0.5
Finland	33	0	2	6	13	1	55	40	95	0.3
Norway	19	3	7	3	17	1	50	37	87	0.3
Greece	41	0	0	0	0	2	43	11	54	0.2
Ireland	24	1	0	1	0	1	27	24	51	0.2
New Zealand	13	1	0	2	0	2	18	28	46	0.1
Ecu bonds	73	0	0	0	0	91	164		164	0.5
Major market totals	8323	2976	1373	2592	2915	2254	20433	13026	33459	100.0
% share	24.9	8.9	4.1	7.7	8.7	6.7	61.1	38.9		100.0

households and the undistributed income of millions of businesses are married up with requests to borrow by governments, government agencies and large industrial corporations and financial institutions. This matching process has become more and more diversified over the past 20 years, to the point where individuals can acquire specific exposure to Asian smaller companies, Japanese companies, US multi-media companies, domestic or foreign money markets, domestic or international bonds, and many more specific categories of investment. Alternatively, they can hand over their savings to a managed fund which attempts to secure a good return from a portfolio of financial investments, thereby spreading the risk. While the extension of consumer choice is to be welcomed, human nature is attracted to investment categories with the highest historic returns (and risks).

Before delving any deeper into the detailed workings of the capital markets, it is necessary to establish one fundamental principle. The households and charitable trusts which make up the personal sector ultimately own everything. Companies, banks, pension funds and other institutions are legal fictions; they exist as conveniences of modern life and as book-keeping entries. In the final analysis, they neither own anything nor owe anything; their net assets or net liabilities are owned by people. Likewise, government is an agent of collective ownership; it operates on behalf of individuals. Its authority to borrow is underwritten, partly by the assets on its balance sheet, but principally by its right to levy taxes on people. The burden of taxation may fall on companies in the first instance, but it is individuals who will pay them eventually. Once again, the government has no wealth of its own. It is a transfer mechanism in the financial system.

ILLUSTRATION OF A NATIONAL CAPITAL MARKET: THE UK

In order to gain a better understanding of the workings of a modern capital market, it is helpful to look at a practical example. Two key concepts lie at the heart of a national capital market: the stock of physical capital (including net ownership of foreign assets) and the net worth of the personal sector. The stock of physical capital is a

---

vital ingredient in the generation of the profits and rents to which the stock of financial assets lays claim. Figure 5.3 illustrates the composition of these two aggregates for the UK at mid-1997. Listed on the left-hand side is an inventory of fixed capital assets, net of depreciation and valued at current replacement cost. The list comprises dwellings, factories, shops, offices, hospitals, schools, roads, vehicles, ships, aircraft, industrial plant and equipment, and all other fixed assets. At the bottom of the list is an estimate of the total value of fixed assets. To repeat, these assets are ultimately owned by UK residents.

On the right-hand side there is a list of the net worth of the domestic private sector distributed among property and other tangible assets, cash and deposits, equities and government bonds. Some of these assets are owned by individuals directly and some indirectly through life assurance, pension and other investment funds. For convenience, all financial liabilities have been treated as if they were loans secured against fixed assets and therefore deducted from their market values. When the two wealth stocks are compared, it is clear that the market value of the financial claims of the personal sector greatly exceeds the replacement cost of the net capital stock.

The full significance of this imbalance will become clearer in later chapters, but for the time being it is important to notice that these two stocks are revalued in different ways. The stock of fixed assets is determined by the pace of net fixed investment and by movements in the prices of capital assets. For buildings, this will be the cost of building materials and labour, not the market prices of houses or offices. In contrast, the net wealth of the personal sector is determined by the net addition to savings and by movements in the market values of property, equities and bonds. There is no practical reason why the value of financial claims on the stock of tangible assets must be equal to the replacement value of these assets.

In the lower part of Figure 5.3, the links are drawn between the markets for capital goods, steel, building materials and other capital items on the left-hand side and the markets for houses, commercial property, sterling deposits, domestic equities and bonds on the right-hand side. Beneath these primary financial markets are the derived markets for futures, options, forwards and swaps. The scope for variation in the valuation of private sector net worth is clearly much

Figure 5.3 Estimated values of UK fixed capital and personal wealth at end-June 1997

Net capital stock

	£bn
Vehicles, ships and aircraft	64
Plant and machinery	477
of which industrial and commercial companies	388
Dwellings	754
of which owner-occupied	612
Factories, shops and offices	436
Government buildings, hospitals, schools, etc.	290
Total	2021

Private sector net worth

	£bn
Direct ownership of:	
Tangible assets *minus* loans	805
Equities	410
Government bonds	69
Sterling liquidity	468
Total directly owned	1752
Indirect ownership of:	
Tangible assets	95
Equities	764
Government bonds	286
Sterling liquidity	115
Other assets	42
Total indirectly owned	1302
Total	3054

Capital goods price index

House building cost index

Other construction cost index

Producer price of transport goods

Property asset returns index

Company securities returns index

Government securities returns index

Sterling liquidity returns index

Sources: ONS National Accounts Blue Book and Financial Statistics

larger than for the valuation of the net stock of fixed capital. In times of apparent prosperity and high investor confidence, the scope to issue fresh securities, or to attach higher valuations to existing ones, is virtually unlimited. However, even at these times it is extremely difficult to increase the physical stock of capital by more than a tiny fraction from one year to the next, particularly since it is continually ageing and depreciating in value. By contrast, equities and bank deposits never wear out. This distinction is extremely important.

RETURNS TO PHYSICAL AND FINANCIAL CAPITAL

While it is quite usual, even desirable, for there to be a small margin of spare capacity, most of the economy's stock of physical capital, comprising buildings, vehicles, plant and equipment, will be busy earning income for its proprietors under normal circumstances. Property will earn a rent; fixed plant, such as an assembly line, will earn profits; equipment and vehicles will earn an implicit hire charge, as they are all used to good advantage. A typical average annual rate of return on the capital stock of the business sector in OECD countries in the late 1990s is 16 per cent, up from 12 per cent at the 1982 recession low. This pattern is consistent with a gradual rise in the share of business profits in national income. Among the larger western economies, the range runs from almost 20 per cent in Canada, 18.7 per cent in the USA and 18 per cent in the Netherlands, down to 15.4 per cent in France, 15.1 per cent in Germany, 14.7 per cent in Italy and 13.3 per cent in the UK. Most western countries have experienced a modest improvement in capital returns during the 1990s, in stark contrast to Japan, where they have fallen in almost every year since 1990.

However, these rates of return on the physical capital stock have been easily outstripped by the rates of return on financial capital employed. The stock of financial capital consists of called-up share capital plus retained profits from previous years plus any other reserves. In the most straightforward example, a firm's financial capital resources would be identical to the replacement value of its physical assets. In this case, the rates of return on financial and physical capital would be equal. In practice, there are numerous accounting devices connected to take-over activities, exceptional charges and taxation which regularly allow firms to declare much higher rates of return on financial capital employed than on physical capital employed. Rather than a typical 16 per cent, returns have ranged between 20 per cent and 40 per cent. The excitement caused by the announcement of such excellent returns often enhances the firm's share price, driving a thicker wedge between the market values of financial assets and the physical asset values.

SEVEN DIMENSIONS OF CAPITAL MARKETS DEVELOPMENT

Since the early 1980s, the connections between saving and borrowing activities within a region, or even within a nation, have become progressively weaker. To give an example, a typical Anglo-Saxon household in the 1960s or 1970s held most of its financial wealth in the form of commercial and savings bank deposits, with a lesser fraction held as insurance policies and pension fund entitlements. At that time, many of the banks still retained a regional bias, lending to local companies, small businesses and householders. Other types of banks specialized in home loans, again with a strong regional identity. Investment funds, depending on their kind, favoured larger or smaller proportions of bonds or equities, but these holdings were predominantly domestic. The global capital market revolution has stretched the choices of savers and borrowers in a number of directions. A total of seven distinct processes have been at work: concentration, diversification, globalization, intermediation, securitization, mobilization and sophistication. Each of these is described in turn.

1. Concentration

Since the beginning of the 1980s, the proportion of household financial wealth under the management or custody of a small number of large banks and investment funds has risen steadily in the USA, the UK and elsewhere. The increasing concentration of these industries is even more dramatic when viewed in terms of household savings flows. As far as commercial and savings banks are concerned, the consolidation of the industry was accelerated by the property-related loan losses at the end of the last decade. Through the strengthening of competitive advantage and through outright acquisition, an élite group of large banks has emerged which accounts for well over 50 per cent of all retail deposits in most western countries. The international fund management industry has also become more concentrated, assembling huge tranches of wealth in the hands of relatively few institutions. Merrill Lynch's absorption of Mercury Asset Management in 1997 raised their funds under management to more than $600 billion. Successful fund management groups have attracted additional clients, while others have chosen the acquisition route. Indeed, given the potential cost economies in global fund management, further consolidation seems inevitable.

2. Diversification

During the past 15 years, long-term savings funds have increased their holdings of overseas assets and commercial banks have undertaken a significant expansion in international lending. Commercial banks are heavily diversified in terms of lending abroad and their dealings in foreign currency. At end-1996, 43 per cent of UK banks' assets were market loans and advances to overseas residents, and 54 per cent of assets were denominated in currencies other than sterling.

While investment funds have always diversified their assets among equities, bonds, property and cash, in most countries they have maintained a strong domestic bias. The usual argument offered in support of this strategy was to match the currency of their assets to that of their liabilities, thus minimizing currency risk. A fund that held a large portfolio of foreign assets would bear the risk of adverse currency movements. However, since most pension funds were still quite immature in the early 1980s, the burden of meeting pension obligations was easily covered by the receipt of current pension contributions. Since dividend income was not required to pay pensioners or insurance policy beneficiaries, investment funds became attracted more and more to the prospect of enhancing returns by investing internationally.

The UK pensions and insurance industry is among the most heavily diversified, with around 25 per cent of its investments in overseas assets. Diversification has moved more slowly in the USA, but holdings of foreign equities and bonds have increased from $409 billion in 1991 to $1.49 trillion at end-March 1998. This represents a jump from 8.8 per cent to 14.6 per cent of US personal wealth held as insurance, pension and mutual funds or direct ownership of overseas securities.

3. Globalization

A feature of the 1990s has been the appearance (or reappearance in some cases) of large populated countries on the global investment scene. China, the former Soviet Union and India provide ready examples of countries in which portfolio investments can be made. International investment fund managers are also poring over the emerging markets of Latin America, Eastern Europe, the Middle East and Africa in search of new investment opportunities. Already there are some specialized regional funds to which retail investors can subscribe. Confronted with this exotic array of investment possibilities, it is easy for the amateur investor to lose sight of the pitfalls of regions where property rights may have only recently been established in law.

4. Intermediation

Pension, insurance and other investment funds operate as middlemen or intermediaries between households or non-profit organizations on one side and the financial markets on the other, to their mutual advantage. For a wide variety of reasons, including tax status, access to market intelligence, economies of scale, dealing costs and so on, individuals are induced to invest their savings through the funds rather than directly into the market. In return, the funds earn fees and commissions for their services. However, the obvious drawbacks for the investor are the loss of transparency and discretion over the use of the funds. Whereas it was once safe to assume that investment funds held only high-grade debt and the shares of blue-chip companies in the country of origin, the modern reality is otherwise. A large investment fund may seek exposure to some emerging market through a specialized fund; it may use derivatives to hedge its currency risk or to protect against a sharp fall in equities; it may lend stock to the market. The task of identifying what a typical pension fund beneficiary actually owns, in terms of an underlying basket of securities, has become much more difficult and sometimes impossible.

In the same way that additional layers of intermediation distance the saver from his or her investment, so lenders have become increasingly separated from their ultimate customers. The demise of regional banks, coupled with the restructuring of banking relationships described in Chapter 4, has turned bank loans and mortgages into commodities, to be bought and sold.

5. Securitization

In its more literal usage, securitization describes the process of transforming loan assets into marketable securities (usually bonds). The clearest example is when a bank wants to release some of its capital to a more profitable use. It decides to package together $100m of mortgages which are in a healthy condition and sell them to the market in the form of an investment-grade bond. As the mortgages are paid off or cancelled, the bond slowly matures. The main reason why banks wish to securitize loans is to avoid regulatory costs. As long as the mortgages are held on the bank's own balance sheet, it must commit capital reserves equal to a certain percentage of their value. If the loans are transformed into securities, then this requirement is avoided. Securitization is most common in the USA, but its use has spread to other countries. It represents a particular example of intermediation, whereby the individual saver and the ultimate borrower are unknown to each other.

6. Mobilization

From around the mid-1980s, a bandwagon has been rolling in the realm of personal savings behaviour. Despite a significant jolt from the 1987 stock market crash, households have displayed an increasing preference for performance-related investments rather than cash or deposits. In relation to the low nominal interest rates available to depositors in the 1990s, investment in various equity vehicles has become increasingly popular. Even bonds have generally yielded a higher nominal return than those on bank deposits, ushering both young and old savers into the financial markets. The young have been induced by tax incentives to channel their savings into collective investment schemes such as mutual funds and unit trusts, while the old have been ushered into higher-yielding investments as a means of sustaining their retirement lifestyles. As consumer awareness of buoyant stock market performance has increased, the commitment of current savings, and sometimes of existing wealth, has gravitated towards the higher returns.

7. Sophistication

In this context, sophistication may be defined as the willingness of the general public to enter into complex financial arrangements based on tenuous projections of future returns or costs. Financial innovations in savings and loan products have mushroomed since the mid-1980s, driven in part by improvements in technology. The marketing of financial products has steered consumers away from plain vanilla mortgages and savings accounts, on which little profit is derived, towards complex transactions on which additional commissions and fees can be earned. In the same way that shoddy building work may take several years to bear fruit in costly repairs, the sale of an inappropriate pension plan or mortgage product may not become obvious for some considerable period of time.

The cumulative effect of these seven distinct, but related, processes over the past 15 years has been to permit the development of a parallel financial system to that which commercial and savings banks offered at the start of the 1980s. The global capital market allows a loan to be originated in Manila, funded in Spain, serviced in New York and held in the portfolio of a Swedish pension fund. For this reason, the consequences of loan default, of fraud or of incompetence can have unexpectedly far-reaching effects. Relatively free from the clutches of the regulator, the financial markets enjoy a liberty much envied by the money markets.

IMPERFECTIONS OF CAPITAL MARKETS

One of the problems of any capital market, even in the example of the self-contained community, is that of unequal access to information. Some savers might accept a low rate of bank interest, or even a zero return, out of ignorance that better returns could be obtained elsewhere. In a competitive capital market, a rival financial institution would emerge to fill this information gap. It would bid away deposits from the complacent bank and re-direct the funds into much more profitable loans or investments. In this respect, the development of liberal capital markets marks a big improvement over a complacent and inefficient banking clique.

But the capital market does not merely serve the function of a clearing house for the investment of the private sector savings flow. There are two other types of activities which are an ever-present feature of the capital market: portfolio balancing and risk arbitrage. Portfolio balancing refers to the ceaseless efforts of the investment institutions to out-perform industry benchmarks by adjusting the mix of assets (between cash, property, equities and bonds) and the mix of specific investments within each category. Risk arbitrage is a general term used to describe all kinds of transactions which move existing wealth from one use to another. The character of risk arbitrage may be conservative (designed to reduce risk at the expense of lower return), opportunistic (prepared to take on modest risk in order to capture a higher return), or aggressive (ready to accept more risk in search of an exceptional return).

Whereas the massive institutional funds manage a stock of wealth on behalf of their clients, the arbs (short for arbitrageurs) usually finance their transactions using borrowed money. Arbs do not necessarily take greater investment risks than the large funds, but their investment performance tends to be more volatile simply because they are much more highly geared. On the most benign interpretation, arbs resemble the tiny fish which feed off the food debris scattered around the mouths of much larger fish. While they perform a useful and complementary function, that of identifying and helping to correct anomalies in the capital markets, they are continuously at risk of being eaten alive.

RISK ARBITRAGE: THE DARK SIDE

However, a description of risk arbitrage cannot be confined to a benign interpretation. During the 1990s there has been an explosion of its aggressive forms, sometimes explicit in the case of the misnamed hedge funds, but more often hidden behind the respectable cloak of a large bank or investment fund. Hedge funds aim unashamedly at high absolute returns. Their clients tend to be wealthy individuals who are willing to place a small proportion of their total wealth at greater risk in return for some excitement. They do not care whether their hedge fund holds 100 per cent in equities or none; they understand that the fund will often use leverage and derivatives to increase the size of a position or sell stock short with the obligation of buying it back later. As long as the fund delivers returns comfortably in excess of those obtained by the mainstream investment funds, then the hedge fund investor is happy.

Less obvious forms of aggressive risk arbitrage are routinely carried out by proprietary traders in large investment banks, multinational companies (usually with some links to the commodities markets) and even government agencies. In other words, these traders have the permission of their managements to use the institution's capital to establish trading positions in the hope of generating extraordinary gains. Notional limits are imposed on each desk's activities or on each security traded, but these can often be blurred or circumvented using derivatives trading and complex instruments. Time and time again, senior managements discover how trading losses can multiply far beyond the intended maximum limits of exposure. So concerned have senior executives in investment banks become, they have committed millions of dollars to sponsor group risk initiatives and Value-At-Risk projects, designed to restore a measure of standardization and control.

These exercises definitely have merit, but there is a sense in which risk monitoring is always playing the catch-up game; financial innovation is opening up new holes in the regulatory fence as quickly as old ones are plugged. Moreover, trading operations that supply a significant proportion of group profit generally have enormous internal political weight; efforts to monitor the group risk profile will necessarily irritate the geese (or, should one say, the geeks) that lay the golden eggs. One of the recurrent themes of modern financial scandals is the length of time over which the problem has developed, usually many months and often years. Such is the character of futures and options trading that the cupboards containing the skeletons may not be discovered for ages. Witness the Belgian government, whose ill-judged decision to support the Italian currency in the ERM crisis of September 1992 matured as a $1.2 billion derivatives loss five years later.

A feature of aggressive arbs is their supreme confidence that all mistakes can be rectified, preferably before they have been admitted or noticed. Even for experienced traders, there is always the danger that the investment risks of an arbitrage opportunity may not be fully understood. Should a trading strategy fail expensively, then it is quite conceivable, even probable, that they will try to compensate for the shortfall by accepting even greater risk. The practice of 'marking to market', that is, valuing the firm's trading positions at prevailing market prices, may occur only at periodic intervals, perhaps only at the end of each year. In the intervening weeks and months, there is the opportunity to turn embarrassing losses into respectable returns. Trading losses are seldom realized deliberately, except for the purpose of limiting tax liability.

To take an extreme example from 1996, one of the best hypothetical deals would have been to borrow yen from a Japanese bank at less than 0.5 per cent per annum interest, swap the yen into US dollars at the start of the year (when the rate was 90 yen to the dollar) and invest the proceeds in the Russian stock market, which gave a return (in dollars) of more than 100 per cent over the course of the year. The Japanese yen fell in value from 90 per US$ to 120 per US$ during the course of 1996, cutting the value of the loan by 25 per cent. The total return on this strategy would have been about 170 per cent over 12 months!

But let's also examine what could have gone wrong with this nifty plan. First, the cost of borrowing might have risen during the year; after all, Japanese call money rates were at an all-time low. Second, the yen–dollar exchange rate could have moved 25 per cent the other way, leading to a corresponding *increase* in the value of the yen to be repaid. Third, given the economic turmoil in the country, the Russian stock market could have halved in value, instead of doubling. On this worst-case scenario, the initial investment would have *shrunk* by 60 per cent during the same 12 months.

Whereas banks are limited by externally imposed minimum capital requirements, any reasonably large company or financial institution with access to borrowing facilities could have attempted this trade. The latent borrowing capacity of the private sectors of the major developed economies is immense; a sizeable fraction of this capacity lies idle all the time. For example, at end-1996, the value of unused credit facilities of the UK private sector represented 20 per cent of the outstanding stock of loans. In addition, individuals and businesses have the potential to borrow against a huge amount of collateral in the form of property assets, should they wish to do so.

In a de-restricted, global capital market, it is very difficult to know whether the allocation and re-allocation of savings dominates the various types of risk arbitrage activities or vice versa. The argument of this book is that the relative weights of these two activities have swung heavily towards risk arbitrage, including derivatives trading. While the primary activity of the large institutional fund managers, the prudent investment of individuals' pension entitlements, insurance funds and so on, receives a benefit from the additional market turnover generated by speculation and arbitrage trades, this comes at a cost in terms of market transparency. The motivation behind a sudden increase in the demand for Peruvian equities, silver or Italian bonds might bear no relationship to the market fundamentals such as profits forecasts, interest rate movements, industrial news or government bond issuance. While frequently deriving enhanced performance from such events, the fund managers remain baffled as to their underlying causes.

CONCLUSION

For 20 years every attempt to stimulate the economy using low interest rates has ended in failure. The banks have lent to excess and companies, faced with buoyant demand for their goods and services, have driven up prices in order to ration supply. Government has been compelled to intervene, raising interest rates in order to quell inflationary pressures or to rescue an adverse foreign trade position. Politicians have longed for a magic potion that would enable companies and governments to borrow, yet without requiring the banks to expand their balance sheets. Interest rates would not need to rise to choke off the expansion of demand, and inflation would remain low because the traditional channel of bank lending had largely been avoided. Enter the global capital market, a market where the supply of savings appears unlimited and where each borrower, however large, is too small to influence the price of credit. At last, it seemed, the link between national borrowing and inflation had been severed!

Thus far, the capital markets revolution is favourably regarded. After some teething problems in the financial markets in 1987, 1990 and 1994, most western governments have become quite relaxed about the enhanced role of financial markets in economic development. They continue to congratulate themselves on excellent inflation control, while ignoring growth rates of domestic debt (which are twice or three times as high as the inflation rate) and the persistence of high real interest rates. Yet the honeymoon phase of this radical transformation of our financial arrangements will not last indefinitely; the side-effects and the social consequences are still poorly understood.

6

Throwing Caution
to the Wind

'To a few alarmed observers it seemed as though Wall Street were by way of devouring all the money of the entire world.'

John K. Galbraith, *The Great Crash, 1929*

'As the old virtues of thrift, honesty and hard work lost their appeal, everybody was out to get rich quickly, especially as speculation in currency or shares could palpably yield far greater rewards than labour.'   Adam Ferguson, *When Money Dies*, 1975

For most of the 1980s and 1990s, cash has been despised as an investment in most Anglo-Saxon countries. It has come to be regarded as a symbol of financial naïvety, tax inefficiency and irrational aversion to risk. Indeed, bank deposits, Certificates of Deposit (CDs) and money market accounts have frequently carried negative returns, after allowing for inflation and taxation. Even when those returns became consistently positive during the 1980s, they were dwarfed by the returns available from investments in stocks or funds. The steady migration of household savings into higher-yielding investments has therefore been vindicated year after year. This is an understandable reaction on the part of hard-pressed senior citizens and others who depend on income from capital to pay household bills. However, heavily indebted young households are equally scornful of liquid savings, preferring saving plans linked to stock market investments.

The warnings in this chapter do not apply with equal force to all western countries. As Figure 6.1 indicates, there are wide differences between nations in the degree to which cash and cash equivalents

Figure 6.1 Estimated proportions of liquid and near-liquid assets in total financial assets ultimately owned by the household sector at end-1995

%	Cash and cash equivalents	Loans and mortgages	Other non-invested assets	Total
Sweden	14	3	1	18
UK	22	0	4	26
USA	20	3	3	26
France	16	2	13	31
Austria	8	6	21	35
Italy	32	1	9	42
Canada	32	6	5	43
Germany	37	4	6	47
Netherlands	8	38	1	47
Denmark	13	36	1	50
Norway	41	8	12	61
Spain	52	4	6	62
Japan	53	13	1	67

Source: D. Miles (1997)

have been abandoned as a store of household financial wealth. Sweden, the UK and the USA are sailing closest to the wind on our chosen definition, but it may be that some of the loan assets and other non-invested assets held on the continent should not really be counted as liquid assets; France, Austria, the Netherlands and Denmark might then be considered equally vulnerable.

THE REAL MEANING OF LIQUIDITY

It is important to be clear at the outset what is meant by the word 'liquidity'. Just as a liquid can be poured from one container to another, so assets that are truly liquid can be transferred readily from one use to another. In this analogy it is assumed that there is no evaporation, condensation or spillage. Provided the requisite measures are available, exact quantities of liquids can be poured out. Liquids are divisible into infinitesimal amounts. Cash, in the form of notes and coins in current circulation (currency, for short), comes the closest to fulfilling the criteria of a liquid asset. It can be handed from one person to another in exchange for commodities, services or assets without any doubts as to its monetary value. Provided a sufficient quantity of smaller notes and coins is available, then currency is divisible into the smallest recognized monetary unit. In the USA and Canada this is a cent; in the UK, a penny; in Germany, a pfennig in 1998 (but shortly to become a euro-cent).

Moving along the spectrum, a cash card or debit card is almost as good as cash in hand, but is limited in its acceptability. Unless the retailer or merchant has the necessary technology, the debit facility will not work. The fallback is then for the user to withdraw cash from an automatic telling machine (ATM) and to return to the point of sale in order to complete the transaction. This represents a marginal loss of liquidity. Similarly, a cheque drawn against an 'instant' bank or money market account is effective in making immediate purchases, but it takes time for the paperwork to be completed and for the cheque to be cleared. If there are insufficient funds available in the payee's bank account, then the cheque will be returned unpaid. Cash cards, debit cards and cheques still qualify as liquid assets, but the liquid is more like syrup than water.

Taking one step further, there is the postal savings account, the bank time deposit and the CD. In return for the payment of interest at a rate which approximates to the short-term money market rate, such accounts require holders to give notice of withdrawal and normally suffer a loss of interest during this notice period. Even where these accounts have a chequing facility, it is clear that the funds are not readily transferable. If the opportunity to purchase was conditional on immediate settlement, then these accounts would not suffice. They are more like jelly than water.

What unites all the financial instruments mentioned above is their fixed nominal amount. There are no quibbles as to the face value of a bank note or a cheque. To move further along the spectrum into government securities, bills, bonds and shares, it is necessary to cross into the territory of assets with uncertain nominal values. The par or redemption value of a bond may well be predetermined in money terms, as indeed may be the coupon. But as a security traded in the market day by day, its current value will change throughout its life. Equities are normally issued with a nominal par value, but this relates only to the share capital which appears in the company's balance sheet. Share prices vary continuously as the financial markets react to general and specific items of news. For this reason, securities and the funds which invest in them cannot be described as liquid assets. In terms of the analogy, these instruments are puddings, varying in texture from mousses to sponges and cakes. They cannot easily be reconstituted in terms of their ingredients.

Under normal circumstances, government bonds and shares can be liquidated (sold for cash) within about 14 days, but with no guarantee of the price which will be realized at any particular moment. This raises the issue of floor or reservation prices, which are common at auctions of fine art and antiques, but which also apply to investments. Most investors hold in their minds reservation prices for the shares and bonds they own directly (rather than through an intermediary). In some cases, this is simply the purchase price; in others, it may be a recent share price peak. The general principle is that investors are loath to realize a loss. Indeed, where the investment has been financed by borrowing, the investor may not be able to afford to crystallize a loss. This aversion to losses, whether real or notional, plays an important part in financial market dynamics. It explains why few investors sell when a share or bond price is less than 5 per cent from its most recent peak, but many seek to sell once the deficit reaches 20 per cent, thus amplifying the collapse.

A by-product of this behaviour is that the ease of purchase and keenness of price which face the investor when buying into a fashionable stock are rarely observed when its popularity reverses. The speed with which prices are marked down in a bear market phase typically allows few investors to sell out above their reservation price. Market-makers exploit this reluctance by introducing deep discounts into unfashionable stocks, thus minimizing the actual amount of selling which occurs. If the company is hit by further bad news, then its stock may become worthless; otherwise, a new source of demand for the stock materializes eventually and the price discount is removed. Either way, investors may have a long wait before the stock regains an acceptable selling price. There is no such thing as a liquid stock in a bear market. What is true of individual company stocks is also true of some stock markets. Christopher Fildes, writing in the *Spectator* a few years ago, defined emerging markets as those from which it was difficult to emerge in an emergency!

One of the biggest crimes of financial terminology is the bastard usage of the word 'liquidity' to mean the fluidity of a market, the ease with which transactions can be executed at the prevailing market price. Thus, the US Treasury bond market has been described as the most liquid market in the world. In other words, the Treasury bond market has a massive daily trading volume, such that even large individual trades are likely to have little influence on the market price. This enables the identity of the parties to large trades to remain a secret until the deal is done. Ease and anonymity of trading are genuinely important market characteristics, but it is very confusing to describe them as liquidity. Treasury bonds and blue-chip company securities are not liquid assets. In this chapter and throughout the book, the word liquidity will be reserved for its primary financial usage.

AGGREGATE MEASURES OF LIQUIDITY

All liquidity originates within the monetary or banking sector of an economy. Whether the originator is the central bank, a commercial bank or a private bank is immaterial. Whether the bank is independent, owned by a foreign parent, owned by an insurance company, an industrial company or a chain of hypermarkets is similarly unimportant. Only banks can create and destroy liquidity; central banks have this authority under the terms of their constitution, and the rest of the domestic monetary sector enjoys a delegated authority from the central bank. Liquidity, in the form of deposits, is created as banks increase their net lending to the private or public sectors; the deposit is merely a parallel book-entry to the loan. Conversely, liquidity is destroyed when banks remove (write off) non-performing loans from their balance sheets, thereby reducing shareholders' capital.

The measurement of liquidity in the large western economies is rather more problematic. Money stocks or aggregates differ in significance between countries. By and large, the broad money aggregates M3 or M4 (which correspond to the liabilities of the domestic monetary sector) offer a reasonable approximation to 'liquidity', but some of these contain large proportions of interest-bearing money which, for practical purposes, are unavailable for transactions use. Where defined, M2 or money of zero maturity (MZM) is probably closer to the ideal. These nuances of definition are not central to the argument. Interested readers are referred to the detailed definitions in the glossary!

In Chapter 3 the distinction between liquidity and purchasing power was introduced. Retail or consumer purchasing power was defined as currency, bank deposits, other monies owed and payable on demand, and unused credit facilities. Credit facilities for the individual consist mainly of loans and overdraft facilities from banks and other financial institutions, credit cards, instalment debt and the loan component of a vehicle lease. Unused credit facilities represent additional purchasing power but not additional liquidity. The borrower is essentially paying for the privilege of using someone else's liquidity. This payment, which may be in the form of interest, fees or commission, can be considered to have three components: one, a payment of the market rate of interest to the depositor in return for the use of the money; two, an insurance premium to the bank or finance company to cover the risk of default by the borrower (i.e. credit risk); and three, a profit margin to the intermediary for providing the service.

SEA-CHANGES IN PERSONAL FINANCIAL BEHAVIOUR

With these necessary clarifications in mind, it is possible to show how consumers in the USA and several other large countries have undertaken two significant transformations of financial behaviour. In the first phase, from 1977 to 1986, they accumulated liabilities (debts) at a rapid pace; and in the second, from 1984 to 1997, they switched from acquiring liquid assets to illiquid ones, such as pension, insurance and mutual funds and direct ownership of bonds and shares. The overall effect of this transition for US households has been to reduce net liquidity from plus 17 per cent of personal after-tax income in

Figure 6.2 Allocation of US personal savings flows (%)

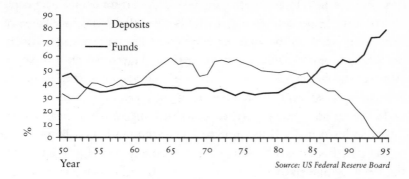

Year   *Source: US Federal Reserve Board*

1984 to minus 25 per cent in 1995. In terms of the allocation of gross household saving, Figure 6.2 shows that the share of new saving held in liquid forms fell from 47 per cent in 1984 to almost zero in 1994. Between these two dates, the proportion of gross saving directed to investment in funds or securities jumped from 41 per cent to 73 per cent.

The traditional rationale for holding cash or instant access bank deposits is a precautionary one. In the event of a crisis or emergency, cash comes into its own. It is universally acceptable in settlement of bills or debts, it is convertible at face value into assets, goods and services, it is conveniently portable and readily divisible. While the loss of appeal of deposits as an investment is understandable, the mass marketing of consumer credit has also lessened the precautionary appeal of cash. Households' average holdings of 'rainy day' savings deposits, bearing little or no interest, have declined steadily in the USA, the UK, Canada and elsewhere. One US household survey in 1997 estimated the average holding of liquid assets for working households as around $1,000.

What began in many countries as a grudging acceptance that equities would yield better returns than bank deposits over long periods of time has become an avalanche. In 1980, 51 per cent of households' gross financial assets were held as bank deposits; by 1994 this had slumped to 35 per cent. For the USA, the UK and Canada, this proportion declined from 38 per cent to 26 per cent, and for the other members of the G7 (Japan, Germany, France and Italy) from 61 per cent to 42 per cent. A corresponding increase in the proportion of financial assets held as equities or in investment funds has occurred. The past ten years (and especially the last five years) have seen a huge expansion in the number of individuals investing in the market directly or in fully invested funds for the first time. The consistency of stock market returns over the past 15 years has clouded perceptions of the risk characteristics of these investments in relation to bank deposits and other money market instruments, leaving a new generation of investors historically vulnerable to a financial markets collapse.

Stepping back from these developments, it is useful to distinguish three dimensions of the change in personal financial behaviour. There has been a cultural dimension. As memories of the inter-war and early post-war hardships have faded, a new generation of adults has abandoned the cautious, thrift-conscious culture of their parents and has embraced new credit opportunities early in adult life. There has been a technological dimension. A revolution in computer technology, data processing capacity and communications has enabled numerous innovations in money handling, payments transfer and personal banking. The availability of new financial products has opened out greater potential for borrowing and investment. There has also been a stock market dimension. The extraordinary performance of North American and Western European stock markets since 1982 has served as a powerful catalyst for the transition from deposit-based saving to market-related saving. At other times, the inherent volatility of stock markets might have deterred investors from undertaking such a dramatic switch.

CULTURAL DIMENSION

In every human lifetime of 70 or 80 years, there is usually at least one episode of extreme financial turbulence. The serious economic depressions of the 1880s and 1930s are the most obvious examples, but the German hyperinflations of the early 1920s and late 1940s were probably more devastating to those who lived through them. The quote from Adam Ferguson which appears at the start of this chapter was written in the context of Berlin in 1924. The force of such experiences, sometimes overshadowed by wars, challenges the assumptions of each successive generation regarding the safety of various forms of wealth. The established pecking order for property, gold, cash, bonds and shares is typically turned upside down. When the price level is rising and the greatest fear is of high inflation, conventional wisdom prefers stock market investments (in companies which possess pricing power) and property to government bonds and cash. The onset of a depression, accompanied by a falling price level for ordinary goods and services, turns the tables on this set of preferences. Gold and physical assets become more highly prized, while the stock market loses its appeal. The transition from stable inflation to a hyperinflation is every bit as traumatic, favouring the accumulation of debt and financial speculation while punishing money holdings.

An economy formed of rational individuals and firms, with equal access to financial information, might adjust quickly to an economic earthquake. But the real-life responses of the general public to such shocks are typically inept and ill-advised. The failure to comprehend the nature of a depression or a hyperinflation amplifies the effects of the initial shock, bringing high rates of unemployment and crime. Perhaps as much as war itself, these economic or financial disasters leave behind a permanent imprint. Those whose wealth has been deci-mated or whose livelihood has been confiscated will carry the experience with them for the remainder of their lives. Inevitably, public attitudes towards financial wealth and debt are moulded by such events.

However, there comes a time when these memories belong predomi-nantly to the older generations. Government policy and financial behaviour soon begin to reflect the priorities and values of a new generation who are unperturbed by the folklore of distant financial disasters. For this reason, western economic and financial liberaliz-ation policies of the 1980s and 1990s would have been deeply unpopular if advocated in the 1950s or 1960s. Post-war austerity demanded that financial institutions were conservative and that governments held the economy in a firm grip. By the early 1970s, a more confident atmosphere had emerged in which private individuals were eager to take more personal responsibility and risk. One manifestation of this was a surge in debt-financed home ownership, particularly in Anglo-Saxon countries. This was viewed as a low-risk investment which would always hold its value. Even so, the supply of mortgage loans was rationed more by quantity than by price. The real explosion in Anglo-Saxon home loans occurred in the 1980s.

One further development which is relevant to the cultural dimension is the access to borrowing by the under-25s. The implicit ethos of bank lending in the 1960s and 1970s was paternalistic: that young adults should prove that they could save before they were allowed to borrow. The penchant for borrowing as much as possible as soon as possible was a later addition. Home loans, credit cards, personal loans and student loans are available in most developed countries to young people from the age of 18. The invitation or temptation to an 18-year-old to borrow against the collateral of future earnings potential would have been unthinkable in the aftermath of the Second World War; yet it has become culturally acceptable in a number of western countries. Much to their credit, Germany and the Netherlands have resisted these cultural trends.

The willingness of young adults to assume significant debts is an important cultural phenomenon. It is either an expression of great confidence in the future or a product of ignorance and complacency towards financial matters. This theme is developed further in Chapter 8. What is absent is the voice of the older generations who have first-hand experience of genuine economic hardship and the consequences of financial ruin. Even the post-war hardships are 50 years old. Apart from the history books, the fading memories of the retired generation are the only source of caution available to today's young adults. It was Nicolai Kondratieff, the exponent of the long wave hypothesis, who remarked that wisdom skips a generation.

TECHNOLOGICAL DIMENSION

Technological advances, encompassing the revolutionary changes in computing power and processing capacity, software developments and electronic communications, have transformed the range and scope of financial products available to the general public. Three developments are of particular relevance to a discussion of liquidity and purchasing power. First, banks around the world are rapidly replacing paper cheques with electronic debiting facilities. In the UK, the market share of automated items in total sterling transactions has risen from 30 per cent in 1985 to 45 per cent in 1995 by volume, and from 20 per cent to 95 per cent by value. The increasing use of plastic cards as a means of payment represents an efficiency gain, harvested principally by the banks but offering greater convenience to their customers as well. One aspect of this gain is a reduction in fraud. Stolen cards can be rendered invalid across the whole payments network once they have been reported as missing. To the extent that plastic cards are more liquid than paper cheques, the electronic payments revolution has been beneficial.

A more recent innovation, but not yet in general use, is that of electronic money or the electronic purse. Instead of withdrawing cash from a hole-in-the-wall machine, the customer transfers cash from a bank account to a smart card, which stores a credit balance. After each transaction, the smart card updates the credit balance. Electronic money has the potential to replace notes and coin in a wide variety of contexts, again reducing opportunities for theft.

This cannot be said of a parallel development: the proliferation of credit channels. Plastic card technology has provided a low-cost route for new entrants into the personal lending market. Foreign banks, multinational corporations, retailers and many others have established credit card subsidiaries, aiming to write profitable loan business. Clearly, plastic cards are only part of the story; bank overdrafts, finance house loans and insurance companies offer alternative channels of personal borrowing. But the seduction of plastic cards lies in the ability to satisfy the spending impulse immediately, without filling out forms and undergoing fresh credit checks. An individual with a good credit reference can accumulate literally dozens of credit cards, representing many thousands of dollars of purchasing power, without triggering any alarm bells from the credit reference agencies. The most extravagant attitudes to the availability of consumer credit are to be found in North America, where household instalment debts equivalent to a year's income are not unusual. Technology has removed many of the practical obstacles to inappropriate and addictive borrowing behaviour.

Another manifestation of technology is the growth of remote banking, whether by telephone, home computer or post. While there are obvious cost savings to banks from closing local branches and centralizing their operations in large conurbations, the loss of direct personal contact between a bank and its customers places an enormous strain on security procedures for funds transfer and on the screening of loan applications. The full implications of the shift from banking based on face-to-face contact to remote banking may not be apparent until the credit cycle turns sour.

STOCK MARKET DIMENSION

According to portfolio theory, there should be a trade-off between investments offering different degrees of risk and reward. To compensate for the greater inherent volatility and riskiness of stock market investment, investors demand an excess return over government bonds, which are deemed to have no risk of default. Various studies of investment performance in the USA and the UK, stretching back to the 1920s, have calculated that this excess, known as the equity risk premium, is approximately 6 per cent per annum on average. It is also normal for ten-year or 20-year bond returns to be 2 per cent or 3 per cent higher than the returns to short-term deposits. In other words, if a safe, risk-free investment in cash generated an average return of 4 per cent per year, then expected bond market returns would be 6 per cent or 7 per cent, and a typical portfolio of stocks would yield around 12 per cent per annum. However, the excess return observed in any subset of the 70-year sample might be larger or smaller than this 6 per cent average. Even over successive ten-year intervals, the excess return might vary from 0 per cent to 12 per cent.

Whereas the sequence of annual returns from government bonds might show little variation from the 6 per cent average, the sequence of stock market returns might read 6 per cent, 21 per cent, −4 per cent, 23 per cent, 37 per cent, 28 per cent, −18 per cent, −3 per cent, etc. The excess return is therefore far from guaranteed in any individual year. In this crude example, stocks would beat bonds comfortably in four of the eight years; one would be level pegging; and in the

Figure 6.3 Morgan Stanley Capital International World ex-Japan equity price index (1970 = 100)

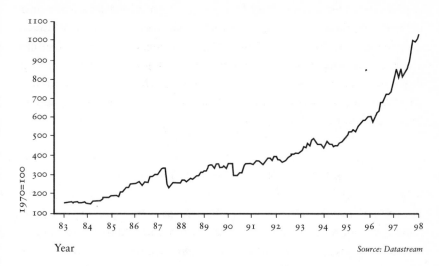

Year

Source: Datastream

remaining three years bonds would outperform stocks. Thus, the probability of a stock market investor gaining a superior return to bonds (or even cash) in any particular year might be only 60 per cent. To increase this probability from 60 per cent to 80 per cent or 95 per cent would require the stock market investment to be held for ten or 20 years in succession, regardless of how bumpy the ride.

In Anglo-Saxon countries with an established equity culture such as the USA, the UK, Canada and Australia, such was the concern that the public would be deterred by the volatility of the stock market that pension and insurance funds have always enjoyed preferential tax treatment. Whether through tax relief on contributions, dividend tax relief on equity investments or by other means, individuals have been coerced into long-term saving vehicles linked to the financial markets.

So much for the theory. Figure 6.3 shows that an index of world equity prices, excluding Japan, enjoyed 15 years of almost uninter-rupted gains between 1982 and 1997. Excess returns averaged more than 10 per cent per annum throughout, with only one year (1990) in which it would have paid to hold a mixture of bonds and currency deposits rather than a portfolio of world (ex-Japan) equities. This extended period of benign stock market performance is remarkable, if not unprecedented. It has fostered a false belief among citizens that equities are a sure-fire bet; that they deliver not only dependable long-term performance but also near-guaranteed short-term performance.

During the 1980s, a small but growing minority of western citizens have participated directly in the stock market's success. Perhaps initially, memories of the deep bear market of 1974–6 or the lesser bear market of 1981–2 weighed heavily on the minds of would-be investors. A return of investor confidence built up strongly during 1986 and the first seven months of 1987, only to suffer the abrupt rebuke of the October 1987 crash. A second shake-up in share values occurred in the autumn of 1990, but of rather less severity. Thus, the popular stock market bandwagon began to gather momentum only in the following year, 1991. Since then, the pace has been breathtaking and the annual returns staggering. The mutual fund movement in North America has promoted mass participation in world stock markets over and above the involvement of insurance and pension funds. In Europe, the most significant catalyst for investor participation has been the privatization of public enterprises and activities. Aware-ness of the stock market's exhilarating performance and enjoyment of its imputed gains have risen on an exponential scale. However, the great majority of today's private investors have no direct experience of a bear market. For them, the implicit choice between an investment in bank deposits or government bonds and a mutual fund or privatization issue is, in the prevailing idiom, a 'no-brainer'. Cash, especially, is despised for its primitive characteristics, the most damning being its low yield.

The question of stock market valuation and the means by which financial assets can become overvalued is deferred until Chapter 12. It is sufficient for present purposes to observe only that an increasing majority of western citizens appear to have overcome their fear of capital loss and to have developed a much larger appetite for financial assets as opposed to property. The consistent out-performance of the stock market has anaesthetized private investors to the pain of wealth destruction. The contention of this book is that individuals are no less concerned about the risks attached to a particular course of action than they were 20 or 50 years ago; rather, it is their perception of the risks inherent in their decisions which has changed.

Two massive mergers between banks and financial companies in the USA during 1998 have all but confirmed the practical irrelevance of the 1932 Glass–Steagall Act which sought to uphold a legal separation between banking and securities businesses. One of the arguments in favour of maintaining a separation between commercial banking and investment banking is that it minimizes public confusion. In the bank, customers knew that the accumulation of their savings was guaranteed and that the bank's deposits were insured with the Federal Deposit Insurance Corporation. In the lobby of an insurance company or in a meeting with a stockbroker, customers knew that projections of future investment values were subject to uncertainty and without guarantee of federal government support. The progress of the *bancassurance* movement in Europe and the marketing of mutual fund products by US banks has dulled the distinctions between capital-certain and capital-uncertain investments and between insured and uninsured deposits and bonds.

In the UK, solicitations to subscribe to financial products in newspapers and magazines are obliged to carry warnings, such as: 'The value of your investment may go down as well as up and you may not get back all the money you invest' or 'Past performance is not necessarily a guide to the future'. However, in the same way that health warnings on cigarette packets seem to enhance their appeal for adolescents, in heady bull markets these admonitions may act as inducements to invest rather than as deterrents. When the public perceives financial markets as a safe place to invest, and every year that passes appears to vindicate this judgement, lectures on portfolio theory and investment risk are destined to fall on deaf ears.

One of the disturbing side-effects of sustained stock market appreciation is the huge amount of publicity it has attracted. As news of the bonanza spread, there was an even faster migration of savings towards the financial markets. There is no better illustration of this phenomenon than the net subscriptions of American citizens to mutual funds over the past 30 years. Between 1966 and 1982, virtually no new money was committed to US mutual funds on a net basis. Yet, by the summer of 1987, these net flows had risen to approximately $120 billion at an annual rate. The crash prompted a few months of small-scale net redemptions, only for the bandwagon to roll forward even more powerfully during 1991. Net subscriptions leapt from $30 billion per annum to $230 billion per annum in the closing months of 1993. A few more anxious months followed as US interest rates doubled from 3 per cent to 6 per cent, but new funds continued to be committed to the market at an annual rate of at least $100 billion. Finally, a third surge in net subscriptions gathered momentum during 1995, carrying the aggregate to a $280 billion annual pace in late 1996. By this time, mutual fund assets had reached 22 per cent of the typical household's wealth. During each of these three phases of mass-buying of financial assets, US and world (ex-Japan) stock market indices rose dramatically.

Another curious – and probably US-specific – phenomenon has been the popularity of stock market investment clubs. Most famous of these clubs is the Beardstown Ladies, a group of novice investors who rose to prominence through their investment successes and who subsequently shared their 'secrets' with the world. However inspired or fortunate their stock selections (and some of their performance claims were later shown to be false), the message from the Beardstown Ladies to every small community in the USA was that you don't need a broker's advice to make money from the stock market. The number of home-spun pooled investment clubs in the USA has burgeoned since 1990. About 1,000 new clubs were formed in 1992, 5,000 in 1995 and around 10,000 in 1996. In one sense, the Beardstown Ladies' success can be attributed to the age-old proverb that a rising tide lifts all ships. The exuberance of a bull market covers a multitude of stock selection sins. However, in less friendly markets, these novice investors in stocks and funds suffer a significant handicap in their endeavours. The intelligence that they receive about companies and market dynamics is usually days – if not weeks – old. Market professionals have already acted on the hot news by the time the private investor hears it; in time-honoured fashion, the belated involvement of the general public provides the last opportunity for the professionals to take their money out.

By any reckoning, the North American and Western European stock markets are overdue a bear market shake-out. In the half-century beginning 1932, there were ten bear markets in US stocks – on average, one every five years. To go 15 years with only one (1987–8) is highly unusual. The average extent of the retracement from the peak value of the stock market index to its nadir for these ten bear markets was more than 50 per cent; in other words, market values were cut in half. Worst of all was the 1929–32 episode, in which the share index declined by 85 per cent, but in three other instances (the lows of 1942, 1970 and 1974) a drop of 60 per cent or more was recorded. In terms of market chronology, a reversal of 60 per cent is akin to turning the stock market clock back from mid-1998 to 1989; a retracement of 85 per cent would cancel out all the gains of the past 15 years.

CONCLUSION

What sets the 1990s apart from other decades is the sheer recklessness of financial behaviour. To believe that there will never be another 50 per cent share price wipe-out requires either great faith in the evolution of more favourable economic circumstances or a blatant disregard for the lessons of history. To run down liquid savings to minimal proportions at the same time beggars belief. Western households whose heads are aged under 50, whether participating directly in the markets or indirectly through investment funds, are hugely under-weight in liquid assets. Most are exposed to the uninsured risk of stock market reversal without even the cushion of three months' earnings in the form of liquid wealth. Given that pension values, government finances and private sector employment would all be adversely affected by such an event, it is easy to predict that the social and economic consequences of the next bear market in equities will be devastating. This is the outcome of throwing caution to the wind.

7

Risk Markets and the Paradox of Stability

'We have no crash at present, only a slight premonitory movement of the ground under our feet.'   Lord Overstone, Governor of the Bank of England, 1845

'I have long believed that growing bank involvement in derivative products is . . . like a tinderbox waiting to explode.'
Henry Gonzalez, US Representative, 1993

Imagine that a private company had developed an explosive ten times more powerful than Semtex. Suppose also that this company planned to increase output by 40 per cent per annum, to sell trading franchises throughout the world and to market the product to all comers. Would not the government take urgent steps to license and regulate this product, perhaps even to the point of nationalizing the company? Yet the financial explosives known as derivatives enjoy virtual freedom in every developed country of the world, and in some emerging nations too. There are organized exchanges for financial futures and options in the USA, Japan, Germany, France, Italy, the UK, Canada, Spain, the Netherlands, Australia, Switzerland, Belgium, Sweden, Austria, Denmark, Norway, Finland, Ireland, New Zealand, Hong Kong, the Republic of Korea, Malaysia, Singapore, Brazil and Argentina. In each country a host of different derivative products are traded, ranging from government bond futures and equity index options to commodity futures and currency options. However, the real action is to be found outside these exchanges in the over-the-counter (OTC) interest rate and currency swap markets.

It should come as no surprise that the financial institutions and companies which operate in these markets are keen for them to remain relatively free of regulatory interference. Similarly, it is unsurprising that there are no reliable, up-to-date statistics for the size of the derivatives markets. Perhaps it is rather more disquieting that the global banking regulator, the Bank for International Settlements (BIS), has abandoned its attempt to extend safety controls to banks' derivatives activities. The regime of capital adequacy that weights the assets on banks' balance sheets according to their degree of risk and assesses the minimum amount of capital they need proved un-workable in its application to derivatives business, because of the complexities. But most surprising of all is the opposition of central bankers, notably in the USA, to greater transparency of accounting standards for derivatives activity. Far from welcoming a framework that would help to prevent derivatives fraud, the authorities objected that the new rules would discourage prudent risk management activities.

No one objects to the use of explosives in quarrying or road-building, but there is still a clear case for proper accounting and secure manage-ment of the detonators and stocks of dynamite. Even if there were no terrorists, the careless distribution of explosives would be sure to lead to accidents. There have already been dozens of accidents with derivatives; some are well documented while others remain corporate secrets. What is striking is how many of these accidents have involved huge sums of money; since 1993, at least ten separate disasters have involved losses of more than a billion US dollars (Figure 7.1). Indeed, as illustrated by the Proctor & Gamble example in Chapter 1, the opportunity for gearing is inherent in the use of derivatives. Gearing describes the power of derivative products to control a more expensive asset (such as DM1 billion) for a low or even a zero cost. It invites the possibility of catastrophic loss as well as explosive gain. As with the mis-handling of Semtex, all accidents are liable to be fatal.

Figure 7.1 Billion dollar losses involving derivatives

Organization	Instruments	$bn
Kidder Peabody	Oil futures	4.4
Schneider Property Group	Derivatives speculation using inflated assets as collateral	4
Sumitomo Corp.	Copper futures	2.6
Metallgesellschaft	Oil forwards	1.9
Orange County	Interest rate mis-matching using structured notes	1.7
Kashima Oil	Oil forwards	1.5
Barings	Japanese equity index financial futures	1.4
Belgian Government	Currency swaps	1.2
Daiwa Bank	US Treasury bond futures	1.1
Balsam Group	Deferral accounting	1

WHAT ARE FINANCIAL DERIVATIVES?

Most types of derivatives have their origins in the world of commodities: agriculture, minerals and metals. Consider the situation of a farmer debating whether to grow a crop of maize. He is aware of the current market price of maize, but he has no idea what the price will be in, say, six months' time when his crop will be ready to harvest. By using futures or options, the farmer can guarantee today the actual or minimum price at which the maize will ultimately be sold, thus enabling him to work out the profitability of the enterprise. If too many other farmers have already pre-committed to grow maize, then the delivery price will have been driven down. This sends a clear message to the farmer that it would be better to grow a different crop, perhaps soybean or rape-seed.

A futures contract is a legally binding agreement to buy or sell a standard quantity of a particular commodity or financial asset on a fixed future date at a price agreed today. In our example, the farmer wishes to hedge (that is, protect himself) against the possibility of an inconvenient fall in the future price of maize. His sole motivation for using the futures market is to reduce risk. Alternatively, the farmer could buy an option to sell his maize when the crop was ready. An options contract confers the right, but not the obligation, to buy or sell an asset at a given price on or before a given date. If the prevailing market price for maize at harvest were higher than the option price, then the farmer would sell into the cash market and abandon the option.

Futures and options are the most clear-cut examples of derivatives. As an aid to transactions, standard contract sizes have been developed, such as 25 tonnes for copper and 125,000 for Deutschmarks. While the value of derivative contracts depends on the price of other assets, the contracts can be traded independently. Most importantly, the price of a future or of an option will typically be a small percentage of the price of the underlying asset. Consequently, the potential to earn profits or to suffer losses is vastly greater for derivatives than for barrels of crude oil or government bonds. Whereas the price of a bond may trade in a monthly range of $102 to $106, the value of a derivative of this bond might move from $1 to $5. The percentage movement in the bond price is 3.9 per cent, but in the derivative it is 400 per cent.

Less obvious examples of financial derivatives are swaps. Currency swaps involve the exchange of loan liabilities in different currencies, whereas interest rate swaps usually consist of the exchange of a fixed rate for a floating rate claim. The main function of derivatives is to enable buyers and sellers to choose how much equity price, bond price, currency rate or interest rate risk they wish to carry. Derivatives have become more popular particularly since the 1973 oil crisis, but much of their development has been enabled by the technological advances in computing. The calculation of futures and options prices goes beyond simple algebra; it requires the solution of complicated algorithms. Powerful computers are needed to provide regular price updates. Without prompt access to these prices, trading possibilities would be very limited.

While options and forward transactions date back at least as far as the early seventeenth century, the trading of contracts on derivatives *markets* dates only to 1972. Indeed, futures are a type of forward contract traded on an organized exchange. The most active of these markets today is in financial futures, with key centres in Chicago, New

York, London and Frankfurt. These centralized exchanges assume liability for the settlement of transactions, thus eliminating counterparty risk and reducing transactions costs for standard contracts. Counterparty risk is the risk that, between the time a transaction has been arranged and the date of settlement, the counterparty (the person or firm on the other side of the bargain) will fail to make appropriate payment or settlement. While counterparty risk has always existed in a paper-based payments system, the increasing interdependence and complexity of financial markets amplify the potential difficulties where there are long transactions chains.

Market turnover on the futures exchanges, that is, the daily value of all the transactions in equity, bonds and currency futures, is in some cases much larger than the average daily turnover in the underlying securities, especially in the US markets. The markets are used by a mixture of corporate treasurers, banks and financial institutions whose job is to reduce risk, by investment banks acting for clients and their own trading books, and by speculators seeking an exposure to certain types of risk. Anyone beginning a career in financial markets since 1980 would not recognize derivative securities as an innovation. Derivative products now dominate the financial markets.

THE SPREAD OF FINANCIAL DERIVATIVES

'OTC trade in derivatives crosses national borders, interconnects previously distinct financial markets and involves a wide assortment of financial and non-financial firms as counterparties.'
Jane W. D'Arista and Tom Schlesinger,
International Economic Insights, May/June 1994

The development of markets in derivatives has been a cause as well as an effect of change; it has helped to integrate different securities and currency markets through the elimination of discrepancies, driving down interest rate spreads and undermining restrictive practices such as the imposition of fees and commissions. Currency swaps are also used to lower international borrowing costs. For example, it might be cheaper for a Spanish company to borrow in pesetas and then swap its loan into US dollars than to borrow dollars in the USA, where the company is relatively unknown. The anonymous counterparty might be a US bank or a US firm needing pesetas. Both parties gain as long as their ability to borrow on advantageous terms in their respective local markets is not the same. The principle of comparative advantage, whereby trade is of mutual benefit provided both parties concentrate on activities in which their relative advantage is the greater, works as well for loans as for regular trade in goods and services. Swaps are handled entirely by OTC arrangements, and banks now buy and sell swaps without the prior matching of counterparties. More than half of all interest rate swaps are between banks.

One of the drawbacks of unmatched swaps was illustrated in early 1997 by the $150 million loss suffered by NatWest Markets in the UK. The precise circumstances of the mis-pricing problem are unclear, but it appears that the bank routinely created a market in options on swaps (effectively, bets or hedges on the future movement of interest rates) in order to provide risk protection for a customer. A typical situation would be that of a mortgage lender wishing to offer a fixed interest rate loan for a five-year term. The presumption in this example is that short-term interest rates are likely to rise. In order to protect the lender from the possibility of rising interest rates during this period, the bank buys options contracts granting the lender the right to borrow at a fixed rate. As it is unlikely that there would be a natural seller of this option at precisely the same time, the bank assumes the role of the seller. This is known as a proprietary trade. If interest rates fall subsequently, then the options contract is 'out of the money'. The further out of the money and away from the specified date the option is, the more difficult it becomes to determine its fair value. Herein lay NatWest's problem: because OTC options each have their own idiosyncrasies, rather like used cars, there is no definitive benchmark against which to price them. The only way of knowing what an OTC option is really worth is to trade it. When the NatWest's star trader routinely valued the option in question, he merely guessed too high. There was no suggestion in this particular case of fraud or deception.

With proper use and in sound hands, financial derivatives enable potential losses arising from unavoidable risks to be limited and controlled. Since every contract has two parties, in theory, derivatives trading encourages the efficient pricing of risks and opportunities regarding unknown future outcomes in foreign exchange, bonds, equity and commodity markets. However, the forces tending to promote stability are strongly opposed by the destabilizing influences of fraud and ignorance. The ease of concealment of large open (unhedged) positions, representing commitments to buy or sell colossal amounts of stock or commodities, has hit the headlines with alarming regularity in the 1990s. Metallgesellschaft, Orange County, Barings, Daiwa Bank and Sumitomo Bank are among the most glaring examples.

Financial derivatives, like insurance contracts, give rise to contingent liabilities, that is, obligations which arise only if certain conditions are fulfilled. In common with insurance, these liabilities can be unlimited and may be influenced or determined by legal judgements. Unlike insurance contracts, the participants may be completely ignorant of the true nature of their exposure. Trades between ever-vigilant and well-capitalized investment banks are one thing; trades between market professionals and corporate treasurers in medium-sized firms or provincial governments are quite another.

HOW LARGE IS THE DERIVATIVES MARKET?

The truth is that nobody really knows. There are many different agencies and exchanges which report statistics and an ever-expanding list of derivative financial instruments. The BIS publishes estimates of the total size of the market in its annual report, but its data are incomplete and six months out of date when they appear. Because derivatives contracts are denominated in a variety of underlying currencies and financial assets, the standard measure of size is the notional principal (or underlying) amount in US dollars. While notional, or contract, amounts are one way of measuring the outstanding stock of derivatives, they are not necessarily meaningful measures of the actual risks involved. The degree of risk for many derivatives varies both by the type of product and by the type of risk being measured.

The BIS end-year data show the aggregate size of the main financial derivatives markets (interest rate, currency and equity options, futures and swaps) as $1.1 trillion at end-1986, $4.2 trillion in 1989, $6.9 trillion in 1991 and $7.5 trillion in 1992. However, the Federal Reserve Board of New York published data in July 1995 showing the total derivatives market value as $10.2 trillion in 1990, $14.0 trillion in 1991, $17.3 trillion in 1992 and $25.1 trillion in 1993. The difficulty of measurement has not eased in recent years. The BIS have estimated that the total outstanding notional value of derivative products was about $55.7 trillion at end-March 1995, comprising exchange-traded derivatives of $8.2 trillion and OTC derivatives of $47.5 trillion. Unofficial estimates suggest that this figure had swelled to between $80 trillion and $100 trillion by the end of 1997. In round figures, the latter figure represents a 40 per cent annual compound growth rate since 1990.

To gain a better grasp of the importance of these large numbers, it is necessary to introduce the concept of replacement value. The replacement value is the unrealized capital gain or loss of a derivatives contract measured at current market prices; in other words, it is the amount of underlying capital that would need to be injected to honour the contract in place of the failed counterparty. The average replacement value of derivatives contracts is estimated at between 2.5 per cent and 4 per cent of the notional principal amounts referred to above. Using the round figure of $100 trillion for the total notional principal amount gives a range of $2.5 trillion to $4 trillion of outstanding replacement or gross market value. There may be some scope to reduce this estimate on the grounds that some banks' derivative exposures cancel each other out. Even so, the total replacement value of derivatives would still be several times larger than the capital base of the 30 banks and securities houses which account for the vast majority of OTC transactions in derivatives.

This is not to say that the banks are necessarily under-capitalized; rather that, in the event of counterparty failure, any bank or securities house would probably be wiped out. It would be highly inefficient for a bank to hold sufficient capital on its balance sheet in preparation for an explosion which may not happen for years, if ever. However, the fact remains that all the large banks and securities dealers that operate in this market have contingent liabilities for which there is no insurance. What is more, the probability of an explosion and its probable size increase dramatically every year, in line with the expansion of derivatives activity. It is quite clear that national and international bank supervisors and regulators would throw a purple fit if they discovered that the commercial banks had expanded their regular balance sheet activities at a 40 per cent compound annual rate. Only the lack of a functional capital adequacy regime for banks' derivatives exposures has permitted this anomaly. As yet, there seems no regulatory mechanism to restrain the unrelenting, event-specific over-commitment of banks' capital resources.

US BANKS' OFF-BALANCE SHEET DERIVATIVES ACTIVITIES

Much of the controversy surrounding bank diversification into peripheral or off-balance activities has centred on the increasing role of banks in derivatives markets. A ranking of the size of off-balance sheet derivative instruments of banks and securities firms at the end of 1995 is given in Figure 7.2. Large US banks in particular have moved swiftly to become world-wide leaders in OTC derivatives. Their motivation has been to replace some of their lost revenues from traditional banking with the attractive returns offered by derivatives markets. In 1994, a handful of US banks held derivatives contracts totalling more than $16 trillion in notional value. Of these contracts, 63 per cent were interest rate derivatives, 35 per cent currency derivatives, and the remainder were equity and commodity derivatives. In addition, most of these were held primarily to facilitate the banks' trading operations as opposed to asset–liability management. In 1994, derivatives accounted for between 15 per cent and 65 per cent of the total trading income of four of the largest bank dealers, namely Chase Manhattan, Chemical, Citicorp and J. P. Morgan. Chemical Bank was subsequently acquired by Chase Manhattan in 1995.

The US Office of the Comptroller of the Currency revealed in August 1997 that the notional principal amount of US commercial banks' derivatives holdings stood at $21 trillion. It stated that the banks had earned $8 billion in a three-month period from proprietary trading, equivalent to a 6 per cent annual return on replacement value.

Figure 7.2 The trillionaires club (as at end-1995)

	Nationality	Notional amounts $bn
Chase Manhattan Corp.	USA	4834
J. P. Morgan & Co.	USA	3447
Bank of Tokyo Mitsubishi	Japan	2869
Citicorp	USA	2590
Swiss Bank Corp.	Switzerland	2581
Société Générale	France	2543
Industrial Bank of Japan	Japan	2071
Crédit Suisse	Switzerland	1959
Fuji Bank	Japan	1891
Paribas	France	1877
National Westminster	UK	1869
Banque Nationale de Paris	France	1814
Union Bank of Switzerland	Switzerland	1781
Banker Trust N.Y. Corp.	USA	1702
Salomon, Inc.	USA	1659
Deutsche Bank	Germany	1651
Sumitomo Bank	Japan	1644
Merrill Lynch & Co., Inc.	USA	1610
Bank America Corp.	USA	1581
Barclays	UK	1569
HSBC	UK	1527
Sanwa Bank	Japan	1495
Lloyds	UK	1435
Lehman Brothers	USA	1209
The Goldman Sachs Group, L.P.	USA	1091
Crédit Lyonnais	France	1053
NationsBank Corp.	USA	1007

N.B. These amounts have not been adjusted for double counting

Source: BIS (1996)

Whether this should be viewed as a good return or a poor one is impossible to judge without some idea of the extent to which these banks placed their own capital at risk. One of the disturbing aspects of the derivatives industry is that all its major participants claim that their activities are consistently profitable. The only sense in which this can be true is if the banks' earnings from derivatives are dominated by arrangement fees and commissions rather than trading profits. Clearly, if the clients bear all the losses from poorly conceived trading, then the mystery is solved. However, it is difficult to believe that the banks have not been trading extensively on their own account; the character of derivatives suggests that some banks must be heavy loss-makers as well.

The increased participation of banks in derivatives markets has been a concern to both regulators and legislators because they fear that derivatives may enable banks to take more risk than is prudent. There can be little doubt that derivatives can be used to increase risk substantially; because of the multi-dimensional scope for leverage, derivatives enable banks to place sizeable bets on interest rate and currency movements. If these bets are wrongly conceived, enormous losses can result. Unlike organized futures exchanges, the OTC markets in which banks predominate offer no clearing house guarantee to mitigate the credit risk involved in derivatives dealing. However, the value of these guarantees is itself open to question. A clause in the UK's Securities and Futures Authority's risk warning notice to private customers states that: 'On many exchanges, the performance of a transaction by your broker is "guaranteed" by the exchange or its clearing house. However, this guarantee is unlikely in most cases to cover you, the customer, and may not protect you if your broker or another party defaults on its obligations to you.'

The culmination of these concerns was the Derivatives Safety and Soundness Act of 1994, introduced by Representatives Jim Leach and Henry Gonzalez. At approximately the same time, a comprehensive report was issued by the US Government Accounting Office (GAO).

THE IMPACT OF THE 1994 GAO REPORT

The 1994 GAO report raised the prospect that a default by a major OTC derivatives dealer (quite possibly, a large bank) could result in spill-over effects that could close down the OTC markets (such as currency and interest rate swaps), with serious consequences for the entire financial system. Two key risks were identified: first, that the sheer size of banks' OTC derivatives activities was excessive in relation to their balance sheets, such that their capital could be wiped out by the bankruptcy of a single counterparty; and second, that regulatory and risk management skills have lagged behind developments in derivatives, leaving open the possibility of unintended and imprudent risk exposure.

While, quite properly, the GAO report highlighted credit or counterparty risk, there are many other potential risk-types to be considered. Market risk arises from an unfavourable movement in the price of the underlying assets, such that derivatives prices could be impossible to calculate. Literally, the prices of these contracts could become mathematically indeterminate. For example, the complex computer algorithms used to calculate derivatives prices are tested over certain ranges of volatility for the underlying financial asset prices. If volatility explodes because of erratic equity price movements, then it may be impossible to calculate the price of the option. Another type of risk is legal risk, by which a derivatives contract may not be legally enforceable because of the nature of a counterparty. A famous example was the legal judgement which found that two London boroughs, Hammersmith and Fulham, had exceeded their authority in entering into derivatives contracts between 1983 and 1989, forcing the losses on to the underwriting banks. Finally, there is technology or operations risk, whereby computer and communications systems fail or operating procedures break down irretrievably. This could arise as a result of sabotage, civil war, software failure (such as the Millennium bug) or simply human error.

On a practical level, the worry is that senior managers do not have an adequate understanding of the internal controls necessary to limit derivatives trading risk in their own institutions. The official inquiry into the collapse of Barings stated that the management had failed at various levels to institute a proper system of internal controls; to enforce accountability for all profits, risks, and operations; and to take effective action in response to a number of warning signals over a prolonged period. A second concern is that the complex mechanisms which link markets, virtually instantaneously, may promote an unhealthy degree of hedging and speculative activity. Where there is no centralized market, and where netting-off procedures are not yet legally enforceable, there are grave dangers of potential failure in the settlement of these huge volumes of transactions.

GAO'S FOLLOW-UP REPORT

Prompted by the concentration of financial catastrophes in 1994 and 1995, the GAO produced a follow-up report in November 1996 in which they warned that many of the weaknesses identified in May 1994 had not been addressed. In each of the cases the GAO reviewed in which major losses had occurred, including Orange County and Barings, serious weaknesses in their risk management, internal control and corporate governance systems were uncovered. They added: 'Compliance with guidelines and recommended risk management practices is essentially voluntary for derivatives dealers and end-users other than regulated entities, and some surveys have shown that firms using derivatives are not involving their boards of directors in risk management.'

The GAO also expressed concern at the slack accounting standards for derivatives, noting the common use of accounting practices which allow delay in recognizing gains or losses on derivative transactions. The use of deferral hedge accounting, as it is known, in combination with historic cost accounting has enabled some investment managers to conceal losses in the market value of derivative securities for extended periods of time. The most glaring example was at Daiwa Bank in New York, where an employee accumulated $1.1 billion of losses in US government bond trading activities over a 11-year period which was predominantly a bull market!

An important step in the direction of a firmer accounting framework for derivatives activities would be to switch from a historic-cost basis to a market-value basis. US academics Franklin Edwards and Frederic Mishkin argued in 1995 that the adoption of market-value accounting would provide a more accurate and transparent picture of a bank's economic condition. At present, regulators and politicians often have an incentive to hide potential problems (to avoid financial panic) when the public interest would be served much better by an early indication of a bank's difficulties.

THE CENTRAL BANKING VIEW OF
DERIVATIVES

Giving evidence to a Congressional Committee on Energy and Commerce on 25 May 1994, the Fed chairman, Alan Greenspan, drew attention to the original GAO report. He highlighted two potential sources of systemic disturbance: 'First, the failure of a major derivatives dealer could impose credit losses on its counterparties that could threaten their financial health. Second, the dynamic hedging of options positions (e.g. associated with portfolio insurance) and certain other risk management techniques lead market participants to buy assets when prices are rising and to sell when prices are falling. In principle, such behaviour could amplify market price movements.'

He added that 'even if derivatives activities are not themselves a source of systemic risk, they may help to speed the transmission of a shock from some other source to other markets and institutions'. However, by mid-1998 at least, the gravity of these concerns had not matured into an effective response. Four years on, Mr Greenspan's speeches display little enthusiasm for any form of restriction on derivatives trading and an increasing confidence in the vigilance of the banks' and securities houses' own internal risk management systems. In 1997, when the US Financial Accounting Standards Board (FASB) sought to make derivative positions more transparent for investors by requiring companies to calculate a fair market value for their positions and to report changes in fair value in financial statements, Mr Greenspan's sympathies were elsewhere. He opposed the valuation proposal on the grounds that it 'may discourage prudent risk management activities and could in some cases present misleading financial information'.

The following is an extract from the BIS commentary on derivatives markets, dated August 1997:

The healthy economic environment, the high credit quality of counterparties, the growing use of collateral and correspondingly low level of credit losses all combined to support market growth. The data also reveal that a greater number of banks engaged in transactions, a development interpreted by some analysts as an indication that the backlash against derivatives that followed a series of corporate losses is waning. The use of derivatives is likely to continue to expand as new users are drawn into the market. Insurance companies, for example, are developing their expertise in the area and are forming joint ventures with investment banks to offer alternative solutions (including derivatives) in management of a variety of corporate risks.

While central bankers in Washington, Basle, London and Frankfurt are greatly exercised by issues of global financial stability, the emphasis is now on risk monitoring systems and disseminating models of best practice. Any sense of collective responsibility as regards the frantic pace of innovation in financial instruments, the overall growth of the value of derivatives or the absence of an accounting discipline (such as marking to market) seems to have melted away.

LOSS OF MARKET TRANSPARENCY

There is an even more serious dimension to the meteoric rise in the use of financial derivatives: the implicit credit system that operates within it. Quite apart from the inherent gearing of futures and options, relative to trades in the underlying securities, it is possible to use unrealized gains in financial assets (including derivatives contracts) as collateral for further purchases. The persistent upward trend in underlying asset prices has amplified these unrealized gains and has enabled and encouraged the progressive doubling-up of 'long' positions, particularly in government bond futures. It is easy to envisage how the cumulative actions of a small minority of market participants over a number of years can mature into a significant underlying demand for bonds. While financial commentators are apt to attribute a falling US Treasury bond yield to a lowering of inflation expectations or a new credibility that the federal budget will be balanced, the true explanation may lie in progressive gearing.

John Succo, formerly a senior executive of Lehman Brothers' equity derivatives trading desk in New York, used the following example of current market practice in his address to an investment conference organized by *Grant's Interest Rate Observer* in April 1998. The example concerns a hedge fund wishing to acquire an exposure to equities; but the mechanics would apply equally for bonds. Noting that swaps are loans in disguise, Mr Succo takes the case of a hedge fund which manages $100 million and wishes to control $100 million in stock. To gain control of $100 million of stock, the fund will typically need to put up a minimum of $8 million, in other words, a maximum gearing ratio of about 13 to 1. The hedge fund effectively buys the performance, good or bad, of $100 million of equities using an investment bank as an intermediary. The investment bank will then borrow money to buy the stock, charging the hedge fund an interest rate 0.2 per cent higher than the cost of borrowing. To quote Mr Succo, 'You're seeing leverage upon leverage at this point.'

The performance of the loan is very highly correlated to the collateral involved; in this example, the collateral is an equity portfolio. As long as the stock goes up, the investment bank is fully protected against loss. Even if the hedge fund goes bankrupt (and some smaller ones have), the investment bank is still protected because it can sell the stock and repay the loan. The real problem comes when the value of the market falls *and* the hedge fund goes bankrupt. The banks that are falling over themselves to execute deals of this nature may appear to be more than adequately capitalized. Upon closer examination, their exposure to a significant fall in the value of their financial market collateral is monumental, such is the implicit gearing in the financial system. It is a sobering thought that the most prestigious bond and equity markets in the world are exposed to the sudden withdrawal of these synthetic sources of demand.

A by-product of the derivatives boom has been an accumulation of concern over the reduced transparency of bond and equity markets. The sheer scale of futures and options trading in relation to the underlying instruments deprives market participants of important information as to the motivation for large transactions. A particularly disturbing development is the extent of programmed or quasi-automatic trades. While loss-limiting actions such as stop-loss sales or margin calls have been around for a long time, the addition of computer programs to secure certain investment objectives (e.g. option hedging, portfolio rebalancing, portfolio insurance and index matching) has increased the volume of quasi-automatic trades significantly. The existence of invisible trigger-points in currency and securities markets, for example a technical support level for the Dow Jones index, invites the possibility that a seemingly trivial price movement could provoke extreme volatility. The coincidence of expiry dates for futures and options contracts also sometimes has this effect.

THE HEDGING TRAP

An increasingly popular use of derivatives by fund managers is as a form of insurance against capital loss in securities or portfolios of securities. Rather than express their concerns that a blue-chip stock or portfolio of stocks may be overvalued by selling into the market, many institutional investors hedge their exposure in the futures and options markets. Essentially, what happens is that the investment fund pays a premium to insure against the risk that share prices will fall below a particular level over a specific time horizon. Meanwhile the bank or securities firm which accepts the risk must prove that it has sufficient funds available to reimburse its client (the investment manager) in the event that share prices fall below the specified threshold. A proportion of these funds is deposited (without interest) as margin. If share prices fall, then the client will be called upon to supply additional margin to the relevant exchange. Conversely, if share prices rise, then margin requirements are reduced and the bank or securities firm can earn a return on the funds released.

All is well so long as only a small proportion of institutional investors share these concerns over falling share prices. Provided the market sustains an upward trend with only temporary downward deviations, then the worries of the minority will not prevail. The banks and securities houses writing the options will make profits at the expense of the institutions seeking protection, and the market's upward trend will be undisturbed. If, however, market fears are widespread and the demand for portfolio insurance becomes very large, then the market will disintegrate. In an obviously vulnerable market, the investment banks that sell these portfolio hedging instruments to fund managers have no choice but to cover themselves by simultaneous sales of the full value of the underlying securities. In other words, the direct selling of securities that the funds sought to avoid proves unavoidable. Under these circumstances, insurance against the erosion of portfolio value becomes either prohibitively expensive or simply unavailable.

Derivatives trading played a key role in the equity market crash of October 1987. It is estimated that $3 billion of portfolio insurance triggered a bigger price move in US equities than $300 billion of direct selling would have done. In the week prior to 19 October, portfolio insurers' sales soared well above their usual levels as investors rushed to protect themselves against the market's decline. Their actions proved self-fulfilling. Unfortunately, the investment banks providing the insurance relied on their ability to sell exactly the amount of stock that their computer models told them to sell. On this occasion, they found that they could not sell the underlying equities fast enough to keep pace with the action their computer models demanded. By the time the stock market opened on 19 October, an $8 billion overhang of selling orders had arisen, equivalent to a typical day's trading volume on the New York Stock Exchange. A severe bout of indigestion in the trading system denied traders access to the market, leading to a breakdown of the normal relationship between the cash price of equities and futures prices. With futures prices remaining below cash prices, portfolio insurance fell apart at the seams.

The paradox is that portfolio insurance supports an ongoing bull market, but it accelerates and amplifies a bear market. A minority of worried institutional investors are able to lay off market risk without suffering the portfolio damage that would result from urgent selling of the underlying stocks. It is rather as if 'bearish' investors are admitted to clinics to receive treatment for their sour disposition. Having cured them of their hypochondria, the clinics then release them back into society. In this way a contagion of market pessimism is prevented. However, when this minority of investors becomes very large, the clinics are overwhelmed with applicants. The facilities available to the few are incapable of dealing with the many. Moreover, the very mechanism which diminishes price volatility in a rising market multiplies it in a falling market. As fund managers act discreetly to lay off market risk, the banks and securities houses observe a one-sided market and are compelled to slash prices.

CONCLUSIONS

The development of financial derivatives is perhaps the most strident expression of the confidence embodied within the global capital markets. Inspired by a global bull market in equities and bonds which has spanned almost a generation, advocates of sophisticated financial innovations have pushed against an open door. Under the guise of risk management techniques and efficient hedging strategies, the increasing acceptance and use of derivative products have galloped ahead of our understanding of their wider implications.

Central banks, and the BIS itself, have abdicated responsibility for the specific task of ensuring that banks' capital is not over-traded using financial derivatives. The capital adequacy safeguards for depositors in the context of the slowly growing balance sheets of the banks should apply equally to their rapidly growing off-balance sheet activities, such as unmatched swaps. However, they plainly do not offer comparable protection. Whereas most on-balance sheet risks are clearly defined, derivatives risks are complex and inter-correlated. By netting off exposures with each of its counterparties, a bank may be able to argue that its capital requirements are trivial. However, many of the risks associated with derivatives do not fall neatly into the categories of counterparty credit risk or market risk. Like inept detectives, the central bank regulators are liable to arrive on the scene of a crime long after the damage has been done. Meticulous post-mortems are no substitute for intelligent anticipation.

A recurrent theme of this chapter has been the participants' desire to conceal and the ease of concealment that financial derivatives allow. Between 1994 and 1997 there was little growth of derivatives activity on the organized exchanges. By contrast, the OTC market activity has grown at breakneck pace. Legal risks encourage the creation of off-shore subsidiaries for derivatives dealing. Accounting standards are as lax as cooked spaghetti. While the GAO and FASB are fighting a lone – and probably losing – battle for tighter reporting standards and monitoring frameworks, the spread of derivatives users becomes wider and wider. What is clear is that when the next global bear market in equities and bonds arrives, the unwinding of highly geared derivatives positions will trigger financial explosions in every corner of the developed world.

8

The Illusion of Unlimited Savings

'Furthermore, the world's capital markets are much more open than they were ten years ago and the US has access to a virtually unlimited supply of funds.' *Financial Times* article, 20 February 1998

'In all, it would appear that the secular rise in the real interest rate is due to a decline in the saving rate – driven largely by fiscal deficits – which has outweighed a parallel reduction in desired investment.' *Saving, Investment and Real Interest Rates*, G10 Study, 1995

There are two age-old questions concerning saving, borrowing and investment for which mankind has failed to find satisfactory solutions. The 18–25-year-old asks, in tones reminiscent of the Prodigal Son, 'Why, if I have excellent earnings prospects, should I not be allowed to spend some of my future wealth now when I am best able to enjoy it?' Similarly, the fifty-something-year-old asks, 'Why should I spend my latter years in drudgery or near-poverty only to leave a sizeable inheritance to my comparatively rich children?' In both cases, the inquirers long for access to a capital market that does not stereotype them on account of their age.

Consider first the case of the young adult who wishes to borrow against the security of his or her potential lifetime earnings. Clearly, there is a material risk that the loan will not be fully repaid. In a civilized society, where slavery and intimidation are illegal, the lender risks the loss of his capital. The problem is that young adults are frequently unable to offer any credentials in support of their credit application other than their education and enthusiasm. Some countries, for example Germany and Switzerland, set stringent limits on credit availability until the applicant reaches a certain age. Other countries insist that applicants develop a consistent savings habit over several years before they become borrowers of significant sums such as home loans. Latterly, the Anglo-Saxon attitude has been to hand the money over and hope to allow for the added risk in the interest rate charged.

The second conundrum is posed by older adults who would prefer to spend more of their lifetime savings while they are still reasonably energetic and healthy. Instead, the actuaries compel them to choose between two less appetizing prospects. In one, they retire early with a diminished pension entitlement and combine a few years of high-quality leisure with many years of subsistence living later. In the other, they work additional years and retire on a full pension but risk the depletion of their energy or health in the meantime. Their wealth is ultimately consumed by medical and nursing bills or is bequeathed to their heirs. The problem here is to balance the entitlements and responsibilities (i.e. benefits and taxes) of successive generations. It is far too tempting for politicians to indulge one generation of pensioners, whose ranks they will shortly join, at the expense of the next generation and their children. Equally, it is desperately difficult to induce younger adults to make adequate provision for their own, albeit distant, retirement.

The interaction of short-sighted decision-making and demographic cycles can be very dramatic. If the dependency ratio is high (that is, there is a large population of beneficiaries relative to the working population), then even high income tax and contribution rates may deliver only modest pensions and benefits in a state-organized Pay As You Go system. Privately funded pension schemes, in which individuals accumulate their own personal pension entitlement, may appear superior but are vulnerable in other ways. What happens, for example, if the pension fund invests the money badly, or is the victim of fraud? Presumably, the government still bears ultimate responsibility for the support of the disenfranchised pensioner. Worse still, there may be a wide gulf between the state's pension liabilities and its perceived ability to raise taxes to fund them, either in the present or in the future. This is sometimes referred to as the pensions time bomb.

PERSONAL VERSUS NATIONAL SAVINGS

These two examples give a flavour of the conflict between personal and national savings preferences. The national interest strongly favours a system whereby individuals have few lifetime opportunities to become technically insolvent, that is, for the market value of their assets to fall beneath the value of their debts and other financial obligations. Where technical insolvency translates into actual bankruptcy, the wealth of other private individuals is wiped out and the state bears an added burden of support costs. The more open a society and the greater the opportunities for individuals to succeed or fail financially, the larger the risks of widespread insolvency and dependence on state support. Paradoxically, in some developing countries, where personal freedom is heavily circumscribed by government and where capital markets are undeveloped or strictly regulated, the national saving rate (adding together the private and public sectors) tends to be higher than in mature western economies.

A fascinating study by the International Monetary Fund of national saving rates in developing countries found that middle-income countries (such as Peru, Sri Lanka, Egypt and Zimbabwe) showed a much greater appetite for saving out of current income than high-income countries (such as Mexico, Hong Kong, Israel and Brazil). Whereas an increase in the ratio of total wealth to national income induced the middle-income countries to save at a faster pace, the reverse was true for the richer developing countries. In almost all countries, the national saving rate fell as the dependency ratio rose. The increase in life expectancy in developed countries over the past 30 years implies that, barring disaster, the dependency ratio will rise over the coming 30 years regardless of the fertility rate. In the absence of other economic stimuli, the national saving rate in the wealthy western economies and Japan is set on a downward path.

Well aware of this savings deficiency problem, western governments have tried two broad approaches. First, they have offered tax incentives and subsidies to persuade individuals to save more. Second, they have increased general taxation or reduced social security expenditures in order to improve the public sector's saving rate. In countries where the public sector finances are in deficit, this means reducing the degree of dis-saving. Unfortunately, as various governments have discovered, there is an interdependence between private and public savings behaviour. If the tax incentives are designed to be popular, they are also expensive in terms of revenue forgone; also, the more the government saves, the less the private sector does. Typically, the net improvement in national saving is only about half as large as the authorities had hoped. Furthermore, the easier the access that young prodigals and greying adventurers have to the capital market, the harder it is to keep the national saving rate from falling.

THE EMERGENCE OF A UNIFIED CAPITAL MARKET

In theory, efficient capital markets should be able to lend the savings of the older generations to the younger ones in exchange for a reasonably stable risk-adjusted rate of return. In practice, these rates of return have been volatile, leading to irregular intervals when one group or the other has enjoyed an unwarranted gain at the expense of the other. In the inflationary episodes of the 1970s and 1980s, real interest rates (nominal rates minus actual or expected inflation) oscillated between −15 per cent and 10 per cent in the G7 countries. During intervals when real interest rates were negative, the advantage lay predominantly with the generation of younger adults whose interest payments were falling in relation to their incomes. Conversely, the era of quite high real interest rates which began around 1981 has conferred a relative benefit on the older generations whose wealth has grown effortlessly.

The notion of a unified global capital market gradually took shape during the 1980s, as we discussed in Chapter 5. Until then, a mixture of institutional rigidities, private capital controls and national oligopolies in the provision of financial services had ensured an effective separation of national savings markets, except that of the USA which was a pioneer in the large-scale import of foreign capital. As the waves of financial de-regulation, privatization and the liberalization of capital flows swept across the European continent, so private capital has become more and more geographically diversified. Aided by improved information sources and technology, and co-ordinated by a growing international fund management industry, treasured secrets become common knowledge and pricing anomalies are straightened out. On 1 April 1998, the last large bastion of financial regulation, Japan, finally opened up its securities markets and abandoned its foreign exchange controls. There is speculation that a sizeable segment of the $2 trillion of lowly yielding bank deposits will exercise the freedom to roam the globe in search of a better return.

Much has been written about the diversion of savings from the large developed economies to the emerging markets of Asia, Latin America, Europe and Africa, but these flows remain of marginal significance to the global capital market. Total capital flows from developed to developing countries rose dramatically from $10 billion in 1970 to a peak of just over $100 billion in 1981 until the Latin American sovereign debt crisis struck. From a base of around $65 billion in 1986, a second wave of capital transfer has lifted the annual flow to $280 billion in 1996 after a hiccup in 1994. Even at 1996 rates, these transfers represent only a small fraction of total capital demands. Moreover, there are several examples of Asian countries with surplus savings that have been reinvested in US dollar assets, particularly US Treasury bills and bonds. The capital traffic has not been all one way.

Perhaps the most important practical implication of capital market de-regulation has been the convergence of the inflation-adjusted cost of capital around the globe. During the 1980s, European and North American real yields on benchmark ten-year government bonds, for which there is a high degree of standardization, began to converge on a single rate. Average real yields for the 1970s ranged from −1.4 per cent in Italy to 3.2 per cent in Germany, but by the 1980s the spread had narrowed considerably, ranging from 2.8 per cent in Italy to 4.6 per cent in Germany. The implication of this convergence is that Italian and German ten-year bond yields, for example, differ mainly because of varying perceptions of inflation expectations in the two countries. As inflation has been brought under control, so benchmark bond yields have converged in nominal terms as well as real. This is not to deny that nominal yields are still vulnerable to favourable and unfavourable shocks to the supply of government debt.

Many imperfections and inconsistencies remain, but there is a genuine sense in which savings and investment are determined in a single capital market with a single real interest rate. For the world as a whole, it is plain that the aggregate flows of savings and investment must be identical in any time period. However, the process whereby the flow of savings offered to the market is matched up with planned investment in capital assets is far from a pure market-clearing process. Real interest rates appear to play a relatively small part in balancing the two sides of the market. At various times there are frustrated savers, who decide to spend more of their income than they had originally intended, and frustrated investor-borrowers, who postpone or cancel their investment plans in the light of market conditions.

THE PERILS OF OVER- AND UNDER-INVESTMENT

Before introducing any further complications into the analysis, it is necessary to dispose of a popular myth about saving and investment. Governments of all shades along the political spectrum are very fond of the word 'investment'. Whatever economic ills are diagnosed, someone will propose a larger dose of investment. For some it will be investment in advanced technology, for some, grand energy projects and, for others, the transport and social infrastructure. The slogan conveys the impression that all investment at all times and in all places is a good thing. This is plainly false. It is equally possible and dangerous to over-invest out of current income as it is to under-invest. Over-investment typically occurs when the cost of borrowed capital is artificially low, the expected returns on capital are exaggerated or capital is appropriated for grandiose projects with little or no commercial logic attached. Ill-timed, ill-advised or merely ill-fated investment earns disappointing returns and may even destroy financial capital. Japan in the late 1980s and East Asia in the mid-1990s are the prime examples of over-investment in industrial and commercial capacity.

Under-investment (or over-consumption) occurs when real interest rates appear discouragingly high to potential investor-borrowers, but comfortably low to consumers and property speculators. This paradox is explained by the fact that producer output prices may be stable or growing only slowly, while property prices are soaring and are expected to increase further. The high cost of capital to the industrial borrower will reflect the low inflation rates for his end-products, while property-owning consumers will be much more relaxed about taking on more debt in order to maintain or increase their expenditures. In many western countries the problem is compounded by the policy of allowing loan interest to be offset against tax liabilities. By contrast, after-tax real interest rates to domestic savers will not be sufficiently attractive to induce them to offer more savings.

Across the global capital market, the proportion of income saved and invested can rise or fall for various reasons. Ratios of gross saving and investment to world GDP contain a large segment of depreciation of the capital stock. Depending on the type of physical asset formation which takes place, there is scope for the element of replacement investment to be high or low. If the bias of productive investment is in power plants and railway networks, then the assumed asset lives will be long and the implied depreciation rates will be low. Conversely, if the bias is towards portable and almost disposable technologies (such as personal computers), then the assumed asset lives should be low and the rates of capital consumption correspondingly high. Only after deducting depreciation is it possible to assess whether the savings and investment trend is rising or falling.

CAN THERE BE TOO MUCH SAVING?

It is harder to envisage a situation of excess saving, but it can certainly happen. At the national level, the most obvious examples are small rich countries with relatively large financial sectors and small industrial and commercial sectors, such as Switzerland, Saudi Arabia, Kuwait, Luxembourg and Brunei. These countries are natural exporters of capital because of the paucity of opportunities for physical investment in their own countries. Another example would be a rich country with limited opportunities for personal consumption or ownership of domestic assets. Japan's high saving rate is in part a product of the lack of land available for private ownership. At the global level, excess saving might occur in the aftermath of a stock market crash as individuals refrain from consumption in order to rebuild their savings. If the financial mood remained over-cautious, then the over-supply of savings would drive down the real interest rate and the required real rate of return on business investment. The outcome would be complementary to the description of over-investment given above.

However, it is not difficult to identify episodes of inadequate aggregate saving; indeed there have been worrying declines in gross national saving among western developed countries at the start of the 1980s and the 1990s. This observation is all the more mystifying when it is contrasted with the conventional wisdom of the global capital market. Received wisdom, as illustrated by the quote at the start of this chapter from the *Financial Times*, holds that the pool of private savings among the large developed nations is so large as to appear unlimited to any single borrower. In any case, the borrowers are mainly sovereign governments and companies with impeccable credit agency ratings, so what could possibly go awry? This complacent and erroneous mind-set is a product of some remarkable capital market circumstances which have evolved during the 1990s. Despite an escalation in capital market borrowing by both public and private sectors of the developed nations, benchmark government bond yields around the world have trended lower. In the first wave of euphoria, which reached its climax at the end of 1993, it was widely supposed that global savings within the developed countries were in abundant supply. The low bond yields, it was claimed, were a reward for the tough anti-inflation measures adopted by most governments during the 1980s; the lower debt service costs were a 'peace dividend' arising from the defeat of inflation.

EXPLANATION OF THE 1994
BOND MARKET CRISIS

After the bond market climax at the end of 1993, the euphoria was dashed by a symbolic US interest rate increase in February 1994. In the following nine months, bond yields rebounded sharply, wiping out most of the capital gains of the previous two years. The logical explanation of the 1994 bond market crisis, which added 2 per cent (200 basis points) to US bond yields and 4 per cent (400 basis points) to Italian bond yields, is that an unsustainable boom had collapsed under the weight of its own contradictions. Gross national savings of the developed nations, measured as a proportion of GDP, fell by 2.4 percentage points between 1989 and 1993 due to a rise in public sector budget deficits that were not fully compensated by a higher rate of private saving. A fall of 2.9 percentage points had occurred ten years earlier, and only 1.1 percentage points were recovered during the subsequent economic upswing. The coincidence of rising capital demands and falling bond yields is explained by two factors: first, a portfolio shift in the savings market away from low-yielding bank deposits into higher-yielding bonds; and, second, a huge tide of speculative investment in the bond markets financed at historically low cost in the US and Japanese money markets and using the opportunities for gearing offered by the derivatives markets (Chapter 7). The surge in capital market issue between 1990 and 1993 was accommodated by dramatic changes in the composition of existing private sector financial wealth rather than an increase in the saving rates of the large developed countries.

The steeply sloping yield curves of the USA, Canada, the UK, Italy, Scandinavia and Australia sucked existing savings out of low-yielding capital-certain bank deposits and money market instruments into higher-yielding and illiquid investments, *whose capital values were not guaranteed*. The nature of this transaction, involving an addition of both risk and return, is central to the argument of this book. It is a tribute to the gullibility of ordinary citizens in financial matters that so few people bother to inquire how investment products generate their seductively high yields. A prime example comes from the USA in 1991–2 when billions of dollars' worth of ten-year CDs, issued in the high interest rate environment of 1981–2 and yielding more than 10 per cent per annum, matured. Finding that the returns for the comparable instruments had fallen to 3 per cent or 4 per cent, investors faced a sharp reduction in their income. Those who had become dependent on this income, especially pensioners, were eager to find a better-yielding alternative. In order to secure these yields, they unwittingly acquired replacement products that embodied much greater capital market and credit quality risk. It is all the more remarkable that, six years later, no accidents have occurred.

As and when these retail investors in mutual funds, private pension plans and individual retirement accounts experience their first bear market (the mildest of which typically involves a 30 per cent retracement in fund values), the effects could be quite devastating. While those in employment have the opportunity to rebuild wealth through accelerated saving, for those in retirement this will be impossible. Nevertheless, in the aggregate there will be a natural rebound in private saving behaviour. But until then, the temptation for young and old is to live well and borrow freely against the security of spectacularly performing funds.

THE NEW BOND CLIMAX OF 1998

Thinking back to the rude awakening that greeted the global bond market in February 1994, it seems like a breath of fresh air, a triumph of analysis over anecdote. But it was desperately short-lived. By the end of 1994, the bond crisis had been overtaken by the Mexican peso crisis and the upward march of US policy interest rates was arrested. As part of the international support package for Mexico, the redemption of $17 billion of its dollar-denominated bonds (tesobonos) was guaranteed without resort to US Treasury bond issues. The combined message of these events was favourable for world bond markets, and yields fell once more. By the close of 1995, the bull market in bonds was fully reinstated. Despite a flirtation with higher US bond yields in early 1997, the downward drift in yields was still intact in October 1998. Paradoxically, the financial turmoil which developed in East

Asia during 1997 has triggered many of the same favourable bond market dynamics that were evident after the peso crisis. Once again, expectations of higher policy interest rates in the USA and Germany evaporated and investors embraced western bond markets as perceived safe havens from Asia's troubles. As a result, in the autumn of 1998, the US 30-year Treasury bond yield dropped to an astonishing 4.7 per cent and benchmark ten-year bond yields in Germany and France fell to 3.8 per cent, the lowest since 1945.

The task of exposing the inconsistencies and dangers which lie behind these record-breaking bond market performances is even more daunting now than in 1994. The illusion of an unlimited savings pool has grown more and more powerful, and it is matched by a new confidence among prospective bond issuers. The World Bank (IBRD) announced a $4 billion bond issue in March 1998, only to be outdone by a $5 billion issue from Fannie Mae, the US mortgage lender, a few months later. These jumbo bonds convey the impression that there is an insatiable demand for government, quasi-government and high-quality corporate bonds. Massive investment funds, whose minimum holding size prohibits them from venturing into all but the largest and most actively traded securities, are eager customers for these huge bond issues. Jumbo meets Mammoth.

UNDERSTANDING THE ROLE OF BUDGET DEFICITS

The temptation to regard the secular decline in bond yields as a reliable and irreversible phenomenon reflects a growing optimism that the government budget deficits have finally been tamed. Lower budget deficits imply a reduced supply of government bonds and, superficially, lend support to higher bond prices and lower yields. Budget deficits have weighed heavily against national saving rates for many years, averaging 2.9 per cent of GDP across 21 OECD countries between 1980 and 1996. A reduction in the budget deficit to GDP ratio in OECD countries from 4.3 per cent in 1993 to 2.6 per cent in 1996 and a projected 1.0 per cent in 1998 has been accompanied by a recovery in the average national saving rate for the developed countries from 19.0 per cent in 1993 to an estimated 20.5 per cent in 1996.

While this is definitely a step in the right direction, there is considerable doubt over its sustainability. Despite the narrowing of the US federal deficit, the US national saving rate is no longer rising. Private saving rates are declining as fast as public saving improves. In Japan, the situation is even less promising. A steady decline in the national saving rate from 34.5 per cent in 1991 to an estimated 31.4 per cent in 1996 reflects a sequence of abortive fiscal packages. In April 1997, the Ministry of Finance restored the consumption tax to its previous level after a period of concession, and economic growth fell apart once more. Taking into consideration the degree of undeclared bad debt problems in the Japanese banking system and the cost to the public sector of its Bank Stabilization Package ($238 billion) in February 1998, a further decline in the national saving rate looks to be inevitable. As a postscript, it should be noted that the budget deficit data include receipts of social security and public pension fund contributions. On the basis that these funds will ultimately be discharged as payments to the various beneficiaries, the underlying budget deficit is understated by about 1.0 per cent of GDP in the USA and by 2.4 per cent of GDP in Japan.

There are also concerns surrounding the sustainability of the public finances of several EU countries. Despite persistently high and rising unemployment, Germany and France have contained their budget deficits within the Maastricht-prescribed limit of 3 per cent for 1997, while Italy has plunged beneath it. However, for some countries there are suspicions that expenditures have merely been deferred and that asset sales and other technical devices have been used to hold the deficits down. These arguments will be fleshed out in Chapter 14. The objective in this chapter is to challenge the prevailing wisdom that savings in the large developed countries are in plentiful supply and will remain so.

AN ALTERNATIVE EXPLANATION OF
FALLING GLOBAL BOND YIELDS

The single most compelling explanation of the multi-year bull market in benchmark government bond yields is the apparent opportunity to generate capital gain at negligible risk. As the parallel bull market in equities has been exploring the stratosphere and offering pitifully low dividend yields, so there has been a migration of institutional funds and retail investment into bonds at the expense of bank deposits and money market funds. The prevalence of an upward-sloping yield curve (with ten-year bond yields comfortably higher than three-month deposit rates) since 1992 has convinced a sizeable majority of professional investors that playing the yield curve is a low-risk activity. Borrowing short and lending long has been the bread-and-butter risk business in traditional banking for over 200 years. It has become the staple trade for the investment management industry also, not to mention the hedge funds and certain central banks.

The fundamental motivation behind ever-lower bond yields is this overwhelming desire to lend long-term. Governments and companies cannot believe their good fortune. Instead of treading carefully in the money markets, to avoid driving up their borrowing costs, or issuing equity capital to wary institutions, they are able to borrow at bargain-basement rates at three-year, five-year and ten-year maturities. This passion for curve-playing has fostered a demand for such exotic offerings as 50-year and 100-year bonds from Disney Corporation and Coca-Cola, although investors pick up only a few extra basis points of yield along the way. The outcome of all this nonsense is that ordinary investors have become exposed to the classic risk of mismatched interest rates. Any sequence of events which causes the US and German yield curves to invert (raising short rates above bond yields) will wreak havoc on investment returns.

Much to their amazement, companies and mortgage borrowers that financed their ten-year debt at 8 per cent have been able to refinance it at 7 per cent and now at 6 per cent. Like small children let loose in a chocolate factory, commercial and financial corporations have indulged their appetites, borrowing well beyond their current and even future requirements for funds. Their willingness to lock in at these rates reflects an instinctive (and historically sound) belief that mid-1998 bond yields are artificially low. For as long as the bull market in global bonds persists, the lenders (investors) are content because their asset is appreciating and the yield is the best that they can find. The borrowers are equally happy because they firmly expect that one day bond yields will rebound and that they will be protected against the higher cost of borrowing. Meanwhile, they are enjoying the cash-flow benefit of lower debt service charges following their last successful refinancing.

What happened in 1994, when the US Federal Reserve raised the funds rate by a mere quarter of a percentage point, was a huge surprise to the bond market. The money and debt markets appeared to have fully discounted a rise in short-term interest rates of this amount. What threw the bond and equity markets into confusion was the degree of highly leveraged yield curve speculation. In an instant, some market participants had suffered a rise in borrowing costs, a loss on their investments and an urgent demand to deposit additional funds or securities to fulfil margin requirements on their derivatives. All this occurred without an actual inversion of the US yield curve. Had the Fed been free to complete their sequence of funds rate increases, then an inversion might well have happened during 1995.

The lessons of 1994 are long forgotten, lost in a mist of boundless optimism about inflation and long-term real interest rates. For the time being, the inflation optimism is well justified but the real interest rate optimism is not. In the final part of this chapter, the role of real interest rates in the global capital market is elaborated.

REAL INTEREST RATES

The emergence of a representative real bond yield which seemed to apply across all the major government bond markets should have heralded an improvement in the efficiency of the global capital market. In an ideal world, this global real yield would signal a prospective shortage or surplus of savings, causing savers and borrowers to change their behaviour. The fundamental rationality of the global capital market was not difficult to assert during the 1980s. A downward drift in national saving rates since 1980 was associated with markedly higher real interest rates for most of the decade that followed. The puzzle of the 1990s is why the global real bond yield has gradually declined without any convincing evidence of a sustainable savings recovery.

Anyone familiar with financial markets will appreciate that there is seldom a shortage of enthusiastic optimism, nor of eloquent rationalizations of abnormally high market valuations. A popular explanation of declining real bond yields in the late 1990s asserts that a technology-induced productivity miracle is unfolding in the Anglo-Saxon economies. Under this line of reasoning, economic growth in North America and parts of Europe will soon rival the 4 per cent annual growth pace of the golden 1950s and 1960s. At much faster growth rates, the public sector will spring back from perennial budget deficits to record budget surpluses and national saving rates will recover strongly. Real bond yields will then fall towards the 1–2 per cent range which prevailed in the 1950s and 1960s, allowing nominal bond yields to fall to 5 per cent or even 4 per cent. *Ergo*, the global bond market has plenty of scope to extend its bull run, which will underpin a rising trend in equity prices into the bargain.

The appeal to a golden era which few can remember is part of the revisionist's stock-in-trade. A moment's reflection should be sufficient to pour a flood of scepticism on the optimist's charter. Is there any similarity between the mind-sets of consumers in the 1990s and in the aftermath of the Second World War? A slight difference in demographics, perhaps? In consumer attitudes to debt and the opportunities to express them? Is there any comparison between the sophistication and complexity of capital markets now and then? And where is the wealth-enhancing productivity growth that has long been heralded? Moreover, in the 1950s and 1960s, political leaders enjoyed much more public trust than they do today, enabling tougher economic decisions to be taken. The budget deficit culture, from which the western world is still trying to free itself, is symptomatic of a loss of political authority.

Once again, there is a much more persuasive and coherent explanation for the fall in real interest rates across the whole yield curve in the second half of the 1990s. If it were necessary to borrow $1 in the money market to lend or invest $1 at a longer maturity, then yield curve manoeuvres would have no influence on real interest rates. In reality, it is possible to establish capital market positions at least ten times larger than the amount borrowed using derivatives, such as bond futures and interest rate swaps. This neat trick has been performed with increasing regularity during the 1990s. As capital gains have accumulated in the bull market, so the traders have acquired an influence over real interest rates. Either an unexpected rise in short-term interest rates in the USA or an independent shock to the global bond market (e.g. a debt moratorium for East Asia or a world grain shortage) is capable of provoking a panic reaction.

CONCLUSION

The conclusion of this extended episode of geared yield curve specu-lation will be spectacularly painful for borrowers. Real interest rates may rise from the 3 per cent region, not only to the market-clearing level of around 5 per cent, but well beyond it in the first instance. High real interest rates are an established market mechanism designed to call forth extra private savings and to curtail capital demands by both public and private sectors. The prevalence of artificially low real interest rates has diverted global capital to unprofitable end-uses, including the construction of excess industrial capacity. It is an obstacle to the recovery in national saving rates and a false signal to bond issuers. When the mist clears, the supreme challenge for the financial authorities will be to foster the confidence of savers in a weak economic environment.

9

The Bloated Bond Markets

'In particular, financial institutions and private investors show repeated tendencies to underprice risk in debt contracts . . . which in turn has been readily accepted by borrowers.'

E. P. Davis, *Debt, Financial Fragility and Systemic Risk*, 1992

The development and behaviour of bond markets lie at the heart of the thesis about debt and delusion. In Chapter 5 the significance of bonds was introduced in the context of the spectacular growth of the financial markets since 1980. Chapter 7 noted the added dimension that derivative products bring to the analysis of government bonds. The evolution of bond yields in the 1990s featured prominently in the discussion of the savings illusion in the last chapter. This chapter throws the spotlight squarely on the global bond market and addresses some fundamental questions. How big is the world bond market? How quickly has it grown? Which countries have the largest bond markets? What is the relationship between budget deficits and the issue of government bonds? Who really owns the bonds? Should bonds be counted as additions to private wealth? Is the bond market out of control? What frightens bond markets? Which countries are in greatest danger if there is a global bond market shock?

Part of the mystique about bond markets results from the fact that so little useful information is readily available, apart from bond yields and the prices of individual bond issues. In stark contrast to monetary statistics, which appear promptly, regularly and in fantastic detail for many countries, bond market information is patchy, awkwardly presented and very slow to arrive. It is as if the authorities wish to emphasize monetary data at the expense of bond market data. The balance sheets of the commercial banks are scrutinized each month by central bank officials and policy committees to gauge whether the money supply is growing too quickly, and whether interest rates should be raised. While most monetary policy committee members pay no more than lip service to the behaviour of monetary aggregates, even this is better than the downright neglect which is shown to bond market data. The closest that most countries come to an analysis of the bond market is an annual review of the management of the national debt. Knowing that the media thrive on timely official data releases, they are careful to publish bond market data late and in obscure places.

From humble beginnings 30 years ago, bonds have developed into the pre-eminent global financial market. With colossal turnover for the benchmark government bond issues and a complex structure of bond derivatives, each with its own high turnover, the centre of gravity of the whole financial system has altered since the mid-1980s. The money markets, particularly the market for short-term deposits and loans, are no longer the centre of the financial universe. The more rapid development of government and corporate bonds has transferred activity and influence away from money markets, up the yield curve into bond market territory. Whereas bond markets used to react primarily to policy changes in short-term interest rates, nowadays the bond markets interpret economic data for themselves. The expectations of bond market participants and their reactions to world economic, political and meteorological news send shock waves to world equity and currency markets. Whether these conclusions and opinions are inspired or indifferent, accurate or wayward, they are authoritative. To an increasing extent, the assimilation of information flows and the formation of consensus economic opinion in the financial markets have become centralized in bond market circles. Shocks migrate as readily from bond markets to the money markets (often transmitted through the relevant futures contracts) as vice versa.

WORLD BOND MARKETS: DEVELOPMENT
AND SIZE

Whereas the quantities of different types of bank deposits can be added together without controversy, bonds can be valued at the price when they were issued, the nominal price that they will achieve at redemption, or at the prevailing market price. The convention adopted here is nominal value outstanding. This is the nominal amount that the bond issuer must eventually repay to the bond holders at the end of the bond's predetermined life span. For example, the price of a five-year bond issued at par ($100) on a coupon of 6 per cent (per year) would stay close to $100 throughout its life, provided bond yields also remained close to 6 per cent. The bond would be redeemed for $100 at the end of the five years. But if bond yields fell to 5 per cent at some stage in its life, the bond price would rise to $120, such that the 6 per cent coupon would be scaled by $120 rather than $100. Bonds which are issued at a discount to par typically offer a smaller coupon or interest payment but include a built-in tendency to appreciate in value.

Unofficial estimates of the size of the world bond market at end-1997 suggest a figure of around $25 trillion, roughly equivalent to a year's GDP of the 20 largest developed countries. This staggering total represents a doubling since 1989, and a six-fold increase since 1982. Almost two-thirds of this debt is owed by governments and their agencies, or backed by them. Quite simply, the public sector segment of the debt mountain is the counterpart to almost 25 years of lax fiscal policy, that is, perennial budget deficits. It is easy to forget that, as recently as the 1960s, the government budgets of the OECD countries were in approximate balance and that net issues of debt were comparatively rare. The outstanding stock of debt in public hands was a meagre $800 billion at the end of 1970. At that time, debt issue was typically reserved for the financing of large construction projects or investment in power generation by publicly owned corporations. Figure 9.1 chronicles the suddenness of the transition from balanced to unbalanced budgets. While Italy, Ireland and Belgium were already experimenting with deficit finance by 1970, the USA avoided its first serious budgetary lapse until 1975.

Figure 9.1 General government financial balances as a proportion of GDP

% of GDP	1960–69 Average	1970–79 Average	1980–89 Average	1990	1991	1992	1993	1994	1995	1996	1997
USA	-0.1	-1.0	-2.5	-2.7	-3.3	-4.4	-3.6	-2.3	-2.0	-1.6	-1.1
excluding social security(1)	..	..	-2.9	-3.7	-4.2	-5.2	-4.4	-3.2	-2.8	-2.5	-2.0
Japan	1.0	-1.7	-1.5	2.9	2.9	1.5	-1.6	-2.3	-3.7	-4.4	-3.1
excluding social security(1)	..	-4.0	-4.3	-0.7	-0.8	-2.0	-4.8	-5.1	-6.6	-7.3	-5.8
Germany(2)	0.7	-1.7	-2.1	-2.1	-3.3	-2.8	-3.5	-2.4	-3.6	-3.8	-3.2
France(3)	0.0	-0.4	-2.1	-1.6	-2.0	-3.8	-5.6	-5.6	-5.0	-4.2	-3.2
Italy	-2.4	-8.6	-11.0	-11.0	-10.2	-12.1	-9.7	-9.6	-7.0	-6.7	-3.2
UK	-0.3	-2.4	-2.0	-1.2	-2.5	-6.3	-7.8	-6.8	-5.5	-4.4	-2.8
Canada	-0.3	-0.8	-4.5	-4.1	-6.6	-7.4	-7.3	-5.3	-4.1	-1.8	-0.2
Belgium	..	-5.1	-9.2	-5.6	-6.5	-7.2	-7.5	-5.1	-4.1	-3.4	-2.8
Netherlands	..	-1.4	-4.9	-5.1	-2.9	-3.9	-3.2	-3.4	-4.1	-2.4	-2.3
Sweden(3)	3.4	2.6	-1.6	4.2	-1.1	-7.8	-12.3	-10.3	-7.7	-3.6	-2.1
Australia	..	0.0	-1.4	0.6	-2.7	-4.0	-3.8	-4.0	-2.0	-1.4	-1.0
Denmark	..	1.5	-2.7	-1.5	-2.1	-2.9	-3.9	-3.4	-1.9	-1.6	0.0
European Union	..	..	-4.3	-3.8	-4.4	-5.6	-6.5	-5.8	-5.2	-4.4	-3.0
OECD	0.0	-1.6	-2.9	-2.1	-2.7	-3.9	-4.3	-3.6	-3.3	-2.9	-1.9

(1) Estimates made by the OECD Secretariat. The coverage of social security systems is dissimilar in the USA and Japan.
(2) Includes balances relating to the German Railways Fund from 1994 and the Inherited Debt Fund from 1995 onwards.
(3) Definition of the financial balance has altered due to the adoption of Maastricht principles. This affects France from 1992 and Sweden from 1995.

Source: OECD Economic Outlook, *various issues*

145

Reactions to OPEC's quadrupling of the oil price in November 1973 were initially responsible for the abruptness of the fiscal deterioration across OECD countries. In 1973, the developed world recorded its last balanced budget, with 12 out of 18 countries in surplus. By 1993, the Republic of Korea (a relative newcomer to the OECD) was the only exception to the tide of red ink. In total, the developed world racked up $2.6 trillion of budget deficits during the 1980s and issued $3.5 trillion of federal, state and local government debt, of which the USA ($1.2 trillion) and Japan ($1 trillion) were the largest elements. These figures exclude debt issued by public corporations and by government-sponsored agencies.

Between 1989 and 1995, the scale of government debt issue expanded relentlessly. OECD countries accumulated another $3.7 trillion of budget deficits and issued $3.9 trillion of central and local government debt. While the USA was still the largest constituent, at $1 trillion, Germany climbed into second place with $600 billion as a result of financing unification. Japan and Italy each issued $500 billion, with France the next largest issuer at $270 billion. An important consequence of this ocean of new debt issues was the broadening and deepening of national bond markets. As more and more bonds were issued in a particular currency, so the maturity spectrum became continuous from short-term (soon to mature) issues through to ten-year or 15-year issues. Potential investors looked on with approval as the issue sizes and market turnover in the bond market increased, facilitating anonymous entry and exit. At the end of 1979, only four bond markets were valued at more than $100 billion: the USA, Japan, Germany and the UK. By the end of 1989, these had been joined by Italy, France, Canada, Belgium and the Netherlands; six years later, Denmark, Sweden and Spain had also passed this threshold.

It is a sobering thought that most of the accumulated government debt stock has been added within the past ten years. Despite the downward drift in bond yields during the 15-year bull market, the burden of debt interest payments for the OECD countries has risen from an average of 1.4 per cent of GDP in 1980 to 3.0 per cent in 1996. In the public debt-ridden EU, the increase is from 2.0 per cent to 4.8 per cent. Of the larger OECD countries, Italy leads the way with a net interest charge equivalent to 9.5 per cent of GDP, followed by Belgium (8.3 per cent), Canada (5.3 per cent), Spain (5.1 per cent) and the Netherlands (4.7 per cent). In other words, each year Italy needs to collect an extra 9.5 per cent of GDP in taxation over and above that which is needed to cover current government spending, in order to achieve a balanced budget. God forbid that bond yields should ever spiral higher; the burden of compound interest would quickly suffocate these indebted economies.

WHO OWNS THE BONDS?

All wealth ultimately belongs to individuals, and this applies no less to bonds. The only real exception is the small percentage of bond issues that reside on the balance sheets of the central banks and which, in a sense, are excluded from general circulation. For example, in mid-July 1998, the US Federal Reserve held $442 billion of US government securities and foreign central banks owned $587 billion. The remaining 90 per cent or so of government and corporate bonds in issue are traceable to individuals, with a tiny slice set aside for charities and trusts. The largest segment represents bonds held directly by the public. If bonds are typical of all financial assets ultimately owned by the household sector, then the proportion of bonds held directly was 43 per cent at the end of 1995. This share varies enormously across different countries, ranging from 10 per cent in the Netherlands to more than 60 per cent in France and Italy.

A further 26 per cent of the bond stock is held by public and private pension funds, insurance companies and collective investment schemes such as mutual funds, investment and unit trusts. Finally, individuals own bonds indirectly via their holdings of company and bank securities. Essentially, everything on corporate and banking balance sheets can be considered as the property of individuals by virtue of share ownership. In the USA, chartered commercial banks hold 22 per cent of their assets in the form of government, municipal, corporate and foreign bonds, equivalent to more than $800 billion at end-1997. US non-farm, non-financial companies hold a mere 2 per cent of their financial assets as government and municipal bonds, but in some European countries the percentage is much higher.

The answer to the question is plainly that *we* own the bonds, whether we like it or not. Moreover, we own proportionately more government bonds than ten years ago. For the majority of western citizens this is not because we have decided to hold more government bonds but because it has been decided for us by pension funds, by insurance companies or by banks. Quite simply, when western governments run budget deficits, they issue debt which is considered to be of the highest credit quality. Most of this debt is marketable and is readily absorbed by large financial institutions on our behalf. All that remains to be determined is the price at which the bonds will be sold.

WHAT EXACTLY DO WE OWN?

Economists have debated this question long and hard without coming close to agreement, but the issue cannot be dodged in the present context. Are governments adding to the stock of private wealth when they issue bonds, or are they merely redistributing the ownership of existing wealth? Just as the money supply is no longer backed by gold or silver, so the stock of bonds is not matched by physical assets. As a British bondholder, it might seem reasonable to request that one's maturing certificates be redeemed for ownership of a staircase in the Victoria and Albert Museum, the gun turret of a warship or a municipal dustcart; in reality, all that is offered is settlement in sterling cash. The government may dispose of some of its fixed assets from time to time through privatizations or agreed sales, but it is scarcely credible that it would ever redeem the national debt by means of asset disposals. Even the determined efforts of the UK Conservative government during the 1980s succeeded only in reducing net financial liabilities from 41 per cent to 22 per cent of GDP. Privatization will always have its limits. Ultimately, there is only one valid explanation for the excellent credit standing of western governments: their unique authority to levy taxation in a politically stable economy.

The systematic rise in the ratio of government net financial liabilities to GDP from 22 per cent in 1980 to 49 per cent in 1997 for the USA, from 9 per cent to 50 per cent for Germany, from −3 per cent to 41 per cent for France, from 53 per cent to 111 per cent in Italy, from 36 per cent to 45 per cent in the UK and from 13 per cent to 67 per cent for Canada represents a decision to tax future generations more heavily than the present generation. In this sense, government bonds are little more than vouchers to be redeemed against certain future tax liabilities. Depending on the circumstances and the apparent ability to pay, the government of the day may choose to tax current incomes, purchases, savings, capital gains or personal wealth. In some countries, governments tax not only the quick but also the dead!

The campaign to arrest the inexorable march of public indebtedness and the accompanying tide of bond issues has become more organized in recent years, with attempts to pass a balanced budget amendment to the US constitution and the enforcement of the Maastricht criteria for the 15 EU countries. However, even under extremely favourable economic circumstances, the task of debt containment is remarkably difficult. After six years of continuous economic expansion, the US federal budget deficit was pared back to $23 billion in the 1997 fiscal year, but Treasury Gross Public Debt still climbed by $177 billion over the year to a record $5.52 trillion. The decline in new borrowing by the federal government has created an opportunity for its sponsored agencies, such as the Federal National Mortgage Association (commonly known as Fannie Mae) and the Federal Home Loan Mortgage Corporation (alias Freddie Mac), to step up their own debt issue programmes. Public awareness of the hazards of sustained government debt accumulation remains at a low ebb throughout the western world. The effective elimination of the inflationary solution to public indebtedness, as an act of policy preference, leaves only the politically unpalatable choices of higher taxation or lower government spending.

MONEY MARKETS VERSUS BOND MARKETS

Whereas the money market deals typically in maturities ranging from a few hours to two or three years, bond market maturities at issue stretch from about three years to 30, 50 or even 100 years. As bonds approach their redemption dates, their maturities overlap with money market instruments. However, the two markets remain distinct because the money value of a deposit cannot vary, while the capital

Figure 9.2 Comparison of money and bond markets 1970–97

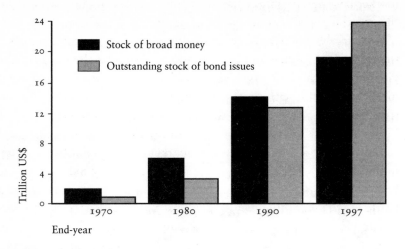

value of a bond can. The world bond market has grown to a prodigious size not only in absolute terms but also in relation to the stock of world money. Figure 9.2 represents the money stock and the bond stock of the developed world by pairs of bars. The height of the bars are in proportion to the size of the financial stocks at various dates. In 1970, the aggregate money stock in the OECD (using the M3 definition) stood at $2.0 billion versus a world bond market of $800 billion, a ratio of 2.5 to 1. By 1980, the money stock had expanded to $5.8 trillion and the stock of publicly issued bonds to $3.3 trillion, a ratio of approximately 1.75 to 1. Ten years on, in 1990, the developed country money stock had risen to $13.8 trillion against a bond market of $12.7 trillion, closing the ratio to 1.1 to 1. Finally, at end-1997, the money stock of $19.1 trillion was overhauled by a bond market total of about $23.5 trillion, giving a ratio of roughly 0.8 to 1.

This transformation in the relative sizes of the markets is the natural but unintended consequence of government policy and corporate preference in the western world over almost two decades. In the case of government policy, there has been a bias towards high real interest rates, offset by slack fiscal conditions and unrestrained bond issues. For the corporate sector, the preference for debt over equity issues has been influenced by favourable tax treatment for debt interest and dividends and by the desire to cultivate institutional shareholder loyalty. It appears that the development of a massive global bond market has been haphazard and expediential. It does not conform to the grand designs of some global planning unit.

Back in the 1960s and for most of the 1970s, governments ruled their domestic money and bond markets, changing the shape of the yield curve almost at will. The massive expansion of world bond markets, in combination with the abolition of foreign exchange controls, has shattered this financial hegemony. Governments are no longer the dominant market players in their own bond markets and cannot prevent international bond market shocks from being transmitted down the domestic yield curve to the money markets. In the brave new world of the late 1990s, governments are engaged in a battle of wits with financial institutions. Some are better armed than others but, in general, efforts to manipulate the yield curve using short-term interest rates are much less likely to succeed than before the financial markets revolution.

As government budget deficits have been financed to a growing extent in the capital markets rather than monetized through the commercial banking system, this has removed a significant source of balance sheet expansion for the banks. After average annual expansion of broad money of almost 11 per cent in the 1970s and 8 per cent in the 1980s, the pace has slowed to a mere 3.9 per cent in the 1990s. The migration of credit expansion from within the monetary sector to outside it is probably the single most important reason why the OECD average inflation rate has fallen to below 5 per cent per annum on a consistent basis since 1983. This is notwithstanding the monetary lapse during the second half of the 1980s in some countries. For completeness, it should be recorded that the stock of bonds in public hands has decelerated as well. After increasing at almost 15 per cent per annum in the 1970s and 1980s, its pace has moderated to around 8 per cent per annum. However, in the current low inflation environment, this still implies that the overall burden of corporate and government indebtedness is rising by 5 per cent or 6 per cent per year in real terms. This growth rate is well in excess of the pace of GDP expansion in western countries (between 2 per cent and 3 per cent per annum), suggesting that the debt service burden is becoming progressively more onerous for public and private sectors alike.

IS THE GLOBAL BOND MARKET
OUT OF CONTROL?

If bond market control has slipped away from the treasury departments of national governments, with whom does it now reside? With pension funds, insurance companies and hedge funds? Is the global bond market efficiently regulated by market forces, or is it on the verge of anarchy? Or perhaps governments have surrendered conventional instruments of control only to seize upon others, for example the covert manipulation of the market using futures and options? To argue that all willing buyers and sellers of bonds are accommodated by the markets is to resolve nothing at all. In that sense, the world's bond markets are plainly efficient and self-regulating. The key issue is whether the demand for bonds has been artificially inflated by a mixture of yield curve speculation (borrowing short and lending long) and aggressive gearing using derivatives. In other words, is there a danger that these contingent demands for government bonds will melt away at some stage, leaving the market to reach a new balance at much lower bond prices and higher yields? Potential sources of demand distortion include the proprietary trading desks of investment banks, the hedge funds and, if they should ever indulge in acts of such breath-taking duplicity, central banks or other government agencies.

Drawing on the discussion of bond yields in the last chapter, there are three reasons to doubt whether the observed prices of bellwether bonds, the benchmark ten-year government debt issues, are the result of an unfettered market-clearing mechanism. First, there is the extra-ordinary behaviour of the market in 1994, when a seemingly innocuous increase in the US Fed funds rate triggered a bond market setback many times larger than expected and numerous derivatives-related losses occurred. Second, there is the increasing reluctance of policy-makers to raise interest rates under any circumstances, as if in fear of a systemic banking or derivatives crisis. Third, the increased popularity and influence of hedge funds seeking an absolute (rather than relative) return has undoubtedly increased the scale and scope of yield curve speculation. Whereas a pension fund manager is judged on the per-formance of his or her fund relative to other similar pension funds, hedge funds are free to be utterly different from each other in their portfolio strategy. According to Tass Management, 1,414 hedge funds had $150 billion under management in November 1997, up from 444 funds and $70 billion in December 1992. However, five funds, including Soros, Tiger and Moore Capital, probably handle over $50 billion among them.

If our suspicions regarding the influence of yield curve arbitrage are broadly accurate, then the evolution of the bond markets can best be described as a series of temporary resting places, each of which is dependent on the preservation of an upward-sloping yield curve and the fulfilment of a certain set of expectations regarding the interest rate outcome of policy committees. Over time, local equilibriums may have moved a significant distance away from the unconstrained or general equilibrium that would prevail in an unfettered capital market in which all participants had equal access to information. This framework of analysis is able to reconcile all the ingredients of contemporary capital markets: a weakening trend in national saving rates, the absorption of an increasing supply of new bond issues and the lowest bond yields in 50 years. These trends would be incompatible within a free market. However, the vested interest in maintaining and rationalizing a low yield environment among companies and governments alike is huge. Reversion to general equilibrium (at higher bond yields) would probably require there to be an external shock. Some examples of external shocks are provided below.

BOND MARKETS: THE STING IN THE TAIL

In the movie *The Sting*, set in Chicago during the prohibition era, a dummy betting shop is established in a disused basement. Everything looks authentic, with one exception: the shop's clocks are a couple of minutes slow, allowing the crooked proprietors time to discover the racing results before the betting is closed and to adjust the house odds accordingly. It may be going a little too far to suggest that the bond market is akin to a fraudulent betting operation, but there are similarities. Like any successful fraud, the financial delusion at the end of the twentieth century operates behind a façade of respectability.

What could be more respectable than the markets in government debt and in the debt instruments of companies with world-wide reputations? Yet these are, without doubt, at the heart of the delusion.

There is an important sense in which the race results (the direction of bond prices) can be known while the betting is still in progress. In Chapters 2 and 3 it was contended that the fight against price inflation in the major developed economies became first the preoccupation of economic policy, during the 1980s, and later its obsession. The attainment of consistently low inflation in most western developed economies in the 1990s has enhanced the reputation of national central banks and has institutionalized an ever-vigilant attitude towards consumer prices. The policy frameworks developed by central banks in their pursuit of inflation targets or ranges have become much too transparent in the process. Interest rates are seldom altered outside a predetermined schedule of policy committee meetings, held every two, four or six weeks. Policy rates are rarely moved by more than 0.25 per cent at a time, and the committees seek to avoid frequent changes in the direction of rate changes. Bond auctions or tenders are also held at regular (usually monthly) intervals with pre-announcements concerning the size and type of stock to be sold.

The actions taken by central bank officials in the money and debt markets, especially after the regular policy-setting committees have convened, can be construed as pointers to profitable trading along the yield curve. Even though money market interest rates are free to diverge from policy rates, under normal circumstances the departures tend to be small. Between policy meetings, short-term borrowing costs are effectively fixed. When the yield curve has an upward slope across the maturity spectrum, this offers the seemingly risk-free opportunity to play the curve, to borrow from the money market and lend to the bond market. For as long as the position is run, the trader pockets the difference between the bond yield and the cost of short-term borrowing while bearing the risk of a fall in bond prices. However, with billions of dollars of capital positioned in precisely the same way, at times there is an overwhelming presumption that bond prices will rise, producing a capital gain as well as a yield pick-up. If desired, the trade can be unwound a week before the next policy meeting.

In order to maintain the credibility of a given short-term rate, the monetary authorities are bound to supply unlimited funds to the market at this rate. This is the price that the central bank pays for asserting its control over short-term interest rates. While there are other policy instruments available that could neutralize this monetary stimulus, central banks have forsworn their use. Over-funding, the practice of selling more government debt than is needed to cover the budget deficit, is a means of mopping up excess liquidity but one that has fallen out of favour. Snap variations in the auction schedule for government debt could be used to punish yield curve speculation, but these also have been ruled out in the name of policy transparency. Meanwhile, bond traders are presented with frequent opportunities to exploit the predictability of official policy operations, placing ever larger bets over ever shorter time horizons.

POTENTIAL BOND MARKET SHOCKS

In the last chapter, a description of the powerful momentum behind bond yield reduction in the 1990s and some of its underlying causes were discussed. The development of this benign environment for borrowers and investors can be traced all the way back to the mid-1980s. However, there have been many bond market shocks in the past, both nationally and internationally, and it is necessary to consider their characteristics. The first type of shock involves a sudden jump in oil or commodity prices. The trigger event might be an earthquake or volcanic eruption, the failure of an important agricultural crop, the exhaustion of grain reserves after a succession of poor harvests, or the outbreak of war, perhaps in the Middle East. Bond markets fear that the commodity price shock will be absorbed into goods and services prices in developed countries via loose monetary policy.

A second shock scenario involves political instability in a wider context. If the markets sense that large countries will go to war with each other, then military expenditures will send government finances into serious deficit. Whether this deficit is financed by bond issue, monetary expansion or higher taxation, there will be an adverse impact on international bond markets which will be compounded by the uncertainty surrounding the breadth of the conflict and the length of the war. Civil wars tend to have a lesser impact, but they can have similar effects since a government's authority to collect tax revenues and maintain law and order is undermined. On a smaller scale, a last-minute decision to delay the starting date for EMU would have sent European bond markets into disarray.

The third class of bond market disaster involves financial speculation or fraud and the reassessment of credit risk which follows hard on its heels. Concern that a large international bank or group of banks might be unable to meet their obligations promptly gives rise to the fear of uninsurable financial losses among the banks' counterparties. The troubled financial institutions or even the government's own debt agency might suffer a downgrade from the various credit agency rating services such as Moody's, Fitch–International Bank Credit Agency, or Standard and Poors. Bond markets dislike the uncertainty over the scope or size of the losses, the damage to financial reputations and the likely degree of support by government agencies or central banks. In the event of a debt moratorium or outright defaults, bond yields could climb in spectacular fashion.

This list is by no means exhaustive, but it should serve as a reminder of the extreme volatility bond markets have experienced in the past and will most probably suffer again. Even where governments have secured several years of low inflation and balanced budgets, there is no protection against external shocks. If bond prices have lost touch with reality as a result of speculative activity, then the market will be extremely sensitive to any unanticipated event. In the event of a discontinuity in bond prices, such as that described for equity prices on 19 October 1987 in the last chapter, the value of certain derivatives may cease to be defined.

THE FINANCIAL STABILITY CONE

This chapter has, unashamedly, peppered the reader with statistics relating to the development of the bond market in two key dimensions: first, the size of the government bond market and its connection to accumulated budget deficits and the size of the economy; and, second, the size of the overall bond market in relation to the national money stock. It is time to summarize this data in a straightforward way. Figure 9.3 combines two ratios which relate to the manageability of domestic debt burdens in 16 developed economies. On the vertical axis is measured the ratio of the national bond to money stocks, and on the horizontal scale the size of the government bond market scaled by nominal GDP. They can both be regarded as measures of the relative sensitivity of the economy to an international bond market shock. The scatter of data, relating to end-1995, falls into the shape of a cone.

A cluster of six countries, comprising the UK, Spain, Austria, Australia, Norway and Finland, lie towards the 'safe' region at the pointed end of the financial stability cone where money markets still dominate local bond markets and the government bond market is relatively small. A second cluster, comprising France, Canada and the Netherlands, have money and bond markets of approximately equal size, but government bond markets twice the relative size of those in the first cluster. Japan also appears to belong this second cluster, but its peculiar off-balance sheet accounting arrangements suggest that its true ratio for the stock of bonds to GDP could be 80 per cent or more of GDP rather than the superficially comparable figure of around 45 per cent. Three countries lie on a straight line close to the upper boundary of the cone, combining bond markets of much larger size than domestic money stocks with moderately large government markets. Germany is the least worrisome of this trio, followed by Sweden and Denmark. The final group of three contains the USA, Italy and Belgium. These are arguably the countries most vulnerable to a bond market accident, having large bond–money ratios and a government debt overload.

CONCLUSION

Agencies of government, ranging from the policy-setting committees of central banks to the detailed supervisory and regulatory bodies for specific financial activities, have turned a blind eye to the bloated bond markets. A curious prejudice has gained favour among the policy-making fraternity to the effect that excessive credit expansion

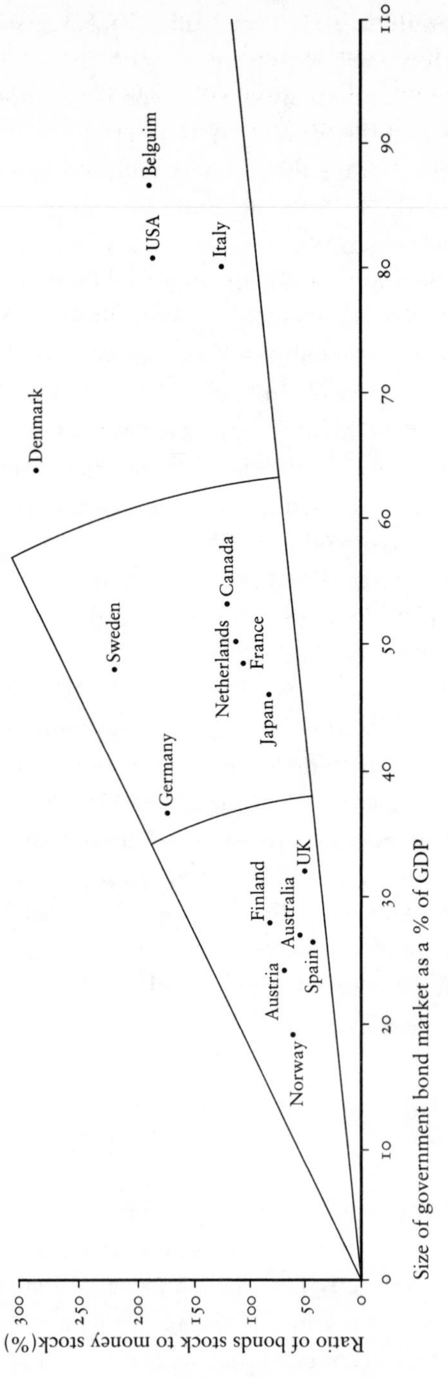

Figure 9.3 Financial stability cone (as at end-1995)

is dangerous only if it fuels rapid growth of the money supply. Therefore, government budget deficits are routinely financed by additional bond issues, while corporations and financial institutions borrow freely in the domestic and international capital markets. As long as this borrowing doesn't show up on banks' balance sheets or, worse still, present an overt inflationary threat, then it is generally presumed that all is well.

In truth, the bond mountain poses a latent threat to the health of the global financial system and to the economic stability of the western world. This inherent danger has been averted thus far only at the expense of compounding one folly upon another. Borrowing from the US, Japanese, German and UK banking systems has gravitated away from industrial and property uses towards the financial markets; unrealized capital gains in bonds and equities now form a significant segment of banks' collateral. Aggressive yield curve speculation and colossal use of derivatives have cast a dense mist around bond market excesses such that the real cost of borrowing has not risen to its logical extent. Indeed, during the 1990s there has been a gradual tendency towards lower real bond yields. Our susceptibility to this delusion has been fostered by its longevity. Wandering deep into the enchanted forest of financial sophistication, we have lost our bearings, ignored our instincts and mislaid our proper sense of danger. Tolerance of rapid growth in bond issuance may not give rise to higher inflation but, ultimately, it must force up the real cost of borrowing and the incidence of debt delinquency. The harmful side-effects of unrestrained credit expansion have merely been displaced from inflation to high real interest rates and declining credit quality.

10

The Erosion of Credit Quality

'Beautiful credit! The foundation of modern society. Who shall
say this is not the age of mutual trust, of unlimited reliance on
human promises?' Samuel L. Clemens and Charles D. Warner,
The Gilded Age: A Tale of Today, 1873

Credit quality, or creditworthiness, describes the likelihood of a debtor
satisfying all the obligations of a debt contract, including the prompt
payment of interest and the repayment of capital. Throughout the
last chapter the discussion was focused on prime quality borrowers,
namely sovereign governments and top-notch corporations. Someone
who buys the treasury bonds of a western government expects to be
repaid in full because of the impeccable credit quality and reputation
of the borrower. The reason that government bonds are used as
benchmarks is that, under normal circumstances, no other borrower
will be able to issue debt of the same maturity and type at a lower
redemption yield. A company or institution of lesser credit quality
than the government is required to offer a higher yield, a premium,
over sovereign debt in recognition of the higher risk level. This is also
referred to as the credit spread, and it is usually measured in basis
points, where one basis point is equal to one-hundredth of 1 per cent.
Nevertheless, the lender still expects to be repaid in full and on time
under normal circumstances.

Moving along the credit quality spectrum, there are debt issues by
medium-sized companies, real estate developers, airline operators,
provincial governments, construction consortia, mining companies,
and so on. In each case, the lender or investor is necessarily exposed

to the risks inherent to the regular business or activity of the borrower. Some of the bonds issued by these entities will be of investment grade (rated A), while others will be of medium grade (B), and still others will be of speculative or junk grade (C or below). In theory, there are two key disadvantages to owning lower-grade debt instruments. One is that the borrower may file for bankruptcy and the administrator or receiver may recover sufficient assets to award only partial repayment of the debt, or even none at all. The second is that, even where there is no particular reason to believe that the borrower is in trouble, the investor may be unable to liquidate his holding at short notice without incurring a penalty. Even if a secondary market exists, and it may not, the bonds may trade at discount to their face value at redemption. In both cases, the lender or investor may realize a capital loss.

GRANDMOTHER'S FOOTSTEPS

A childhood game, which is probably still played, involves a group of infants creeping up on a 'grandmother' without her knowing it. Periodically, grandmother will suspect that someone is getting close to her and will turn around to check. If she sees any who are moving or have come too close, then they are sent to the back of the group. The winning child is the first one to touch her before she turns around.

This seems an apt analogy for the debt market, where the credit spread between two instruments of different investment grades, or even of the same grade, may display wide variations over time. When the bond markets exude confidence and the incidence of corporate bankruptcy and debt default is low or is perceived to be low, then it is tempting to consider all debt instruments to be alike. If, for any reason, one bond offers a higher yield than another of similar grade, type and maturity does, then investors will be attracted to the first. Very quickly, investors' preference for the higher-yielding bond will translate into a rise in its price and a fall in its yield, relative to the second bond. The yield spread between them will be smaller than before. In this way, the debt instruments issued by poorer quality borrowers outperform those of higher quality. Sometimes this convergence process continues until the yields of the two instruments look certain to cross over. However, with uncanny timing, grandmother has a habit of turning around at this moment and dispatching the usurper to the back of the class. In the next section, three examples of this mechanism are examined.

1. Government debt markets in North America and Europe, 1992–4

Long-standing participants in the international financial community, with first-class credentials, have taken for granted their preferential access to global capital markets. Specifically, the US economy has imported foreign long-term capital for most of the past 20 years, without attracting a noticeable credit risk premium, or spread. By and large, foreign investors in US Treasury debt and private sector debt instruments have been satisfied by the huge market value of US fixed assets, the political stability of the country and the reputation of the Federal Reserve Board as an independent central bank. Similarly, European governments, with sizeable deficits to fund, have come to expect that their frequent debt issues would be absorbed effortlessly. As they have shed their inflationary skins, even the less prestigious economies of southern Europe and Scandinavia have become used to the erosion of the risk premiums attached to their benchmark bonds.

Figure 10.1 summarizes government bond data for 12 countries at three critical dates between 1992 and 1994. The beginning of 1992 represents an early stage of the bond market's speculative run. The start of 1994 marks the point by which the bull run had terminated in all the countries; for some, the actual peak came two or three months earlier. By November 1994, the bear phase initiated by the February rise in US short-term interest rates had worked itself out and yields had stabilized. There are several points to notice from the table. First, taking all the countries together, there is a near-perfect symmetry between the extent of yield convergence (narrower yield spreads) in the first time interval and the degree of yield divergence (wider yield spreads) in the second period. The key difference is that the convergence phase took 24 months and the divergence phase only ten months. In general, bull markets last longer than bear markets in financial assets.

The second critical distinction is between countries for which

Figure 10.1 Benchmark ten-year bond yields at selected dates (% p.a.)

	1 Jan. 92	1 Jan. 94	1 Nov. 94	Basis points I	II
USA	6.70	5.80	7.90	−90	211
Germany	8.05	5.71	7.62	−235	191
France	8.52	5.60	8.28	−291	267
Italy	12.90	8.66	12.02	−424	336
UK	9.73	6.10	8.68	−363	258
Canada	8.09	6.61	9.18	−147	256
Spain	11.26	8.12	11.15	−314	303
Australia	9.39	6.68	10.54	−271	386
Netherlands	8.58	5.50	7.61	−308	210
Switzerland	6.37	4.07	5.51	−230	144
Sweden	9.89	6.99	11.07	−290	408
Denmark	8.76	6.09	8.97	−267	289
Differentials (basis points)					
Germany–US	136	−9	−28	−145	−19
Canada–US	139	82	128	−57	46
UK–US	303	31	78	−272	47
France–Germany	46	−10	66	−57	76
Italy–Germany	485	295	440	−189	145
UK–Germany	167	40	106	−128	66
Spain–Germany	321	242	353	−79	112
Germany–Switzerland	169	164	211	−5	47

Key: I: Yield shift between 1 Jan. 92 and 1 Jan. 94
II: Yield shift between 1 Jan. 94 and 1 Nov. 94

the yield movement was larger in the convergence phase versus the divergence phase. Germany, France, Italy, the UK, the Netherlands, Spain and Switzerland belong to the former group, while the divergence phase was dominant for the USA, Canada, Australia, Sweden and Denmark. There are three characteristics that help to discriminate between the two groups. The first is the national saving rate that was introduced in Chapter 8. The 1994 average, unweighted national saving rate was 20.7 per cent for the first group and 15.6 per cent for the second. The only real anomaly from a national savings perspective is the low-saving UK, which would seem more at home in the second group. A second characteristic is the extent of foreign ownership of its public debt, although the globalization of bond markets in the 1980s has removed some of the historic contrasts. In the USA, foreign holdings amounted to a little over 20 per cent of the stock of government debt at end-1994; this proportion has since risen to more than 34 per cent. Foreigners also hold significant shares in the Canadian (28 per cent in 1992) and Australian government debt markets. By contrast, the European bond markets have had lower rates of foreign ownership historically. However, overseas investors owned 32 per cent of French government bonds in 1992 (from zero in 1979) and 26 per cent of German bonds (from 5 per cent in 1979). For other European countries, the foreign proportion is around 10 per cent. Thirdly, a distinction can be drawn between countries with a firm commitment to budget deficit reduction and those with less rigorous policy stances. European countries participating in the ERM and preparing for the start of EMU were credited with high marks for policy commitment in 1994, whereas Australia and Sweden were still locked into high public deficits and relatively weak regimes for containing inflation.

If these three discriminants can be assembled into a straightforward story, it is that countries with low national saving rates and a high foreign ownership of domestic public debt tend to suffer most when global bond markets are under pressure. In the predictable circumstance that foreign bond holders decide to repatriate their wealth in a nervous market, it stands to reason that the domestic bond market will falter unless domestic savers step in to support it. The difficulty is compounded if government policies imply that sizeable future bond issues will be needed, or if they fail to provide reassurance on inflation control. With a persistently low national saving rate (around 16 per cent in 1995–7) and soaring foreign ownership of US Treasury bonds, the largest economy in the developed world is also one of the most vulnerable to a bond market shock. Should the financial markets ever perceive that the Federal Reserve Board had failed to make an effective response to an inflationary threat, the penalty in yield divergence could be enormous.

It is far from fanciful to suggest that the US government will one day be forced to borrow at premium interest rates embodying an adjustment for credit risk. Indeed, it is possible to argue that such a situation is already close to becoming a reality. In May 1998, a ranking of 20 government bond markets, in ascending order of yield, revealed that US ten-year bonds lay in eighteenth place, ahead of the UK and New Zealand only. Disregarding the oddities of Japanese and Swiss bonds, the credit quality standard in the international bond market in the late 1990s is set jointly by Germany, France and the Netherlands. However, it astonishing that countries of lesser credit quality, such as Italy and Spain, should sport ten-year benchmark bonds only 20 or 30 basis points above those of the leading pack, as they have consistently during the first half of 1998. The convergence in nominal European bond yields conveniently ignores the fact that national characteristics will remain important after the single currency begins.

The latest convert to the cause of low inflation and budgetary discipline is Greece. In isolation, the March 1998 devaluation of the drachma by 12.1 per cent would have been interpreted as a warning of inflationary danger and a reason to widen the yield spread between Greek and German benchmark bonds. Yet, because it was accompanied by the decision to join the ERM in mid-March 1998 and to participate in monetary union by 2001, its yield spread over Germany dived from 5.3 per cent to 3.6 per cent in a single day. There are two possible explanations. Either investors judged that the implied commitment of the Greek government to pursue responsible inflation and budgetary objectives was more significant than the devaluation, or they simply spotted an opportunity to make easy short-term profits for their bond funds.

2. Emerging debt versus US Treasury bonds, 1994–7

The 1980–82 recession in industrialized countries triggered a debt crisis in middle- and low-income emerging countries around the world. A combination of high oil prices (after the Iran–Iraq conflict in 1978–9), depleted international demand and painfully high US short-term interest rates tipped dozens of poor countries into debt default and many others into debt service problems. On Friday, 13 August

1982, Mexico stunned the financial world by temporarily suspending its bank debt payments and the developing country debt problem was born. There followed ten years of debt re-negotiations, rescue plans, bank bail-outs, debt–equity swaps and eventually debt forgiveness for some of the poorest nations. The failed Baker plan of 1985 gave way to the partially successful Brady plan of 1989.

In order to qualify for debt reduction, debtor nations, in consultation with the IMF and the World Bank, had to carry out policy measures designed to promote economic growth, to encourage foreign invest-ment flows, to strengthen domestic savings and to promote the control of flight capital. The new element in the Brady plan was official support for the conversion of commercial bank loans into new bonds with reduced principal or reduced interest rates, and for debt buy-backs. The principal payments on Brady bonds are backed by US Treasury bonds, while the interest payments are the obligations of the individual countries concerned. While 39 debtor nations were originally identified as potential candidates for the Brady treatment, only eight had completed deals by the end of 1991 and 14 by mid-1997. However, at $175 billion, the market in Brady bonds is sizeable and actively traded. Roughly 70 per cent of the stock comprises Latin American debt.

Given that Brady bonds were created in the context of a debt crisis which prompted the intervention of western governments, it should come as no surprise to learn that their yield spread over US Treasury bonds has always been wide enough to place them in either the medium or junk bond categories. A weighted average of Brady bond spreads in recent years traces a journey from 5.2 per cent in January 1993 to 2.7 per cent in December 1993, to almost 10 per cent in April 1995, and back to 3 per cent in May 1997. In comparison to the government bonds of developed countries, the potential for capital gains and losses is very much greater. Whereas the Mexican currency crisis of late 1994 proved to be a positive event for the US bond market, because it bailed out US investors in Mexican bonds, the impact on emerging debt markets was quite the opposite. By April 1995, the vulnerability of emerging markets to interest rate and credit risk was much better understood. However, the bond market rally that followed was spectacular.

Over-eager lenders, comprising commercial and investment banks and specialist funds, whittled away at the risk premium in the belief that emerging markets had shaken off the Mexico experience. By May 1997 it was possible to argue that emerging market debt was an accepted asset class, providing high US dollar returns and less volatility than comparable market indices. It offered global diversification and had out-performed emerging market equity. As credit quality recovered in developing countries, so it was argued that Brady bonds deserved a lower risk premium. It was soon after that grandmother turned around and stared investors in the face once more. The onset of the Asian financial crisis sent the emerging market bond spread scurrying back up to 6 per cent, from 3 per cent in May 1997. The clear message from the emerging debt markets is that prudent risk assessment will always be swept aside by tides of global capital. As long as the banks believe that their solvency and liquidity have been guaranteed by the central banks, there is little reason for the traders to pay attention to credit risk.

3. US corporate debt, 1960–97

Most corporate bonds are issued by multinational businesses or by national corporations that are household names in a particular industry. In general, most medium-sized and smaller companies prefer to borrow from banks and other financial intermediaries rather than to issue their own debt instruments. There are fixed costs to raising money in the capital markets that make it uneconomic to raise, say, less than $10 million. Moreover, the smaller and less well-known the issuer, the greater the credit quality premium required by investors. The US corporate debt market offers the best example of credit quality behaviour because it is composed of a large number of issues and it is the most mature.

Over the past ten years or so, the capital markets have insisted on an average yield premium for investment-grade ten-year corporate bonds over comparable US Treasury bonds of around 30 to 40 basis points. A yield premium of 70 basis points in 1986 was transformed into a small yield discount in the early months of 1989, as the US markets were flooded with property-backed bank credit. Japanese

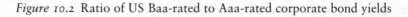

Figure 10.2 Ratio of US Baa-rated to Aaa-rated corporate bond yields

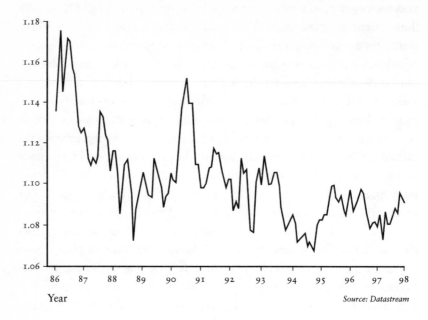

Year   *Source: Datastream*

banks were particularly active in bidding away US credit quality spreads at this time. As the US property boom turned to bust and the aggressive lenders withdrew, the corporate risk premium rose steadily through 1990–92, reaching a peak of 75 basis points. The crisis passed only as the US monetary authorities pursued an easy credit policy that allowed the banks to rebuild their capital reserves. Corporate yield spreads over Treasuries have settled down in the 30–50 basis point range since 1994.

A longer-term perspective on US corporate debt can be gained from Figure 10.2, showing the ratio of medium-grade (Baa-rated) to high-grade (Aaa-rated) bonds. When looking across periods of great variation in inflation rates and interest rates, the ratio of yields is more informative than the absolute difference between them. Over the course of the past 40 years there have been many phases of yield convergence and of yield divergence. As noted above, in the convergence phases economic prosperity blurs the underlying credit quality distinctions between bonds, while in the divergence phases nervous investors scramble into assets that are of proven quality.

From a position of extreme convergence in 1966, there were three successive cycles in which the point of maximum divergence increased. The culmination of the OPEC-induced recession of 1974–5 was a dramatic flight to quality as corporate bankruptcy rates exploded.

Within a matter of three years, a powerful convergence phase had closed the gap between medium and high-grade corporate debt once more, as the mid-1970s inflation provided an escape route for over-indebted corporations. The next five years witnessed the most erratic movements in the yield ratio as the second oil price hike and the emerging market debt crisis sent the US economy lurching into a double-bottomed recession in 1980 and 1982. However, the yield ratio peak of 1983 marked the end of the credit quality scare; each successive credit quality cycle has recorded a lower peak than its predecessor. Since 1995, the ratio has not risen above 1.10, and it has hovered in the range 1.07–1.10 during 1997 and the early months of 1998. These are among the lowest credit spreads in at least 40 years. By mid-1998, there were already signs that US corporate bond quality was deteriorating; bond defaults (where companies fail to pay the interest due to the holders) doubled in the first six months of 1998, as compared to a year earlier, to reach their highest level since 1991.

NARROWING OF CREDIT SPREADS IS NO COINCIDENCE

In each of the above contexts, there has been a very recent and extreme illustration of narrowing credit spreads. For Italy, Spain and Sweden, in the case of government bonds; for Brady bonds in relation to US Treasury bonds; and for medium-grade US corporate bonds to high-grade bonds. Another example is the collapse of the credit spread between Canadian long-term corporate and government bond yields from 120 basis points in 1992 to 55 basis points in 1997. In the words of *Grant's Interest Rate Observer* of 6 June 1997: 'Thus, Canadians have snapped up provincial debt and lower-rated corporate debt, in the process bringing about a remarkable compression of credit spreads (for instance, causing Alberta's provincial obligations to trade at a premium of just five basis points to the national government's, even though it is Ottawa alone that could print its way out of a jam, assuming there would ever be the need).'

Many financial institutions and large corporations rushed to borrow from the capital markets in 1992–3 at low bond yields, only to find that their investment and other exceptional expenditures could be financed out of the strong profits earned from existing businesses. Finding themselves with spare funds, large enterprises inside and outside the banking sector cast around for profitable ways of putting this excess to work. Meanwhile, other financial institutions borrowed additional capital in order to participate in the more exotic expressions of yield convergence, as if engaged in a game of riskless arbitrage. If anything, this process has accelerated since the mid-1990s.

This coincidence of narrow credit spreads in so many contexts is a phenomenon of the 1990s. Whereas past cycles in credit quality spreads were focused on the specific circumstances and prospects of the borrowers, the yield convergence phase that petered out at the end of 1993 applied almost universally across diverse and disparate debt markets. There have been two very predictable consequences to global yield convergence: first, an increase in the issuance of investment-grade debt; and second, the appearance of scores of debutant issuers of extremely dubious pedigree. Having reduced the credit spreads of investment and middle-grade bonds to wafer-thinness, market interest has turned towards the junk end of the spectrum, where potential profits from yield compression are still lucrative.

Even among the actively traded US junk bond issues, yields have been tumbling. In the 23 March 1998 edition of *Barron's*, it was reported that Globalstar LP 11.375 per cent, maturing in February 2004, yielded 10.22 per cent, down from 11.56 per cent a year earlier; Lear Corporation 9.5 per cent, maturing July 2006, yielded 7.13 per cent, down from 8.7 per cent; Southdown Inc. 10 per cent, maturing March 2006, yielded 6.97 per cent, down from 8.82 per cent in just 12 months. During the same interval, medium-rated corporate bond yields fell from 7.76 per cent to 6.86 per cent, implying an average reduction in the junk-to-medium credit spread from 193 to 125 basis points.

From junk bonds to emerging market sovereign debt to consumer loans to store cards, the excess funds of industrial and financial companies have been chasing high-yielding opportunities. Whereas in the 1980s it was still possible to look across a spectrum of bonds with ascending degrees of business risk and observe an approximate progression of market yields, this is seldom the case today. The elimination of the risk spread is all too familiar. It has been arbitraged away by eager traders, armed with razor-sharp financial software and ample spare capital. Worse still, these traders have the full approval of their superiors as they trade away the credit spread. The consequences of disregarding the fundamental risk characteristics of any investment are not difficult to predict. This is the road to delinquency.

DEBT DELINQUENCY: CAUSES AND CONSEQUENCES

Debt delinquency, the failure of a borrower to honour the terms of a debt contract, can arise for many reasons, but the dominant explanation is the over-extension of debt based on an unrealistic expectation of future revenues. The risk of delinquency is minimized in the case of government borrowing because of the statutory right to raise taxes. However, for poor countries dependent on agricultural produce, even the government's ability to generate revenue is constrained by the behaviour of commodity prices. Provincial governments typically have much less scope to levy taxes, and companies must expose themselves to business risks in order to generate revenues.

The credit spread or yield premium appropriate to a given point on the risk spectrum should act as a buffer, allowing ordinary losses from business activities to be absorbed without great disruption to production. Alternatively, the risk premium can be viewed as the implicit cost of a creditor insurance policy. A risk-averse investor should be able to lay off the additional risk of holding a corporate bond in return for the excess return promised. The compression of credit spreads removes the safety margin in the credit system and cancels the insurance policy for the risk-averse. All investors are forced to travel along the risk spectrum, whether they wish to or not and whether they know it or not.

Furthermore, the hierarchy of credit spreads attached to varying degrees of credit risk serves a fundamental purpose: it is to discourage outrageous borrowing requests. In the absence of an effective system of price-rationing in the capital markets, there is a danger that poor-quality issuers, masquerading as reputable companies, will obtain funds. Credit rating agencies are of no real help here, since they assess the quality of a bond only after it has been publicly issued. Without a healthy two-way market in the risk spread, it is almost inevitable that capital will flow into the hands of those who promise the highest return, regardless of whether they are in a realistic position to deliver it. Thus, the seeds of debt delinquency are sown at the very outset. A theoretical framework for understanding the relationship between the quantity and quality of credit is outlined in Appendix 1.

US PERSONAL DEBT DELINQUENCY

One of the surprising developments of the mid-1990s in the USA was a dramatic increase in the incidence of personal debt delinquency at a time of steady economic growth, falling unemployment rates and falling interest rates. Normally, credit card delinquencies (accounts in arrears of 30 days or more) and personal bankruptcy rates increase only in the context of a weak economy and mounting job-losses. Previous peaks in the bank delinquency rate occurred in 1974, 1980 and 1991–2, following this pattern. The other key predictor of personal loan delinquency is rapid growth in bank loans, roughly two years prior. Indeed, the contraction in personal bank debt in 1991–2 pre-saged the lowest delinquency rates for bank borrowing in the USA for more than 20 years, in 1994. While this result held for the dominant proportion of consumer bank debt, mortgages and personal loans, the downturn in credit card delinquencies was less impressive. Since then, delinquency rates have climbed steeply, reaching 4.5 per cent for credit card debt and 3.1 per cent for all personal bank loans at end-1997.

A number of factors appear to have contributed to the rise in debt delinquency. One explanation lies in the wide variation in bankruptcy laws in different states in the USA, with some states allowing the full discharge of debt even when some repayment is feasible. In states with tough bankruptcy codes, the proportion of delinquents tends to be higher because lenders use the law as a substitute for their own assessment of credit risk. A second explanation, and perhaps the most significant, is the behaviour of the consumer credit industry. The growth of asset-backed securities (ABS) over the past ten years has made the lending business highly competitive, with new entrants providing services that used to be the preserve of the commercial banks. After the securitization of personal loans, including home loans and credit card debt, the assets are sold to yield-hungry life insurance and pension funds. This operation leaves the original lender (e.g. a bank, an insurance or finance company) with excess capital to commit to new loans. In the rush to exploit the seemingly ample returns to personal lending activity, financial companies with little or no credit industry experience have assembled loan books of dubious quality. The process of securitization merely transmits latent credit quality problems into the bond market. Government has not helped matters either, by promoting home ownership linked to 'slow start' financing for low-income families, where debts are designed to accumulate in the early years of the mortgage.

A third explanation of the surge in personal bankruptcy filings lies in some profound changes in attitudes towards debt and related matters among large swathes of the population since the early 1980s. By and large, affluent households in America (those with incomes in excess of $100,000) have a good understanding of financial management. Their average debt service burdens, measured as a percentage of income, were not appreciably higher in 1995 than in 1983, despite the frenzied borrowing activity that occurred in between. In contrast, the debt service burdens of households with annual incomes of under $50,000 have become steadily worse. Those receiving less than $30,000 annually had increased their average burden from 10 per cent of income in 1983 to 17 per cent in 1995; for those in the income range $30,000–$50,000, the average rose from 11.4 per cent to 22.4 per cent of income over the same period. These burdens had continued to worsen despite the recovery of the US economy after the brief 1991 recession. It is little wonder that so many households, predominantly in the low income groups, are filing for bankruptcy. Filings reached 1.2 million in 1997, well above the recession-related peak of 930,000 in 1992.

The USA is not alone in its unusual experience of personal debt delinquency amid economic prosperity. Banks' bad debts relating to personal loans and mortgages rose in the UK during 1997 and there have been reports of a deterioration in credit quality in Canada and Australia too. In the absence of a resurgence of wage and price inflation, the regular cycle of rising and falling debt service burdens has been interrupted. Even though nominal interest rates are remarkably low, this has not been sufficient to compress the relative importance of debt service payments. Research undertaken at the Federal Reserve Bank of New York suggests that consumers worry about the burden of their debts only when they suffer a loss of income or are starved of access to additional credit. This helps to explain why personal consumer spending seems to be relatively unaffected by the rise in the debt service burdens of so many households. Personal credit quality can deteriorate for a long period before latent problems reach the surface.

CONCLUSIONS

The concept of credit quality is fundamental to an understanding of the western financial system. Like George Orwell's animals, all borrowers are equal but some are more equal than others. The virtual elimination of the credit quality spread, in all its dimensions, ought to be regarded as a source of fear and trembling, not a celebration of capital market efficiency. Efficiency argues for the equalization of borrowing costs and bond yields, while equity argues for a well-defined hierarchy of yields. To all intents and purposes the yield convergence movement has succeeded in its bid to treat all borrowers as if their credit quality were identical. The infants referred to earlier are queuing up to tap grandmother on the sleeve; yet, deaf though she may seem, one day she will spring to life, scolding the children for being so presumptuous. As in 1994, but perhaps on a much greater scale, the manifest stupidity of treating different credit risks alike will wreak havoc in the government, corporate and personal debt markets.

Inevitably, the wonderful capital gains obtained from trading away the risk spread will, one day, come to an end. As noted above, the most direct connection between personal debt delinquency and financial markets occurs where credit card or mortgage debt is securitized and sold to fund managers. As delinquency rates rise, so the value of the bond falls and its implied yield rises. The highly developed consumer credit and securitized loan markets of the USA provide an acid test of credit quality developments throughout the western world.

II

The Phoney Auction
of Private Savings

'A golden bait hung temptingly out before the people, and one after the other, they rushed to the tulip-marts, like flies around a honey-pot. Every one imagined that the passion for tulips would last for ever, and that the wealthy from every part of the world would send to Holland, and pay whatever prices were asked for them . . . People of all grades converted their property into cash, and invested it in flowers.'   Charles Mackay,
*Extraordinary Popular Delusions
and the Madness of Crowds*, 1841

'Charles Ponzi was the archetypal confidence man, a swindler who in the space of eight months raised nearly 15 million dollars from 40,000 investors by promising to "double your money" in 90 days. While Ponzi claimed to be taking advantage of arbitrage opportunities in international postal coupons, he was in reality operating a financial chain letter, using funds from new investors to pay off earlier investors . . . The final bankruptcy report, issued in 1931, showed Ponzi's firm to be insolvent to the tune of over two and a half million dollars.'   Stephen O'Connell and
Stephen Zeldes, in
The New Palgrave, 1992

The focus of this chapter is the process whereby capital is allocated between competing uses. In the absence of a global policeman to wave ahead certain capital-raising exercises and to turn away others, who decides which applicants are successful? Is there a genuine sense in which the markets clear of their own accord, or is the capital allocation process more like a theatrical performance than an auction? When companies offer shares for public sale for the first time, only for the share price to tumble shortly afterwards, how can it be determined that important information was not withheld from investors before the issue? How do large institutional investors allocate the funds entrusted to them among different types of assets? What proportion of private wealth is actively managed by intermediaries, rather than by its owners?

MARRIAGES OF CONVENIENCE

In the ideal world of a global, free and fair capital market, blushing brides, representing savings past and present, are united with noble suitors, the most deserving capital projects and investment opportunities. The varying risk profiles of investors are simultaneously matched with the shades of business risk inherent in the various requests for capital. Bound up in this perpetual ceremony are the notions that all the grooms are of good character and sincere intent, and that all the brides have done their homework and studied past form. In the real world, things happen a little differently. Brides take surprisingly little interest in the personalities and particulars of their grooms, normally delegating the choice to an agent. Likewise grooms, bored by the inconvenience of searching for worthwhile partners, employ intermediaries to round up a posse of beauties who appear to satisfy certain important criteria.

The agents and intermediaries, in turn, go about their business with due diligence. Many years of experience have shown that the brides prefer to see lots of pictures and are readily impressed by grooms' assurances about their excellent prospects. The agents have learnt that to dwell on character defects, dysfunctional behaviour and past misdemeanours is a mistake. The grooms, on the other hand, are more concerned that there is money in the bride's family and that she will turn up for the wedding. Once the agents and intermediaries have fulfilled their mandates, an army of clerks ensures that all the forms are properly filled out, the documents are signed and that the cheques don't bounce. Dissatisfied parties are referred to the lawyers.

This caricature of the operation of the global capital market could be developed further, but it should suffice for present purposes. The striking features of the western savings and capital markets are the disinterestedness of individuals in the way that their wealth is invested and the unaccountability of investment firms towards their ultimate customers. In Chapter 5 a list of seven dimensions of capital markets development was suggested, among them concentration, inter-mediation and mobilization. These processes have a particular rel-evance to the questions posed above, and a brief reminder is in order. The term 'concentration' is used in a variety of contexts to describe the degree to which a few producers dominate the market for a good or service. There is a high and rising level of concentration in the investment banking industry, which raises funds for borrowers, and in the fund management industry, which allocates funds among com-peting assets. Intermediation refers to the distancing of the individual saver from his or her investment. For example, the investment activities of a pension or insurance fund are so diverse as to make it very difficult to determine what a typical fund beneficiary actually owns in terms of the underlying assets. Mobilization, the opposite of inertia, is the term used to express the consumer's heightened awareness of the returns available on different types of assets, coupled with a willingness to act upon this information. This applies not only to new savings flows but also to accumulated wealth. Consumers have become increasingly dissatisfied by low returns on deposits and are much less influenced by a sense of loyalty to a particular provider of financial services than in previous generations. Private wealth has a new-found mobility. In the next section, the characteristics of the borrowers and the savers in the capital market are examined.

WHO ARE THE ISSUER-BORROWERS?

In 1994, new funds raised through national and international bond and equity issues and net international bank lending approached $3 trillion, of which $2.3 trillion represented bonds. In 1995, the total of net new issues moderated but it still exceeded $2 trillion, and total

Figure 11.1 Net addition to the stock of bonds in 1995

$bn	Government bonds	Federal agency	Non-agency mortgage	Municipal bonds	Bank debentures	Corporate bonds	Foreign bonds	Eurodollar bonds	Total public	Private placements	All bonds
USA	124	207	37	-45		223	18	52	615		615
Japan	154	11		11	-16	33	11	36	241	78	319
Germany	18	-4	8	7	121	0		43	184	90	274
Italy	68	-3				0	0	10	82		82
France	62	0		-1		-3	-1	6	62		62
UK	33					2	0	9	43		43
Canada	17			5		4	0	-2	23		23
Belgium	32				-4	3	7	0	38		38
Netherlands	19	0		0		17	-2	16	49	-4	45
Denmark	7		8					3	17		17
Switzerland	2			3	5	0	6		16	10	27
Sweden	25		-7	0	0	-2	0		17		17
Spain	31			3	1	-2	1		34		34
Other countries	51	1	-2	0	5	-7	1	9	58	-3	55
Totals	643	212	44	-18	112	269	40	179	1480	171	1651

Source: Derived from R. Benavides, 'How big is the world bond market?'

borrowing has remained at least as strong as this in 1996 and 1997. For what grand purposes are these funds required and who are the investors who subscribe such vast amounts each year?

Taking 1995 as a more typical year for global capital markets than 1994, the following paragraphs attempt to answer these questions in some detail. First of all, it is necessary to show how the total figure for net new issuance is derived. Using an investment industry source for the world's major bond markets, Figure 11.1 derives the net addition to the stock of bonds as $1.65 trillion in 1995, measured at constant exchange rates. The BIS source for net international bank lending estimates an addition of $330 billion for 1995. Finally, gross issues of domestic equities are estimated from OECD sources as $250 billion in 1995. After subtracting $50 billion of equity redemption, this leaves net equity issue at roughly $200 billion. Our crude aggregate is therefore $2.18 trillion.

The distribution of this total among different instruments is as follows. Bonds of all kinds account for the lion's share of net new issues. In 1995, our calculations indicate that bonds had a market share of 76 per cent, international bank lending 15 per cent, and equities 9 per cent. A decomposition of bond issues reveals that 77 per cent were domestic and publicly issued bonds, 10 per cent were domestic and privately placed bonds, and 13 per cent were international bonds. The final subdivision reveals that this dominant category, domestic and publicly issued bonds, is made up of central government bonds (51 per cent), central government guaranteed or sponsored bonds (17 per cent), municipal or state bonds (−1 per cent), bank debentures and mortgage bonds (12 per cent) and corporate bonds (21 per cent).

This implies that about $640 billion was borrowed from the capital markets in 1995 simply to finance the budget deficits of OECD countries. On a rough calculation, this amount is almost equivalent to the net interest payments of OECD governments, which was 2.9 per cent of a nominal GDP of $21.6 trillion in that year. In other words, around 30 per cent of annual capital issuance represents the cost of servicing existing government debt. Other agencies, such as mortgage associations in the USA, borrowed against the government's good name to the tune of $200 billion or so. A further $150 billion of mortgage bonds were issued, mainly in Germany, by banks and other financial intermediaries. The remaining $270 billion was issued by companies and financial institutions to finance take-overs, research and development, to install new capacity, to purchase new capital equipment and to acquire financial assets (e.g. stakes in other companies). Most corporate bonds were issued in US dollars or Japanese yen.

Gross funds raised on the international markets in 1995 amounted to $832 billion, of which 88 per cent was borrowed by the rich OECD countries, 10 per cent by the developing world and 2 per cent by international aid agencies. Even if industrial and commercial companies were responsible for 90 per cent of all the net financing in international markets and all the net domestic equity issues, then the corporate share of new funds raised would only reach 37 per cent in 1995. In practice, their share was probably between 30 per cent and 35 per cent. Governments (47 per cent) are the biggest borrowers on the capital markets, with financial intermediaries (such as investment funds, securities dealers and credit companies) wrapping up the remaining 20 per cent market share.

AND WHO ARE THE MAJOR INVESTOR-SAVERS?

The most direct approach to this question is to examine the flows of funds of the largest borrowing nation in the world, the USA. In 1995, net domestic capital issues of US Treasury and agency securities, corporate and foreign bonds and corporate equities amounted to $656 billion, roughly 30 per cent of the world capital issue. These borrowings were financed to the tune of 40 per cent by non-US savings, another 40 per cent by domestic long-term savings (insurance companies and pension funds) and 15 per cent by brokers, dealers and funding corporations. The remaining 5 per cent covered direct acquisitions of securities by households, businesses and the banking system.

The USA is not typical in depending so heavily on foreign savings, but it is worth delving a little deeper into the identity of these purchasers of US assets. In fact, there are three distinct groups of investors. First, there are funds which correspond to Asian trade surpluses with the USA, especially Japan's trade surplus. For better or for worse, the bulk of Asian wealth (the counterpart to America's net external debt of more than $1 trillion) has been reinvested in US deposits and securities. Second, there are the offshore funds that operate out of centres such as the Bahamas, the Netherlands Antilles and the Cayman Islands. Much of this wealth belongs to US citizens but is channelled into US investments via tax havens. Third, there are the professional fund managers around the world, but mainly in Europe, who have custody over the pension, insurance and savings assets of individuals in dozens of developed countries. Their asset allocation decisions help to determine the extent of foreign demand for US securities.

What is particularly noticeable in this example is the remoteness of the savers from their investments. On a net basis, the official statistics suggest that households contributed nothing to the financing of US capital issues in 1995. Large purchases of mutual funds were offset by direct sales of equities, partly in the context of exercising stock options. Domestic long-term savings institutions contributed 40 per cent of the total US capital requirement, but at least a quarter of the total capital raised by the USA in 1995 was provided by financial intermediaries other than long-term investment funds. The offshore funds, the brokers, dealers and funding corporations are not noted for their lasting commitment to any particular securities; they also tend to be much more highly geared than long-term savings institutions. The key point is that a large fraction of the financing of US capital requirements has been derived from marginal and relatively unstable investors. Moreover, from whom have they borrowed in order to purchase these securities?

THE ROLE OF INVESTMENT BANKS IN CAPITAL ISSUANCE

Apart from government debt issues, which are handled by treasury departments, most private issuance requires the services of an investment bank. While there are corporate brokers, venture capitalists and a few private banks which also arrange finance for companies, investment banks occupy the dominant position in the marketplace. Investment banks perform various functions in relation to capital issues. These may be syndicated loans, issues of corporate debt, initial offerings of equities, secondary issues or placings of stock. In the first instance, the investment bank may have advised the company to raise the capital in order to make an acquisition. The bank may then underwrite the issue of stock or bonds, ensuring that the full amount of capital is raised.

A third function is the marketing of the issue prior to launch. The local stock exchange will require certain due diligence procedures to be followed in order to certify the soundness of the issue. Furthermore, the leading investment bank will normally prepare a detailed prospectus as part of its own marketing drive. Finally, in its role as the lead manager of the issue, the bank is committed to attracting subscriptions from high-calibre investors who are likely to want to hold on to the shares or bonds rather than sell them on immediately. Where the issue is of a certain size, say, above $500 million – and some can range into the billions of dollars – even the largest investment bank would normally assemble a syndicate of other banks to assist with the underwriting and distribution of the issue.

There is a brief period between the announcement of the price and the issue of the stock where the underwriter places his own capital at risk. If some shock political or economic news arrives in this critical interval, then some of the large funds who had agreed, in principle, to subscribe to the issue might well decide to pull out. There is then the risk that the issue would be under-subscribed and that the underwriters would be left holding a sizeable portion of the stock or the debt. This explains why investment banks are prepared to share the fees and commissions connected to a capital issue with their rivals; in the rare event of a disastrous issue, the pain would be shared. The management of an equity issue may also include a responsibility to stabilize the share price during the following few weeks, or even to increase the size of the issue if demand remained strong.

As the scale of domestic and international capital issuance has expanded, the leading investment banks have accumulated a wealth of experience in the issuing, placing and flotation processes. Whereas, in the early 1980s, an investment bank would have had to work quite hard to persuade companies to use the capital markets, nowadays it is often the companies which search out the banks. Corporate strategy may stand or fall on the success of a capital markets manoeuvre; the choice of investment bank can be extremely important. Rather like a theatre company with celebrated actors, the capital markets teams of the major investment banks have their own stars. Whereas, for them, one subordinated bond issue is just another performance, for the customers it is their special occasion. Woe betide the investment bank that does a shoddy job for a blue-chip company.

The importance of a particular bond or equity issue for the client, and the consequences of a badly handled issue, have promoted the cause of an élite group of perhaps 20 banks world wide. This group includes such names as Morgan Stanley, Merrill Lynch, Goldman Sachs, Salomon, J. P. Morgan and Chase Manhattan in the USA, Deutsche Morgan Grenfell, Dresdner, Société Générale, SBC Warburg, Crédit Suisse First Boston in Europe and Jardine Fleming, HSBC and Barings in Asia. As the industry has become more concentrated through mergers, acquisitions and surrenders, prospective issuers have found their effective choice of investment bank much reduced. While there is no shortage of smaller banks and specialists who would love to take on the business, there is a genuine risk that the minnows might launch an issue at an inopportune time. Only the giants really know what other corporate news and prospective capital issues are in the pipeline.

The pattern that is forming, year by year, is of a cluster of massive investment banks. Each has vast capital resources and each has its own particular comparative advantages in certain types of instrument, geographical regions and industrial sectors. Although none of the banks would claim a global market share of fees and commissions as high as 10 per cent, and competition between banks is often fierce, this does not deny their powerful market positions in sub-sectors. In extreme circumstances, these élite banks can virtually guarantee that even a poor-quality issue will be fully subscribed. The issuer will pay higher fees for the privilege, but this may seem a worthwhile price for the added degree of protection against a failed issue.

How can an investment bank persuade institutional funds to subscribe to a mediocre bond issue or to the privatization of, say, an unknown and unpronounceable Croatian gas company? One way is to let it be known that a really attractive issue of stock in a well-known company will be offered soon afterwards. Only if the fund manager takes a slice of the doubtful first issue will he or she be offered a share of the lucrative deal that follows. The closeness of relationship between the capital markets teams of investment banks and the large investment funds provides ample scope for such persuasion to succeed. Peer group pressure ensures that most capital issues are fully subscribed, even where the track record of the management is poor or non-existent. Not that private individuals are likely to complain at this; when they commit their savings directly in the financial markets, they seem attracted to the most ill-judged and disreputable ventures. Two famous examples were quoted at the beginning of this chapter.

THE PRACTICALITIES OF MANAGING VAST INVESTMENT FUNDS

Such is the concentration of power in the hands of about 50 global fund managers that some now have discretion over assets worth over $500 billion. The merger of the Swiss banks, SBC and UBS, has gathered $920 billion of managed assets under one roof. Fidelity, the largest US mutual fund company, Merrill Lynch, which took over Mercury Asset Management in 1997, and Axa, the French insurance group, have also reached the $500 billion threshold. Barclays Global Investors and State Street Global Advisors are not far behind. In the USA, the top 20 asset managers of all types controlled 43 per cent of the assets of the top 200 managers in 1986; by 1996, this proportion had grown to 49 per cent. Meanwhile the value of assets under management by the top 200 grew from $2.5 trillion in 1986 to $9.2 trillion in 1996. The compound annual growth rate of 14 per cent reflects the rate of appreciation of financial assets during this decade.

What is involved in the management of global assets of $500 million; $5 billion; $50 billion; $500 billion? Whereas a $500 million fund can be managed comfortably by a small office with, perhaps, no more than six staff, a $500 billion fund would be a significant company in its own right, with thousands of staff in offices scattered around the world. In the US magazine *Business Week*'s analysis of 1997 data, Merrill Lynch was ranked the 22nd largest company by sales and Morgan Stanley, Dean Witter, was 33rd in the rankings. In the $500 million fund, there is little scope for individuals to develop specialized skills. The functions of asset allocation, client liaison, compliance with regulations and general administration tend to be handled jointly by a closely knit team.

At the opposite extreme, the $500 billion mega-fund is compelled to employ hundreds of specialists to undertake these distinct tasks, and the executives of the business spend much of their time in conference with these specialists. Scores of administrators ensure that diaries are co-ordinated, conference calls are booked, meeting rooms are available and so forth. But there is a more telling distinction between funds of such different sizes: the tiny fund can buy and sell stocks and shares at will, tip-toeing anonymously between investments, whereas the transactions of the massive fund leave behind large footprints. Their dealings are extremely difficult to disguise within the normal trading patterns of the financial markets, except in the government bond markets and in a few dozen actively traded shares. This difficulty has lent powerful support to a passive style of fund management in which investments are programmed to track the progress of a familiar stock market index or industry benchmark.

Somewhere between the $5 billion and the $50 billion fund sizes, a metamorphosis in organizational structure must occur. Below this threshold, the fund can operate almost like a family firm in which everyone knows everyone else and there is a high degree of internal scrutiny. Business secrets, good or bad, are difficult to protect. The small fund is very discriminating in its asset selection and is rewarded by good investment performance for its clients. Word soon gets around and the fund attracts new clients and expands organically within the same cosy structure. Fee income grows more rapidly than the cost base, and profits benefit accordingly. If the firm continues to manage its affairs well, one of two sequences of events is likely to unfold: either a larger fund buys out its owners and absorbs its operations, lock, stock and barrel, or the firm experiences a quantum leap in funds under management as a result of some spectacular success and is forced to reorganize.

Within a very short time, the family-firm atmosphere is destined to be replaced by a corporate culture. In the former case, it will be the existing culture of the parent company and, in the latter, an evolving culture of its owners' design. New management positions will be created, better information systems developed and more attention given to issues of corporate governance, product development and company-wide policies. These changes are essential to enable the fund to cope with its enlarged client base without compromising the quality of its asset allocation and investment performance. However, in a majority of cases, fund performance does suffer from the traumas of this transition and it is common for long-serving personnel to leave at this juncture.

The gulf between the $50 billion and the $500 billion fund management company is greater still. As the number of separate funds increases, it becomes more and more difficult to ensure that consistent decisions are being taken across the whole company. One equity fund manager may be selling European chemicals stocks just as a colleague sitting on the opposite side of the Atlantic is buying them. Each fund will incur transactions costs while, in aggregate, the parent fund management company has a similar exposure as before. At every stage of the investment management process, the tasks become more complicated. The asset allocation process begins with quarterly evaluations of all the major countries in terms of their economic and financial prospects, together with agreed assumptions about currency movements and commodity prices. The stock selection committees divide into larger stocks and smaller stocks. They receive presentations from brokers and even from the companies themselves. Finally, when all these decisions have been made, there is the problem of securing the desired shares or bonds without signalling the fund's intentions to the whole market. Selling a significant holding of company shares is no easier; it may prove sensible to ask a broker to work the order at a reasonable discount behind the scenes, so as not to bomb the share price.

Very large investment management companies tend to grow more by acquisition than by attracting new business or by achieving exceptional fund performance. Indeed, the larger the funds under management, the more likely it is that performance will gravitate towards the industry averages in each asset class. However confident the asset allocators may feel about their investment selection process, there is a tendency for their good decisions to be partially or totally cancelled out by their careless ones. In the intensely competitive world of fund management, the risks of under-performing industry benchmarks provide a powerful argument against bravery in asset allocation or stock selection. The herd instinct that has proved so costly for commercial banks over the years is no less prevalent in fund management circles. Second-guessing the strategic portfolio decisions of rivals can, at times, appear more important than having a clear strategy of one's own. In particular, those investment companies most concerned to protect the accumulated gains of their pensioners and policy-holders in a mature bull market are the most vulnerable to under-performance.

The journey into mega-fund territory requires the successful company to make huge investments in technology, back-office systems and expensive personnel. After so much time, energy and money has been spent on systems and procedures, the logical step is to swallow up some smaller funds in order to rationalize their operations and spread the fixed costs across a wider base of fund values. No matter how large the mega-funds become, they do not seem to lose their appetite for aggrandizement. Their managements are convinced that economies of scale and scope have not been fully exhausted. The gulf that has opened up between the giants and the minnows is so large as to permit their peaceful co-existence. Rather, it is the medium-sized funds whose future is under threat.

In fact, the average size of the top 50 global fund managers has grown at a prodigious pace during the 1980s and 1990s, typically between 15 per cent and 20 per cent per annum. The proportion of private financial wealth placed with investment intermediaries, rather than deposited at banks, has increased steadily. In the USA, this proportion has risen from 19 per cent in 1980 to 26 per cent in 1986 and to over 35 per cent in 1996. The fund management industry has become more international and more concentrated as a result of frequent mergers and take-overs. Moreover, the long bull market in bonds and shares has added a powerful dynamic to fund values. The fusion of these three trends has created an array of mammoth funds that are large enough to digest the jumbo debt and equity issues of the late twentieth century but which have ceased to be sufficiently discerning in their appetites.

WHAT IS MEANT BY A PHONEY AUCTION?

Effectively, there is a global savings auction in progress all the time. In the world of syndicated loans, international bond issues and book-building exercises, tens of billions of dollars of private savings change hands every day. Depending on the relative strength of funds flow forthcoming (either from genuine savings or from speculation using borrowed money) and net capital demands, world bond and share prices rise or fall. A persistent rise in bond prices relative to share prices will persuade fund managers to allocate a higher proportion of their total assets to bonds, and vice versa. If bond prices or share prices perform badly, this may lead the marginal borrower to postpone or cancel a planned issue, although this has become a rare occurrence.

However, as far as the overall direction of the market is concerned, the real contest is between invested funds and liquid assets. In Figure 6.1, the varying propensities of households in different countries to hold cash and other liquid assets in their wealth portfolios were noted. The extent of diversification away from cash, bank deposits and other uninvested assets appears to have been the greatest in Sweden, the USA and the UK. In Chapter 6 the increasing abandonment of cash as a worthwhile financial asset was examined in more detail, noting that for long periods the inducements to invest in equities and bonds have been extremely powerful. With the exception of the 1970s, there has been an almost overwhelming attraction of invested funds as compared to liquid assets ever since the 1950s. From 1982, the returns from bond and equity portfolios in the developed world have tended to be positively associated. Only rarely has either failed to outscore the annual returns available from bank deposits and CDs by 8 per cent or more.

Essentially, the mobilization of western household financial wealth into equities and bonds, increasingly acquired through intermediaries, has been driven by this wide discrepancy in investment performance. The varying speeds of migration of personal savings from the safety of bank deposits into securities investment can be explained largely by institutional features of the financial systems of Anglo-Saxon versus continental European economies. There is very little evidence to suggest that individuals in different countries have fundamentally different attitudes to investment opportunities.

Returning to the scene of the hypothetical savings and capital auction, there are two distinct groups of agents, each with scores of consultants and advisers vying for their attention. The first group of agents represents millions of individual investors in pensions, insurance and savings products. The second represents thousands of companies and financial institutions seeking to issue shares or debt instruments. Brokers offer advice to fund managers as to the content of their portfolios. Analysts write recommendations for the equities and bonds they believe to be the most attractive investments. Trustees of pension funds and charities hold fund managers to account for their funds' performance. Benefit consultants and actuaries produce league tables of comparative fund performance and advise trustees on which investment companies to select as the manager of their pension fund. Newspapers, magazines and a host of audio-visual media offer their own incessant stream of commentary and opinion.

All this activity may give the appearance of free and open access to information at this perpetual auction, but this is far from the reality. Behind the scenes, most of the really important capital transfers are arranged in great secrecy. The huge investment banks on one side and the mega-funds on the other realize that large-scale transactions are better handled well away from the public gaze. Hostile take-overs are necessarily clandestine affairs, but the results of these battles are often decided by the casting votes of two or three investing institutions, each with significant stakes in the target company. Information services, purporting to identify the ownership of a company's shares or of the stock of government bonds in issue, frequently find it impossible to trace the holders of 10 per cent or 15 per cent of the total. Other sizeable holdings may be in nominee accounts that conceal the identity of the ultimate owners. Drug barons and other inhabitants of the criminal world are also believed to be significant holders of bearer financial securities as well as of US dollar bills. Bearer securities are those for which no ownership register is maintained; possession is sufficient proof of entitlement to interest or dividends.

In particular, there are two aspects of the capital–savings matching process which should give rise to investor concern. First, the derivatives markets have come to play a significant role in obscuring the ultimate ownership of securities, especially bonds. Levels of open interest in government bond futures contracts have grown steadily during the extended bull market of the 1980s and 1990s. As was discussed in Chapter 7, derivatives are used to secure the control of a more expensive asset from a much smaller commitment of capital. The use of derivatives by the hedge funds and the proprietary trading desks of large banks in relation to government bond markets represents itself as a grossly inflated demand for the underlying bonds. This acts as an artificial support mechanism for both bond and equity markets, keeping yields lower and asset values higher than would otherwise be the case. This synthetic source of demand is critically dependent on the downward progression of bond yields and on the slope of the yield curve. While there is a sense in which all demands for financial assets are contingent on their expected performance, this is especially true of geared and unhedged derivatives positions. Only a tiny disturbance to the structure of interest rates may be required to undermine the profitability of these positions, triggering dramatic underlying sales of bonds and equities, such as occurred in 1987.

The role of the arbs, or arbitrageurs, in this process was described in Chapter 5. In a bull bond or equity market, arbs chase after higher-yielding stocks in the belief that the market has over-estimated the credit risk attached to them. Their activities are clearly visible in the whittling away of credit risk spreads (detailed in the last chapter), in periodic commodity price bubbles and in the manic behaviour of the shares in highly fashionable technology companies, for example. Risk arbitrage describes a different kind of auction from the one discussed at the beginning of this chapter: an auction of promises. Whoever is prepared to disregard the most risk can afford to promise the highest returns, thus attracting funds from competing uses. The net result of this phoney auction is that the individuals, on whose behalf these investments are made, acquire a more risky portfolio than they bargained for. The double-digit percentage returns available on stock market investments in recent years do not come free; high returns are dependent on the acceptance of significant and sometimes exceptional risk. Investors may be shocked to discover how adversely the performance of their equity portfolios can be affected by a single failed company.

Second, the concentration of global capital issue and global fund management in the hands of the few has undermined the painstaking process of independent risk assessment. Whereas the bank branch manager of the 1960s committed the bank's money to a customer on the basis of personal conversations and in the knowledge that his or her own competence was at stake, the global fund management committees struggle to maintain direct links with companies in which they have substantial investments. More often than not, the fund manager relies on a few key intermediaries to keep in touch with corporate developments. In other cases, the investing institution may own shares on the personal whim of a senior investment officer, who takes a keen interest in the company concerned. The extent to which individuals are held responsible for faulty decisions or poor stock selection varies greatly from one fund management company to another. Much as medical practitioners distance themselves emotionally from the patients they examine, most investment officers have a professional detachment from the consequences of their actions for the beneficiaries of the funds they manage.

The most vulnerable times for investment companies in terms of controlling investment risk are periods of rapid expansion of funds under management. A prime example is the US mutual funds during the 1990s, where inflows have followed a stellar trajectory. Some funds have literally closed their doors to new investors because of the risk of damaging their track record by making hasty investments. In a steeply rising market, there is enormous pressure to stay fully invested. Even a month spent with an excessive cash balance can prejudice a fund's relative performance. In a bull market there is a temptation to pursue almost every investment opportunity that presents itself, for fear of missing out on a wonder stock such as a Microsoft or an Intel. Poor risk control in phases of rapid fund expansion may not be immediately apparent, but ultimately it shows through. The only sure bet is that individual investors will pay for poor fund performance in lower pension entitlements, insurance bonuses and investment returns.

CONCLUSION

The allocation of private sector savings among competing uses is a highly stage-managed affair, despite the apparent openness of stock and bond markets and the relatively free exchange of market information. This situation has evolved since the mid-1980s in the context of increased concentration of issuance expertise in investment banks and of funds under management in large investment institutions. Investment banks are very skilful in bringing unfamiliar country and company names to the capital markets; all too often, the mega-funds solve their asset allocation problem by buying the stream of new issues offered to them by the investment banks. The upward march of share and bond prices between 1982 and 1998 has rewarded this indiscriminate approach, delivering ample investment returns to pensioners and savers in the process. Equally, these consistently pleasing returns have fostered a high degree of trust on the part of individual pension fund beneficiaries and investors. Throughout this period of accelerated development, the mega-funds have rarely been challenged by adversity. Their managers have become increasingly removed from the individual investors they serve. Layers and layers of financial intermediation have accumulated, forming an effective barrier between investor-savers and the managers of their wealth.

12

The Separation of Financial Value
from Economic Reality

When, lo, as they reached the mountain's side,
A wondrous portal opened wide,
As if a cavern was suddenly hollowed;
And the Piper advanced and the children followed,
And when all were in to the very last,
The door in the mountain side shut fast.
Robert Browning, *The Pied Piper of Hamelin*

'There is nothing so disturbing to one's wellbeing and judgment
as to see a friend get rich.'   Charles P. Kindleberger, *Manias,
Panics and Crashes,* 1978

A popular acronym of the 1980s was 'WYSIWYG': what you see is
what you get. Early versions of personal computer software had
the annoying property that the printed version of a file bore little
relationship to the format in which it appeared on the screen. WYS-
IWYG was the proud boast of the programmers who restored transparency to their software products. Capital markets are ripe for
a similar revolution. Earlier chapters have addressed the lack of
transparency in the bond and derivatives markets, the phoney auction
of savings and the distancing of individual saver-investors from the
ultimate deployment of their wealth. This chapter examines the murky
relationship between the valuation of company shares (equities), the
profits that companies report and the economic assets that they own.
Anglo-Saxons hold a substantial proportion of their financial wealth
as equities rather than as bonds, loan assets or cash; but why? How

are equity values determined? Are equities more risky investments than bonds? What are the linkages between the valuation of bonds and of equities? Are equities overvalued, and does it matter if they are? Of necessity, the explanations offered here are all too brief, but it would be impossible to complete the argument of this book without taking a closer look at the stock market phenomenon. At the outset, there are some important contrasts to be made between the organization of personal and corporate financial affairs.

CONTRASTS BETWEEN HOUSEHOLD AND CORPORATE BALANCE SHEETS

Most individuals have relatively straightforward balance sheets. Western households typically own property, vehicles and household goods, against which there may be outstanding borrowings. They also hold wealth in the form of cash, deposits and investments. For most of these items, current values can be obtained readily from the financial press. The exceptions are pension entitlements, which may be bound up in a group scheme or may be in the form of an individual retirement account, with-profits insurance policies and investments in unquoted securities and private businesses. However, even these will be valued at routine intervals. In principle, individuals could calculate their household's net worth, that is, the market value of total assets minus total liabilities. For most households or individuals, this exercise should not be too difficult or time-consuming, although few may attempt it in practice.

The transparency of personal balance sheets can give rise to powerful emotions and abrupt changes in behaviour. When UK residential house prices fell by 20 per cent, and even 40 per cent in some regions, between 1989 and 1991, this represented a dramatic loss of net worth for millions of households whose principal asset (excluding pension entitlements) was their home. For a sizeable minority, the fall in the market value was sufficient to leave them with negative equity in their property. This phenomenon occurs when loans secured against an asset exceed the market value of the asset. On one large Bristol housing estate, Bradley Stoke, the incidence of households with negative equity was so great that locals re-named it Sadly Broke. Despite having little or no understanding of balance sheets and financial analysis, these householders soon became fully aware of their predicament. They had invested unwisely and had fallen into a trap. Some gritted their teeth and took a second job; some threw in the towel and surrendered ownership of their property; some had their properties taken from them in the courts, but the majority muddled through in diminished circumstances. Although UK commercial property values, particularly of offices, recorded a similarly steep decline during this period, comparatively few companies of any size suffered embarrassment. Unlike households, they were able to choose when to re-value property assets in their accounts, thus concealing their insolvency.

Corporate balance sheets and financial accounts are far from transparent. As Terry Smith, the former head of UK company research at securities firm UBS, has argued, accounting profit is a guess, not a fact. Many large companies, not to mention tens of thousands of small ones, have folded despite reporting a consistent record of profitable activity. If beauty is in the eye of the beholder, profit is in the eye of the shareholder, the corporate treasurer, the auditor and the taxman, to name but a few. Declared profit is an opinion, not a fact. To comprehend why large companies' financial affairs are so opaque in comparison to those of households, consider the following list:

a. households don't make hostile bids to acquire other households;
b. households don't have a depreciation policy for their assets;
c. households can't use neighbourhood goodwill or family names as collateral;
d. households can't create legal off-balance sheet accounting vehicles;
e. households don't run their own pension schemes;
f. households are seldom allowed to run unmatched currency positions;
g. households' capital expenditures (other than property) do not qualify for tax relief;
h. households can't issue stock, let alone convertible stock with put options;
i. households don't dispose of other households;

j. households can't capitalize costs in order to turn an expense into an asset.

WHAT IS THE RELATIONSHIP BETWEEN PROFITS AND SHARE VALUES?

Viewed in the simplest terms, companies add value when they apply inputs of labour, land and capital services to bring about the transformation of materials, energy and other consumables into an output that has a commercial value. The sales value of the outputs of goods and services minus the cost of the consumables is the value added by the company; it is divided between labour costs, rents and hire charges, and profits, which may be positive or negative. The stream of profits arising from corporate activity, after the deduction of income tax, is commonly referred to as the earnings attributable to shareholders. After division by the total number of shares in issue, this becomes earnings per share (EPS). The conventional method of valuing shares is to discount all future expected EPS to the present using an appropriate discount rate. The price of the shares is considered to represent the sum of all expected future earnings plus any residual discounted value of the company at the distant point of the calculation. This is usually expressed as a multiple of current EPS: the price to earnings ratio (P/E) represents the stock markets' collective judgement on the ability of the company to earn profits in future years. The P/E ratio measures the number of years taken for a shareholder to recover his initial investment (assuming that all earnings are distributed). Alternatively, it measures the price (in dollars) that an investor has to pay to buy $1 worth of income in the company. A P/E of 1 implies a complete lack of confidence in the prospects of the firm to generate further profits, while a P/E of 100 suggests the utmost confidence in the company's future earnings potential.

Consider the following illustration: TFN mining corporation announces its latest annual results, declaring EPS of $2. If its cost of capital is 8 per cent and the life span of its mines is expected to be 20 years, then the only remaining variable is the average growth rate of EPS over this long horizon, taking into account the likely inflation rate of its products as well as the probable growth rate of sales volumes over the 20 years. If EPS growth is taken as 10 per cent per annum, then the P/E is 25.4 and a rational value for TFN shares is $50.80; using 5 per cent EPS growth, the P/E becomes 16.1 and the valuation drops to $32.20; if there is no growth in EPS, then the P/E is 10.8 and the implied value of the shares is $21.60.

Suppose now that the government's geologists produce a report saying that all TFN's mines will require extensive capital expenditures in ten years' time if they are to continue to receive the health and safety permissions that they need. Rationally, the analysts will re-work their calculations on the basis of a ten-year lifespan for the mines. This yields P/Es of 12.1, 9.6 and 7.7, respectively, for the three different assumptions about earnings growth, with implied share values of $24.20, $19.20 and $15.40. Whether TFN shares change hands for $15 or $50 depends much more on assumptions and guesses about the future than current earnings; it also depends on the company's skill in managing the flow of news relating to its activities. Even where there is utter transparency in the means by which profits are generated and the manner in which they are reported, the market value of a company is subject to huge variation.

CREATIVE ACCOUNTING AND THE CLEVER USE OF SHARE OPTIONS

The euphemism 'creative accounting' has been used to describe the degree of latitude available to treasurers and accountants engaged in financial reporting activities. An exceptional charge for restructuring, an interest rate swap, a timely asset disposal or a bit of off-balance sheet gearing will work miracles for even the dowdiest set of corporate results. Small wonder that the great majority of publicly quoted companies report consistent annual progressions of pre-tax profits and EPS when so many smoothing and sterilization techniques are admissible.

A popular incentive scheme in the USA and elsewhere involves the creation and distribution of company share options to directors and employees. Without paying out any extra cash, the company provides an additional staff benefit which may be worth tens of thousands of dollars in years to come. At a stroke, the company secures the loyalty of its staff and harnesses them to the objective of corporate success. The higher the productivity of the directors and staff, the more share options they are granted year by year. All being well, the benefits to profitability of rising productivity will show through in the appreciation of the company's shares, which obviously enhances the value of the share options.

Employee share options confer the right, but not the obligation, to purchase shares in the company at a fixed price (usually close to the prevailing price when the options are granted) on a future date, typically between three and five years hence. These options have been especially prevalent in banking, finance and hi-tech industries, but their use has become widespread. In 1998, it was estimated that US households owned $800 billion worth of company share options, a tenfold increase over the previous ten years. The attraction of share options to the company is that they are a means of deferred remuneration, exercisable only as long as the individual is loyal to the company. To the recipient, share options offer the prospect of immense capital gains as long as the company's share price keeps rising.

Under the prevailing accounting standards in the USA, when the share options are created companies are not required to make any charge against current profits. While the share options may have no marketable value when they are granted, they do have a specific value to the person that receives them. They are contingent liabilities of the company. If the employee leaves the company before the waiting period is over, the options cannot be exercised and are valueless. If the company's shares perform badly during the life of the options, then they will not be exercised because they have little or no value. In the event that the employee stays long enough to exercise the options and it is in his or her interests to do so, the company's shares will be sold and a (taxable) capital gain will be realized. However, it is common practice for the company to buy back the shares in order to avoid any dilution of EPS. The balance sheet is weakened in the process and other shareholders' interests are disadvantaged. The beauty of share option schemes is that they secure the loyalty of key employees without damaging reported profits.

Like many other technical devices, employee share options are legal and remarkably clever. There is, however, an important snag; they drain cash from the company. To quote Terry Smith: 'It must be obvious by now that profits can be manufactured by creative accounting, but creating cash is impossible. Moreover, *profits are someone's opinion (or true and fair view) whereas cash is fact*. And cash is more important than profits – it pays the dividends, and lack of sufficient cash is the reason businesses fail, not lack of profits' (*Accounting for Growth*, 1992).

If the preoccupation of central banks has been the separation of borrowing from its unpleasant inflationary side-effects, then the corporate equivalent is the separation of profits from underlying financial performance, of which net cash flow is one key indicator. Without the help of the company's finance director or investor relations department, financial analysts sometimes find it impossible to deduce the underlying movements in cash flow from the published accounts. For their part, companies are often evasive and resentful towards securities analysts whose written reports are critical of their accounting policies. Terry Smith's controversial book cost him his job. Analysts who prefer the quiet life will accept the management's view of corporate performance unquestioningly.

THE RELATIONSHIP BETWEEN THE FINANCIAL VALUE AND THE ECONOMIC VALUE OF COMPANIES

For an extended discussion on the improvements and innovations in equity valuation techniques that have occurred since the mid-1980s, interested readers are referred to Appendix 2. The general argument does not require a familiarity with these accounting ratios. To assess the relationship between financial market value of companies and the economic value of their fixed assets, it is necessary to describe only one other ratio, known as Tobin's Q.

Q is popularly defined as the ratio of the market value of a firm, represented by its financial market capitalization, to the post-tax replacement cost of the firm's existing fixed assets. One of the virtues

Figure 12.1 Tobin's Q for the USA: the ratio of stock market value to corporate net assets at replacement cost

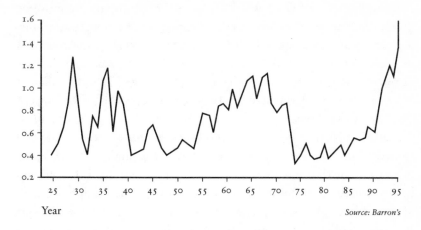

Year   Source: *Barron's*

of Q is that it does not rely on the valuation of fixed assets shown in company accounts and usually measured at historic cost. In theory, the stock market value of the corporate sector should bear a reasonably close relationship to the value of its fixed assets. It would be unrealistic to expect them to be identical, because companies use their fixed assets with different degrees of intensity and effectiveness. However, when large companies are treated in aggregate, it is reasonable to expect the ratio of market value to the replacement cost of fixed assets to oscillate around some long-term average. As Figure 12.1 reveals, this is not what has been observed during the 1990s for the USA. The ratio has risen inexorably since the mid-1980s, and parallel developments have occurred in the UK and elsewhere. Back in Figure 5.3, in mid-1997 the UK private sector was estimated to have net worth of £3.05 trillion when the value of the net physical capital stock was only £2.02 trillion, giving a ratio of financial to economic value of 1.51. What does this mean?

It might mean that companies have deliberately undervalued fixed assets in their accounts, or that the gulf between stock market value and economic value represents a huge investment in intangible assets (such as business goodwill, brand names, drilling rights, broadcasting rights, legal entitlements, etc.). But in the circumstances, it is far more likely that stock markets seriously overstate the true economic value of income-generating corporate assets.

Long before Tobin's formalization of Q, John Maynard Keynes mused: 'For there is no sense in building up a new enterprise at a cost greater than that at which a similar existing enterprise can be purchased; whilst there is an inducement to spend on a new project what may be seen as an extravagant sum, if it can be floated off on the Stock Exchange at an immediate profit' (*The General Theory of Employment, Interest and Money*, 1936). When financial valuations are very high, there should be a great incentive for new companies to be formed from scratch, involving plenty of fixed capital formation. By the same logic, take-over activity should be discouraged by historically demanding levels of Tobin's Q, but this has not been observed.

The prevailing corporate wisdom of the late 1990s is to finance acquisitions using debt, sell off unwanted business assets, rationalize the remaining activities to create an additional revenue stream and, in time, buy back some of the outstanding equity capital from the proceeds of the disposals. The motivation for corporate acquisition has switched from the desire to buy cheap assets to the desire to secure a stream of income from cost-reduction. More and more financial capital is being raised with the express purpose of enhancing the near-term value of shares and share options, rather than to undertake an organic expansion of the business. Mature, slowly growing western economies can no longer generate the rapid profits growth which shareholders have come to expect. The focus of corporate funds use has gravitated away from organic business expansion towards the prospect of deriving high returns from financial engineering and even from successful investments in the shares of other companies. Financial value and economic reality are being driven further and further apart.

THE RELATIONSHIP BETWEEN
EQUITIES AND BONDS

There is a sharp distinction between the typical structure of house-holds' financial balance sheets in continental Europe and in the Anglo-Saxon countries. The portfolio allocation of financial assets ultimately owned by the household sector leans heavily towards bonds on the continent and towards equities in the USA, the UK, Canada and Australia. At end-1995, the ratio of bonds to equities varied from Germany (3.33), Italy (2.11), Denmark (1.88) and France (1.72) down to Austria (0.85), USA (0.54), Canada (0.51) and the UK (0.23). These contrasting preferences are, to a large extent, a reflection of profoundly different institutional structures and tax systems. Whereas Anglo-Saxons invest a substantial proportion of their savings through equity-orientated pension and insurance funds, continental Europeans, particularly the Italians, hold the bulk of their financial assets directly, mostly in the form of bonds and cash.

The emergence of vast global fund management operations, described in Chapter 11, has reinforced the relationship between the valuation of equities and bonds in a particular country or region. In countries with small equity markets and very few private pension funds, the valuation of equities and bonds used to be quite separate; there were few investors with an interest in both types of asset. The advent of global fund managers has increased the degree of switching between equities and bonds even in these countries. As foreign owner-ship of bonds and equities has increased in virtually all western countries during the 1980s and 1990s, so have the linkages between local equity and bond market performance. The difference between the dividend yield on equities and the redemption yield on bonds is known as the reverse yield gap, although some investors prefer to use the ratio of the bond yield to the dividend yield. Most institutional investors monitor the yield gap or ratio very carefully, and some will rebalance their portfolios between equities and bonds when the yield ratio reaches critical upper or lower values. The sharp increase in the yield ratio in the summer of 1987 gave an early warning of the trouble ahead. Turning points in bond prices and yields normally precede turning points in equity markets.

In Chapter 6, reference was made to portfolio theory and the balance between risk and reward. It was noted that the equity risk premium, the excess return required by investors to compensate for the greater volatility of equity returns in comparison to bond returns, has been estimated at around 6 per cent over several decades. Studies of the more recent past have scaled this estimate down to 3 per cent or 4 per cent, claiming that the extreme volatility of the pre-First World War and inter-war eras is irrelevant to the assessment of equity risk today. Yet the most strident attempt at revisionism comes from an even longer-term study of bond and share performance, using rolling 20-year samples between 1802 and 1992. Professor Jeremy Siegel of the University of Pennsylvania reports that the ranges of real returns for US equities and bonds were virtually identical at 11 per cent or 12 per cent. Since equities delivered a mid-point real return of 5.7 per cent, twice that of bonds, it is suggested that, over very long time horizons, investors have received greater rewards from equities at no extra risk.

The emphasis in the last sentence should be placed on the phrase 'over very long time horizons'; for those who are prepared to commit their savings to a long-term contract, such as a pension plan, a reasonable case can be made for a bias towards equities over bonds in a portfolio. Bear in mind, however, that it took 18 years for the US stock market to recover its old level after the Great Crash of 1929. The shorter the investment horizon, the greater the potential volatility of equity returns versus bonds. In keeping with the theme of flattening risk spreads in Chapter 10, it should come as no surprise that the justification for an equity risk premium is under siege. One of the curious features of equity market performance in the 1990s has been the infrequency with which Anglo-Saxon stock market indices have fallen by more than 5 per cent. Not only have these equity markets maintained a consistent record of appreciation, they have displayed remarkable resilience in the face of bad news. The popular investor psychology of 'buying the dips' is reinforced by the programme trading activities of institutional investors. Whenever stock indices fall or rise by more than a given amount over a short interval, powerful computers issue automatic instructions to buy or sell huge volumes of stock. Low equity index volatility feeds the illusion that the equity risk premium is obsolete.

During the 1980s, global equities out-performed global bonds by a wide margin, vindicating the Anglo-Saxon model of asset allocation. Between 1990 and 1993, the contest between equities and bonds was much closer, but the clear superiority of equity returns over bonds has been reasserted since 1995. Such an extended period of equity out-performance has opened up a wide gulf between the relative importance of national stock markets in the various countries. At the end of 1997, London's Stock Exchange was capitalized at 160 per cent of national GDP and New York's at 120 per cent, as compared to the Paris Bourse at 50 per cent and the Frankfurt Stock Exchange at 39 per cent. At the peak of the Japanese share boom in 1989, the London Stock Exchange was capitalized at 17.5 per cent of Tokyo's; during the early months of 1998, market capitalization in London overtook Tokyo!

WHY ARE EQUITIES SO POPULAR AS AN INVESTMENT?

If published profits are so easily manipulated, why are company shares such a popular form of investment? What can explain this Anglo-Saxon stampede into equities, which has, at last, enveloped continental Europe also? There are three widely canvassed explanations. The first is principally a demographic argument; the second has come to be referred to as the 'new paradigm'; the third is based on a mixture of greed and over-confidence in the capacity of the central banks to underpin financial asset values. It is for the reader to decide which of the three is the most compelling, for they are not mutually exclusive.

Demographics are like super-tankers in the economic ocean: they move slowly and silently, but very powerfully towards their destination. When they change course, they create a great deal of disturbance for miles around. If some financial commentator resorts to a demographic argument, it is as well to swallow his opinion with plenty of salt. In peace-time, the composition of the adult population of a developed country does not change materially from one year to the next. Anyone who tells you that there is going to be a recession next March because of demographics is selling you a lemon. However, this is not to diminish the potential importance of demographic changes over five- and ten-year intervals. Cohorts of individuals (e.g. those aged between 25 and 34) in the population hold many financial characteristics in common; as they grow older and become wealthier, the habits of spending, borrowing and saving which they developed in their young adult lives will shape their behaviour in later years. To the extent that succeeding population cohorts have differing financial attributes, demographics are worthy of consideration.

For example, ebbs and flows in the difference between birth and death rates create periodic dips and bulges in population growth. At the end of the 1990s, the baby boomers, born between in the late 1950s and early 1960s, are now in their late thirties or early forties. This cohort is close to its peak earnings capacity and is disproportionately influential in consumer spending and savings decisions. By 2015 or 2020 this group will be on the verge of retirement and looking to receive pensions and benefits. Ahead of them are the post-war babies who are probably the most affluent generation that has ever lived. They were born between in the decade or so after 1946, and have ploughed vast amounts of savings, directly and via pension, insurance and savings contracts, into the stock market.

The demographic patterns vary from one country to another, but there are some broad similarities between western economies. The age band 40−59 is sometimes referred to as the prime savers cohort. For the USA, this group has risen as a share of the adult population from little more than 25 per cent in 1985 to 31 per cent in 1997. Barring human disaster, this share will peak at almost 36 per cent in the year 2006, although the pace of increase has already begun to slow. The proportion of dis-savers, those entering retirement, is rising slowly at the moment but will increase more steeply between 2005 and 2030. By the latter date, all the baby boomers will be in their dotage. The essence of the demographic argument is that the demand for equities has increased substantially since the 1980s because the prime savers cohort has become larger and more affluent. Its proponents would also draw attention to the coincidence of the last trough in the prime savers growth rate with a severe bear market in equities (1974–5), the inference being that there were insufficient prime savers to support the price of equities.

The difficulty with this argument is that it implicitly assumes that the savings propensity is constant in each age group. In other words, if there is a disproportionate increase in the numbers of people in the prime savers group, the temptation is to impute to them the same savings characteristics as the prime savers who occupied this position five or ten years ago. Unfortunately, the labour participation ratio for the over-fifties has fallen quite markedly since the early 1980s, reducing the capacity of the prime savers cohort to save. Moreover, a smaller proportion of the over-fifties is free from debt as compared to ten years ago; this is a further limitation on their savings propensity.

Second in line, there is the new paradigm. The gist of the new paradigm – for its very newness precludes an exact definition – is that knowledge or information has superseded fixed assets as the dominant basis for company valuation. Knowledge-based industries include information technology, research and development, biotechnology, financial services and management consultancy. There may sometimes be a physical end-product, such as a pill or an integrated circuit, but knowledge-based industries tend to be service industries. The new paradigm laughs at conventional measures of valuation based on the book value or replacement value of fixed assets. Knowledge is power.

The role of high-speed communications technology is deemed to be of central importance to the new paradigm. Consumers are abandoning local, regional and national tastes for global brands. The prize for coming first is a bigger prize than ever before. If a product or a talent or an experience is the best, then everyone will want to enjoy it. Multimedia technology places excellence within reach of all who can afford it, for the very best is available only at a premium. There is a polarization of rewards for excellence versus third-best or tenth-best, justifying incredible ratings for a multinational corporate élite. Nearly everyone wants a Pentium personal computer with an Intel chip and Microsoft software. In medicine, law, design, fashion, management consultancy and many other professions, consumers look for proven star quality. Also-ran and me-too products have to be heavily discounted if they are to survive.

The impression given by the new paradigm school is that these knowledge-based industries have catapulted their host economies on to a higher GDP growth trajectory. Moreover, the vicious deflationary trends which are pervasive in the world of personal computer technology, communications and design have removed the threat of inflation which has so often interrupted economic progress in the past. The USA is held up as exhibit No. 1 in this regard; seven years of solid, if unexceptional, GDP growth since 1991 and barely an ounce of inflation to show for it. So what's the catch?

Proponents of the new paradigm gloss over a fundamental distinction between fixed assets, such as plant and equipment, and knowledge. Companies can assert their ownership of the former much more readily than of the latter. Secrets can be lost as well as found. The only effective way of dissuading a top-level employee from sharing the company's secrets with others is to persuade him or her that it is not in his or her interest to do so. This means distributing the firm's value added in fancy salary packages to this inner core of innovative and trusted employees and in maintaining strict security of premises, equipment and personnel. Failing this, the company must resort to litigation to protect its information.

The ongoing cost of preventing the defection of prima donna employees is a serious drain on company cash. As discussed earlier, employee share options can secure loyalty without denting reported profits. Only where the top-level employees are of strong personal integrity, or are frightened by the threat of litigation, or are ignorant of the value of the secrets they hold will there be the opportunity to earn extraordinary profits in knowledge-based companies. All too often, new technology raises consumer expectations without raising corporate sales revenues; continuous quality upgrades are becoming the norm, not the exception. The hoped-for productivity miracle is as elusive in the USA as in Europe; the extended growth sequence in the USA has absorbed a massive amount of additional manpower and may ultimately run aground for this very reason.

The third possibility is the thesis of this book. It is that the developed world has taken leave of its collective senses so far as financial matters are concerned, led astray by its central bankers and its own foolishness in roughly equal proportions. No matter how elaborate the justifications for the kind of stock market valuations reached in mid-1998 may be, the truth is that these prices rest on a shaky pyramid of debt. Low inflation, through its beneficial effects on bond prices, ably assisted by derivatives markets, has created an illusion of plentiful saving in western countries when the opposite is true. Knock away the pillar of bond market support, and the whole edifice of equity prices will come crashing down.

CONCLUSION

After the 1995–8 surge in western stock markets, the real-life P/E ratio for the 30-stock Dow Jones Industrial Average (DJIA) reached 23.3, for the broader Standard and Poors Industrial index it reached 30.6 and for the Nasdaq Composite, 67.5. Among the constituents of the DJIA, the prospective P/Es for 1998 ran from 8.5 for General Motors to a stunning 37.6 for Disney and 46.4 for Coca-Cola. The ease with which cash is exchanged for shares might suggest that the reverse transaction is equally straightforward, but generations of investors have learnt that it is not. When financial markets, and equity markets in particular, undergo a serious correction of past excesses, a tiny fraction of those who desire to sell their shares are able to do so. For most investors, there is no practical opportunity to sell until the majority of the price fall has occurred. Like the children of Hamelin, they will discover that the wide portal through which they entered has slammed shut behind them. Equities are illiquid assets; there is no guarantee that, when equity prices fall, they will fall gradually.

The separation of financial values from economic reality cannot be sustained indefinitely; equities are financial claims on the earning power of real assets. No amount of take-overs, accounting wheezes or super-brands can alter that.

13

Diminishing and Vanishing
Returns to Debt

Neither a borrower nor a lender be:
For a loan oft loses both itself and friend;
And borrowing dulls the edge of husbandry.
William Shakespeare, *Hamlet,*
Prince of Denmark, Act I, scene iii

'Give careful thought to your ways. You have planted much, but
have harvested little. You eat, but never have enough. You drink,
but never have your fill. You put on clothes, but are not warm.
You earn wages, only to put them in a bag with holes.'
Haggai 1: 5–6

Debt can be thought of as a short cut to a desirable destination. It
facilitates the immediate satisfaction of a want or need without regard
to current income. It enables large construction projects, such as
hydroelectric dams or rail tunnels, to be undertaken despite the absence
of current revenues. In poor countries, international loans fund irri-
gation and water treatment programmes, saving lives and improving
public health long before the host country could otherwise afford
them. The presumption of each debt contract is that the borrower
will use the proceeds of the loan in such a way as to derive an ongoing
future benefit. In the case of a consumer loan, the benefit is usually
in the form of services rendered by houses, cars and household goods.
Here, the loan must be serviced out of unrelated income flows and,
if necessary, secured by independent wealth. In the case of a commercial loan, the future benefit equates to a stream of profits or rents.

Under normal circumstances, this stream of income will be sufficient to service the debt and to pay all the other costs of production or trading.

There is a fundamental connection between the increased absorption of debt and the expected expansion of incomes and outputs in the economy. Why else would the lender be willing to enter into the debt contract in the first place? Yet, in most developed countries, the growth of debt has taken on a life of its own. It is seemingly unconnected to the pace of growth of national income. As if enveloped in a thick mist, borrowers appear to have lost sight of the desirable destination and lenders pay little attention to the way that their funds are deployed.

DEBT AND SPENDING

A shopper enters a fashionable department store carrying nothing but a bank charge card. The bank account is empty, but there is a credit facility of $1,000. Forty minutes later, the individual emerges clutching several brightly coloured carrier-bags containing $730 worth of merchandise. There is no mystery here. Private sector bank debt has increased by $730 and expenditure on goods and services has increased by $730. However, this is not the end of the story, since part of this $730 will become income for other individuals, who will spend it a second time, and so on. If, taking into account all the ripple effects, the total effect on national income is $1,095, then the debt multiplier is 1.5 (that is, $1,095 ÷ $730). Assuming that no other transactions take place in the economy, then the national accounts will show that private sector debt increased by $730 and the current money value of incomes, outputs and spending rose by $1,095.

There is no guarantee that the interest on this particular $730 debt will be paid promptly or that the debt itself will ultimately be cleared. At this stage, it is unimportant so far as the measurement of economic growth is concerned. If the bank ultimately has to write off the $730, then this will detract from its profits (and from GDP) in a later year. The basic principle is that, in this example, the use of debt has stimulated the economy and provided incomes of a higher value than the debt itself. A phase of rapid borrowing growth of this nature will lead typically to an over-expansion of demand in the economy and a build-up of inflationary pressures. This inflation serves the useful function of swelling borrowers' incomes, enabling them to meet their obligations more easily, and of reducing the real burden of their debts. This corresponds to a situation in which debt delinquency rates tend to fall and lenders' profit margins are likely to improve.

DEBT AND FINANCIAL INVESTMENT

To take a second example, let's suppose that a salesman intercepted the shopper in question en route to the department store, persuading the person to invest $730 in shares through a mutual fund. This payment is charged to the bank account in the same way as before. The fund issues the shares and uses the proceeds to invest in the stock market. Somewhere in the financial system, these funds are handed over to companies making new issues or to investors switching into other assets, goods or services. The proportion of the $730 likely to be spent on goods and services will probably be between 25 per cent and 50 per cent, reflecting the spending characteristics of companies or financial institutions rather than households. Even after allowing for multiplier effects, it is probable that national income and production will not increase by as much as $730. The investor will receive a tiny income from the mutual fund, or even no income at all.

What is the lender to make of this? When the credit facility was granted, no restrictions were placed on the use of the funds and therefore the bank must have realized that a proportion of its loans might be invested in financial assets rather than spent on capital or consumer goods. However, the income from the mutual fund is not sufficient to service the loan. Either the interest is paid out of other income or it is added to the loan. The practice of rolling up, or consolidating interest as part of the outstanding loan, is one of the strongest dynamics behind debt accumulation. While the rate of capital appreciation of the mutual fund may be sufficiently rapid to outstrip the value of the loan, the bank does not hold the mutual fund as security for the loan. If the loan were secured against the borrower's existing assets, this would probably represent a claim against a property asset rather than a financial asset.

In this example, the accumulation of debt exceeds the addition to national income, over a given period. There is still plenty of income growth from which to service the new borrowing, but there is no longer a presumption that debt burdens will ease with the passage of time. The use of the loan to make a financial investment has minimized the degree of demand pressure on the real economy, stoking up asset price inflation rather than consumer price inflation. At low rates of inflation, the real burden of debt erodes very slowly and the real interest rate tends to be very high. This corresponds to a situation in which lending appears to be very profitable, but the incidence of debt delinquency is liable to increase steeply.

These two examples illustrate the difference between socio-economic groups that are focused on the production and consumption of goods and services and those that are focused on the accumulation of financial wealth, as a proxy for power, status and security. In so far as all socio-economic groups are willing to use debt to bring their objectives closer, they share some common misconceptions. Both segments of society have made the implicit assumptions that there will always be access to affordable credit facilities and that there will never come a time when they will be called upon to repay debt on demand. Alas, these assumptions have no basis in historical precedent or prospective reality.

THE ANATOMY OF THE US BORROWING BINGE

Once again, one of the best examples of a country displaying diminishing returns to debt accumulation is the USA. A popular metaphor for the US economy in 1997 was the little bear's porridge in the Goldilocks story: not too hot and not too cold. Between the final quarters of 1996 and 1997, the US economy expanded by an above-average 3.8 per cent and its inflation rate was a modest 1.8 per cent. The financial markets' preoccupation with these two summary measures of economic health (GDP growth and price inflation) has insulated their thinking from many other disturbing statistics. Why, for example, did the value of national income and expenditure increase by only 5.6 per cent or $439 billion over the previous year, when the personal, corporate and public sectors amassed $759 billion of new debt during the same period? Households accumulated an extra $364 billion of debt, non-financial businesses added $312 billion of debt and the government sector, an extra $83 billion.

On the face of it, the borrowers appear to have been robbed since, on average, each new dollar of debt enabled only 58 cents of extra spending. However, as the second example in the last section showed, the borrowers may have acquired second-hand property or financial assets as an alternative to consumer goods and services. Bricks and mortar yield no income (unless rented out) and US equities offer a paltry 1.5 per cent of dividend yield. In other words, these assets deliver their investment returns as expected capital gains rather than as dividend payments; they make little contribution to the current value of national income.

An examination of US data for the previous 30 years confirms that 1997 was no flash in the pan. Looking back over the 1980s and 1990s, there were no years when the addition to GDP was greater than the value of net new borrowing. The last year for which the net addition to private sector debt was smaller than the annual gain in the money value of GDP was 1976. If public sector debt is included, then the relevant date is in the 1950s. In the USA, the ratio of private debt to GDP has been rising inexorably for more than 30 years. It is a matter of simple arithmetic that, once the value of outstanding debt exceeds the annual value of GDP, each year's increment to debt will exceed the increase in national income unless the debt grows at a slower pace than the value of GDP.

THE CRITICAL ROLE OF THE US FINANCIAL SECTOR

Yet the attraction of financial assets is complicated by another feature of the US credit markets, namely the accumulation of debt by the domestic financial sectors. The more highly geared these sectors have become, the greater the internal momentum of US property and

Figure 13.1 Debt accumulation in the USA ($bn)

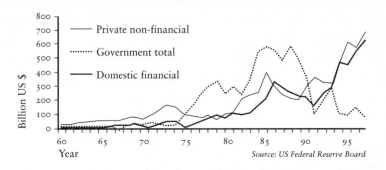

Source: US Federal Reserve Board

financial asset prices. Figure 13.1 catalogues the annual growth of financial sector debt as compared to that of households and non-financial businesses. The largest domestic financial sector borrowers are federally related mortgage pools (e.g. Fannie Mae, Freddie Mac, etc.), asset-backed securities (ABS) issuers, government-sponsored enterprises, funding corporations and finance companies. At the end of 1997, the structure of financial sector debt by instrument was split among federal government related securities (54 per cent), corporate bonds (28 per cent), money market securities (12 per cent) and loans (6 per cent).

To counterbalance this $5.4 trillion debt mountain, the domestic financial sector invests in home mortgages (51 per cent), consumer credit (9 per cent), government bonds (7 per cent), money market securities (5 per cent), other loans (12 per cent) and other assets (16 per cent). The financial sector exerts an influence on property prices through its demand for mortgage assets and on financial markets through the stimulus to consumer credit, the direct investment in corporate bonds and equities and the provision of capital to security brokers and dealers.

The emergence of such a large financial sector since the early 1980s is linked inextricably with the upward march of US equity and bond prices. With property loans to individuals and companies as its major asset and bonds as its principal liability, the domestic financial sector has made easy profits in a bull market. As bond yields have fallen and risk spreads have become compressed, the cost of borrowing has decreased for financial companies. While competitive forces have dictated that the bulk of these gains are passed on to new borrowers, comfortable profits can be earned from older loans where the borrower has neglected to refinance. At the same time, the enhanced availability of loans to the consumer sector and the reduction in borrowing costs after a refinancing have helped to boost demand for investments linked to stock market performance at the expense of deposit accounts. This virtuous circle has encouraged financial companies to expand their market borrowings at breakneck pace. It has also heavily influenced households in their willingness to accumulate illiquid financial assets and debt, hand in hand.

The USA has become an unstoppable debt machine. The demand for and use of debt in the economy no longer bears any obvious relationship to economic growth. An economy in which debt was the servant of production and income would require a fraction of the net new borrowing that occurs each year in the USA. Yet it would be wrong to conclude that debt accumulation is unimportant to GDP growth. Financial sector debt has oiled the wheels of the property, equity and bond markets, enabling a massive increase in household participation in the stock market. The percentage of shareholders among the US population has risen from 14 per cent in the early 1980s to 35 per cent in the mid-1990s, and the share of equity mutual fund assets in total US market capitalization has jumped from 4 per cent to 17 per cent between 1984 and 1997. A by-product of soaring financial asset prices is a powerful wealth effect on household balance sheets. As financial wealth has increased more rapidly than personal incomes, the personal sector has reduced its saving ratio and increased its consumption rate.

THE RELATIONSHIP BETWEEN DEBT AND ECONOMIC GROWTH

Since the mid-1970s, the USA, Japan, the UK, Canada, Sweden, Australia and a few other large developed countries have allowed the ratio of corporate and personal sector debt to GDP to escalate. This group of countries experienced a burst of economic growth during the 1980s, but in most cases this has faded during the 1990s. It appears that a given percentage addition to private sector debt is associated with less and less economic growth with the passage of time. A second group of countries, comprising Germany, France, Italy, Spain, the Netherlands, Belgium, Greece and others, has sanctioned a significant increase in net public sector debt to GDP since the 1970s. This group has generally sought to promote and sustain economic growth through the expansion of public sector consumption and investment, rather than through the growth of private sector credit. For different reasons, these economies have also encountered diminishing returns to domestic credit creation.

A. Anglo-Saxon economies and Japan

Looking first at the mainly Anglo-Saxon countries, the common feature of the late 1970s and the 1980s was the rise in both household and corporate debt as a proportion of income. Between 1983 and 1990, the ratio of household liabilities to nominal after-tax income rose from 74.3 per cent to 117.8 per cent in the UK, from 84.6 per cent to 116.5 per cent in Japan, from 75.2 per cent to 95.1 per cent in Canada and from 73.5 per cent to 92.4 per cent in the USA. With the exception of Japan, the increase in the ratio of corporate debt to GDP was much less dramatic than for household debt to income. However, to grasp the true significance of corporate developments, it is necessary to choose a measure that captures changes to both sides of the balance sheet. In the interval 1984–92, the net interest-bearing liabilities of enterprises rose as a percentage of GDP from 52 per cent to 81 per cent in Japan. The increase for Sweden was from 45 per cent to 68 per cent, for Canada from 39 per cent to 44 per cent, for the UK from 10 per cent to 25 per cent, and for the USA from 16 per cent to 23 per cent. In every case, mortgages and other bank loans secured against property assets played a significant role in the private debt accumulation process.

There can be no disputing the fact that the absorption of additional debt by the private sector spurred economic growth in the 1980s. The Anglo-Saxon economies exploded out of recession in 1982–3 and began uninterrupted sequences of strong economic growth lasting between four and eight years. Over a seven-year stretch, Canada's economy expanded by 33 per cent; both the USA and Australia managed 31 per cent, and the UK 29 per cent. New Zealand's GDP rose by 20 per cent in a four-year burst. In Scandinavia, Finland raised GDP by 34 per cent over eight years, Norway lifted GDP by 21 per cent over 1983–7, Denmark gained 19 per cent between 1982 and 1986, and even Sweden recorded a respectable seven-year gain of 19 per cent. Japan, which did not suffer an early-1980s recession, picked up the pace in 1984 and increased real GDP by 41 per cent over the next eight years. Despite the less impressive growth on the European continent, the G7 club of large developed economies sustained economic growth of at least 3 per cent per annum in *every* year between 1983 and 1989, a feat that was not repeated in *any* of the subsequent eight years. Whatever the bank follies and excesses that lay behind the 1980s boom, there was a keen sense that debt gave a positive stimulus to economic activity.

In the 1990s, the growth of bank lending to businesses and individuals has been much slower and the pace of indebtedness of the household sector has stabilized. The transition from feast to famine was particularly abrupt in the UK, where corporate bank borrowing of $46 billion in 1989 became a small repayment two years later. The displacement of bank borrowing by capital market borrowing during the early 1990s revealed some important contrasts. Of the $18 billion of equity (rights) issues in 1991, the 25 largest accounted for more than two-thirds of the total. Whereas thousands of companies of varying sizes would have shared in an equivalent expansion of bank credit, the funds borrowed from the capital markets were concentrated in the hands of a few large corporations.

A second contrast was the tendency for capital market borrowing to be used for different purposes from bank borrowing. When UK companies issued equities or bonds, the proceeds were liable to be used in repayment of debtors or to restructure the balance sheet. They were seldom used to finance fixed investment or other forms of organic business expansion. Balance sheet manoeuvres during the recession of the early 1990s may have helped to keep cash-starved businesses afloat, but they made little contribution to GDP growth. Whereas the bank borrowing of the 1980s was closely identified with organic or acquisition-led expansion, the capital market finance that followed was not. Even where capital market borrowing was linked to acquisitions, there was a presumption that net job losses rather than job gains would be the result.

In Chapter 1, an attempt was made to sketch out the course that western economies might have followed in the absence of the capital markets revolution. While any such exercise has to be extremely tentative, the conjecture was that the length and depth of the recession in the 1990s would have been greater if the capital markets had not offered an alternative source of borrowing to the banks. The capital markets distributed new credit via the issuing companies and financial institutions to a mixture of financial intermediaries, companies and individuals (consumer loans). In other words, borrowed money that was effectively lost in the wake of the fall in Anglo-Saxon property prices was replaced by new borrowing in the capital markets. As a consequence, the banks lost only a fraction of the amounts that would truly have been lost if this replacement finance had not appeared. Insolvent borrowers, including quite large companies as well as individuals, would have become forced sellers of property and financial assets. This would have dragged down the value of the banks' collateral still further, prompting them to call in an even larger number of customer loans in order to shore up their capital. The ascendancy of the capital markets saved western banks from this nightmare, but at an unspecified future cost.

The extent to which future economic growth was mortgaged in exchange for a swifter conclusion to the recession of the early 1990s is incalculable. All that can be said with any confidence is that the relationship between debt accumulation and economic growth has undergone a radical transformation since the 1980s. Figure 13.2, courtesy of Robert Zielinski, an expert on Asian banks, is an attempt to place the credit expansions of several countries in a wider context. This is a complicated chart and it needs careful interpretation. The vertical axis is a linear scale of the ratio of the stock of debt in the economy expressed as a percentage of nominal GDP. The horizontal axis is a logarithmic scale of real GDP per capita, measured in constant 1990 US dollars. The evolution of these two variables over time is

Figure 13.2 Ratio of the domestic stock of credit to nominal GDP versus real GDP per capita

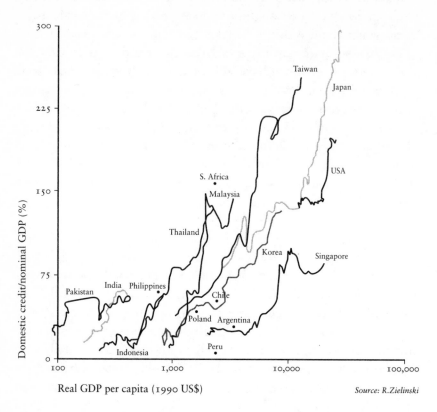

shown as wiggly lines. The data run from approximately 1960 to 1996. For a few countries, only the 1996 data point is shown. The data points for each country are joined up in chronological order, but there is nothing to stop the line from folding back on itself or looping the loop. This is merely a side-effect of squeezing three dimensions into a two-dimensional chart!

The interpretation of the chart is as follows. A line that moves from bottom-left to top-right represents an expansion of the debt to GDP multiplier in association with an increasing standard of living for the country's population. A line that moves horizontally from left to right indicates an economy in which real income per head is rising in the context of a stable debt multiplier. Both of these circumstances are praiseworthy. The steeper the line, the smaller is the benefit to living standards; in the extreme situation of a vertical line, the credit system is expanding wildly without delivering any benefit to real income per head. Finally, a line that is moving from right to left is indicative of a debt deflation. Here, the credit system has broken down, probably as a result of credit quality problems, and living standards are falling.

Both Japan and the USA appear to have reached the point in 1996 where the expansion of debt to GDP was delivering very weak benefits to real income per head. Economic growth has all but evaporated in Japan since 1993, and the East Asian countries may pay an even heavier price for their credit excesses. On the current course, it is only a matter of time before a credit quality disaster overtakes the Anglo-Saxon economies.

B. Continental European economies

The continental economies have behaved in a sufficiently different fashion to warrant a separate analysis. There was hardly any build-up of household sector debt in the 1980s in Germany or Italy, although France was closer to the Anglo-Saxon model. Between 1984 and 1992, net interest-bearing liabilities of enterprises as a ratio of GDP rose only slightly in France (from 33 per cent to 38 per cent), held steady in Germany (from 22 per cent to 23 per cent) and fell in Belgium (from 23 per cent to 12 per cent). The annual growth rates of domestic private credit expansion were comparatively subdued and economic growth rates were quite ordinary on the continent until 1988, when these economies finally caught alight. By then, the Anglo-Saxon nations had exhausted their own productive potential and were increasingly dependent on imports from other developed countries. The initial impetus to continental European economies came from export demand and a weakening Deutschemark, but this was complemented in 1991 by German unification.

German unification necessitated much higher levels of public expenditure and borrowing than before, but this rise in the ratio of public expenditure to nominal GDP was not confined to Germany. As the Anglo-Saxons led the developed world into the recession of the early

1990s, politicians in the continental nations pumped up public spending in an attempt to keep their economies on track for membership of the European single currency. In the interval 1989–93, the share of government spending in the economy jumped from 44.8 per cent to 49.5 per cent in Germany, from 49.1 per cent to 54.6 per cent in France, from 51.5 per cent to 57.1 per cent in Italy and from 40.9 per cent to 47.7 per cent in Spain. Between 1989 and 1995, the net debt of the public sector as a percentage of GDP leapt from 18.5 per cent to 45.0 per cent in Germany, from 14.8 per cent to 36.1 per cent in France, from 82 per cent to 110 per cent in Italy and from 30.9 per cent to 49.8 per cent in Spain. These increases were typically much larger than those observed in Anglo-Saxon countries.

A further distinguishing characteristic of the continental Europeans is the high level of debt servicing costs. In 1996, net interest payments as a percentage of nominal GDP were 11.5 per cent in Greece, 9.5 per cent in Italy, 8.3 per cent in Belgium, 5.1 per cent in Spain, 5.0 per cent in Portugal, 4.7 per cent in the Netherlands, 3.8 per cent in Austria, 3.4 per cent in France and 3.1 per cent in Germany. Of the Anglo-Saxon countries, only Canada (5.3 per cent) had a comparably high burden. The accumulation of public sector debt over at least 20 years, capped by the Maastricht dilemma and the cost of German unification, leaves the continental economies with an extraordinary net interest burden. Despite the dramatic bond yield convergence that has occurred among the EU countries and the persistent bull market in government bonds, the prospective debt service costs for 1998 still range between 3.1 per cent and 8.7 per cent of GDP. Who knows what these burdens would be if the bull market were to come to an end, or if a phase of widening sovereign risk spreads were ever to replace the fashion for yield convergence?

WHAT ARE THE RISKS OF EXCESSIVE DEBT ACCUMULATION?

For the first group of countries, economic growth comes under pressure when the providers of credit suffer a sharp rise in the incidence of defaults and arrears on existing debts, causing them to tighten their screening procedures. Unless a way is found to reflate the economy (through credit, monetary or fiscal policy), a recession is likely to occur. The second group of countries is much less exposed to personal debt problems, but they also end up in recession because of the draconian spending cuts or tax increases that national governments are forced to impose in seeking to eliminate the budget deficit. Short of nationalization, the commercial banks cannot be compelled to expand their balance sheets through the purchase of government bonds or bills. Asset sales are another potential remedy, but one which is very dependent on the buoyancy of the equity market. In both cases, it is the inability to regenerate the inflationary process that spells disaster for economic growth. Debt is irreducible and real bond yields spiral upwards uncontrollably. It is the onset of debt deflation that will ultimately explode the bomb.

WHAT IS DEBT DEFLATION?

The phenomenon of debt deflation is introduced in Appendix 1, in the context of credit quality. For Irving Fisher, its most eminent proponent, the two key features of the debt deflation dilemma are an abundance of debt contracts that are fixed in nominal value and a falling price level. Fisher's work does not address the origins of over-indebtedness during an economic expansion, but concentrates instead on the interaction between debt and prices in the down-swing. His story begins at the point where price inflation is falling and asset prices are dropping. Over-borrowed firms and speculators discover that their cash flows are dwindling while their debt service costs are fixed. Their instinctive reaction is to sell assets and to repay some of their debts. Panic sales of assets lead to reduced asset values, a general loss of confidence and the curtailment of speculative activity. At the same time, falling asset prices lower the value of banks' collateral, making them reluctant to renew loans.

As the banks draw in their horns and begin to recall existing loans, so the money supply begins to contract. This compresses wages and profits still further, pushing up the real interest rate for would-be borrowers. The paradox is that rational acts of asset liquidation exacerbate the problem of high indebtedness and stagnant or falling prices in the economy. Banks cancel loans and individuals hoard money, depriving businesses of the capital and liquidity they need. As businesses become overwhelmed by the cost of debt service, the incidence of bankruptcy and unemployment also rises. In this way, seemingly rational and sensible responses can amplify a downturn into a depression.

Hyman Minsky developed Fisher's hypothesis into a more general theory of financial instability by offering an explanation of initial over-indebtedness. Minsky contrasts the situation in which businesses finance their investment using retained earnings or equity issues rather than loans or bonds. The classical theory of finance claims that economic growth and employment are unaffected by changes in the debt–equity ratio of the corporate sector. However, Minsky argues that a high debt–equity ratio increases the inherent instability of the financial system. Businesses are tempted to borrow to excess when interest rates are low in relation to anticipated profits growth or asset price inflation. Whereas dividend payments on equity can be reduced or suspended, debt contracts must still be serviced, and thus the risk of bankruptcy increases. Presley and Mills summarize Minsky's controversial thesis as follows: '. . . when asset values are appreciating faster than debt service costs, profits are maximised by leveraging purchases as much as possible. Banks and bond-holders are able and willing to supply credit, possibly at declining real interest rates, as risk premia are reduced when collateral values are appreciating. As investment expands and prices rise, profit expectations will be validated and further investment encouraged' (J. Presley and P. Mills, *Islamic Banking: Theory and Practice*, forthcoming).

What brings the party to an abrupt conclusion is a rise in real interest rates, whether prompted by a dearth of liquid savings or by the monetary authorities' fear of inflationary pressures. Minsky highlights the role of declining profits, rather than falling prices, in forcing over-indebted businesses to close. He attributes the absence of financial collapses in the USA, post-war, to large government expenditures and over-lenient attitudes by the monetary authorities in seeking to pre-empt crises. An ever-expanding stock of government debt has been required to stave off the debt deflation process. Arguably, the USA's most severe post-war crisis took place in 1990–91, when the state honoured the liabilities of the bankrupt Savings and Loan institutions and acted, perversely, as *borrower* of last resort.

Critics of the debt deflation hypothesis argue that it requires borrowers and lenders to behave irrationally, or for them to have unequal access to information. This book cites many examples of irrational behaviour, from the South Sea Bubble onwards. There is ample evidence that crowds are as easily captivated by fashions, fads and crazes in matters of investment as in their choice of clothing or restaurants. As to the assumption of unequal access to information, this accords well with observations in earlier chapters concerning the increasing lack of transparency in the financial system. On the contrary, the Fisher–Minsky thesis offers an eminently feasible and potentially relevant analysis of the western world at the close of the twentieth century.

COULD DEBT DEFLATION REALLY HAPPEN IN THE 1990S?

In April 1994, the City University hosted a conference on Debt Deflation in London. While many illuminating papers were presented on the topic, the tone of the speakers and the discussants was dismissive of the hypothesis. However, the director of the research and statistics department of the Bank of Japan did venture the opinion: 'So far, a deflationary debt spiral has not been observed in Japan. Of course, it is extremely difficult to measure the influence of debt-deflation quantitatively. It has never really been experienced since the 1930s, and we have not yet confirmed even the bottoming-out of the Japanese economy. In this sense my report is quite tentative. What is clear now is that the cost of accommodating the economic boom, which saw tremendous land price hikes in the second half of the 1980s, was very high.'

Four years later, land prices in Japan's major cities were still falling. A flurry of economic growth in 1996 gave way to a new recession in 1997–8. The spokesman was wise to say that the bottoming-out of the economy was unconfirmed. The cost of the debt-financed asset price bubble in the 1980s has risen much higher than even he imagined. The principal costs are the loss of economic momentum, the rise in unemployment and bankruptcies and the insolvency of a large proportion of Japanese banks and financial institutions. Late-1990s Japan is the closest example for many years to an economy suffering from debt deflation. Irving Fisher's tick-list of diagnostic symptoms sounds all too familiar. At various times, there have been debt liquidation efforts by businesses; the contraction of the money supply; a fall in the domestic price level; a fall in the net worth of businesses; a fall in profits and a reduction in output, trade and employment. The prevalence of pessimism and loss of confidence, the hoarding of currency and the slowing down of the velocity of currency in circulation came to a head in the latter months of 1997, in the wake of the East Asian debt crisis. Nominal interest rates of virtually zero have combined on occasions with rising real interest rates.

Japan is a rich country that can amply afford to deal with these troubling symptoms of debt deflation. Its predicament, even in mid-1998, had not reached the stage where a depression was inevitable. However, if radical remedial action is not taken to heal the wounds of a diseased credit system, then the prognosis will deteriorate. The west has no cause for complacency in this matter.

CONCLUSION

One of the most important insights into the 1990s concerns the substandard economic performance of most developed countries in the west. During the 1980s, rapid debt growth was an expression of confidence in our economic future; there seemed to be plenty to show for all the borrowing. In the 1990s, the borrowing binge has been no less frantic, but the economic returns are much reduced. The huge expansion of public debt has not been associated with a noticeable improvement in economic performance. All that the Anglo-Saxon and some continental European countries have to show for the credit expansions of the 1990s are the huge improvements in the valuation of their bond and equity markets. On the contrary, the increase in overall indebtedness has constrained and complicated national and personal economic life. A turning-point in the exposure of our foolish attitudes to debt will be an open admission of economic failure.

14

Confronting Economic Reality

'If EMU does come into existence, as now seems increasingly likely, it will change the political character of Europe in ways that could lead to conflicts in Europe and confrontations with the United States.'   Martin Feldstein,
Foreign Affairs, Nov.–Dec. 1997

'The opacity of public sector accounting in Japan is such that the public finances are regarded as a mystery wrapped up in an enigma.'   John Plender, *Financial Times*, 11 June 1998

Economists are called upon all too frequently to offer predictions. A lamentable success rate has proved no discouragement. A popular adage among business economists is that it's safe to predict events and times, but never both together. Yet the debt disorders catalogued in earlier chapters cannot be viewed merely as an intellectual curiosity; they point to a conclusion, a showdown with economic reality. For all our financial sophistication and cleverness, there is a sense that this confrontation with reality cannot be postponed indefinitely. If the analysis presented in this book is even broadly accurate, then there lies ahead an economic and financial event of awesome proportions, one that will overturn the prevailing perceptions and priorities of the western world. This chapter considers four potential triggers for this defining event, although no list can pretend to be exhaustive.

The first is the tensions between European nations created by the formation of a premature Economic and Monetary Union (EMU). The second is a shock to the US bond market, and the third is a financial meltdown in the Asia Pacific region, centred on Japan. Fourth, and of less importance than the first three, is the possibility of chaotic disruption to the financial system as a result of computer-programming anomalies or techno-terrorism. Each of these deserves careful consideration.

TENSIONS WITHIN EMU

It is highly likely that the timetable for establishing the European single currency, the euro, will play a critical role in exposing the hidden consequences of debt accumulation and financial sophistication. The 11 original participants in the single currency project (Germany, France, Italy, Spain, the Netherlands, Belgium, Austria, Portugal, Finland, Ireland and Luxembourg) are all committed to phasing out their national currencies by 1 July 2002. To participate in the single currency project, each of the successful applicants was supposed to have fulfilled certain conditions, known as the Maastricht convergence criteria.

The criteria covered exchange-rate stability, the convergence of consumer price inflation and government bond yields, and some upper limits for government borrowing and public sector debt in relation to GDP. The purpose of these conditions was to set a standard of economic and financial management that was acceptable, primarily, to the Germans. For a long interval between the signing of the Maastricht Treaty in 1991 and the critical year for economic assessment, 1997, it was commonly assumed that the southern European states (Italy, Spain and Portugal) would not qualify for EMU. Their unsuitability stemmed from inflation rates that were excessive, bond yields that were far too high, budget deficits that far exceeded 3 per cent of GDP, and gross government debt to GDP ratios that were well above the arbitrary limit of 60 per cent. However, so great was the prize of sharing a common currency and enjoying broadly similar costs of government borrowing with the hard-headed Germans, that very strenuous efforts were made to comply with the convergence criteria.

By the spring of 1998, when the official reports on Maastricht convergence were prepared by the European Monetary Institute and the European Commission, the only obstacle to Italy's participation was its high government debt ratio. But since Italy's ratio was scarcely any worse than Belgium's (and there was never any question of excluding Brussels from the single currency zone), Italy could not be excluded either. Spain and Portugal had also converged in remarkable fashion, and with much lower public debt ratios than Italy. Ireland, by virtue of generous EU rebates and incentives and a competitive currency, stormed through the EMU obstacle course with several years of strong economic growth leading up to 1998.

Thus the 'wide and weak' version of EMU came into being at the start of 1999. Greece has indicated its intention to join EMU at the start of 2001, and there is a chance that Denmark, Sweden and the UK will all have joined by the middle of 2002. The determination of a political élite to bring the single European currency into being has swept aside all forms of opposition, both superficial and fundamental, sentimental and objective. However, the gravity of the commitment that these politicians have made on behalf of their electorates will take time to become fully apparent.

A rude shock awaits the inhabitants of the Eurozone (one of many suggested names for the group of countries in which the euro is planned to replace national currency as legal tender). They have been led to believe that their economic lives will become more straightforward and that a single currency will enhance the economic standing of Europe on the world stage. The replacement of their national currencies, such as the DM and the French franc, by the euro is presented as a technical matter of no greater significance than the re-denomination of old French francs into new francs that took place in 1959. On the contrary, the political independence of the constituent countries is at stake in this bold venture. The freedom to conduct national diplomacy, to declare war or to refrain from war, to protect the banking system from collapse and to overspend the government budget under conditions of national emergency are all compromised by the adoption of a European single currency.

Under strong Germanic influence, the original objective of the Maastricht Treaty was to close off all the escape routes for national financial profligacy. Having suffered the traumas of two hyper-inflationary episodes this century, German politicians and bankers have insisted throughout that the European single currency project must be constructed on the basis of sound money and price stability. However, there is evidence that some countries used extraordinary tax or capital receipts and accounting fudges to bring their budget deficits down in 1996 and 1997. The pressure to sustain fiscal discipline is likely to intensify in these countries as politically unpopular strictures on public spending replace the cosmetic ones. Having qualified for EMU – albeit spuriously – there can be no question of relaxing these policies after joining. While the convergence of inflation rates and of bond yields prior to the creation of EMU may be seen as part of the illusion, the strictures on budget deficits and public sector debt laid down by the Stability and Growth Pact represent the chilling reality.

The Stability and Growth Pact was finalized at the Amsterdam summit in 1997. Among other things, it lays down the rules and the penalties for countries whose government budget deficits exceed the permitted limit of 3 per cent of GDP. The 'Excessive Deficit Procedure' has a particularly Teutonic ring about it. Professor Tim Congdon, in a pungent critique of EMU, describes the procedure as follows: 'After receiving a report from the Commission, it is the task of the ECOFIN-Council – taking a decision by qualified majority voting – to confirm or deny that the deficit is indeed excessive. If ECOFIN decides that the deficit is excessive, it makes recommendations about fiscal policy in the country at fault and "requires that effective actions have to be taken within four months". If the country fails to take such action, ECOFIN imposes a fine. The fine takes an unusual form, with the offending government having to lodge a non-interest-bearing deposit at a European banking institution, presumably the ECB. It forfeits the interest until its finances again comply with the Stability Pact' (*The single currency project and European political union*, 1998).

Consider the predicament of a country in which a sizeable majority of the electorate rejects the imposition of this fine and the economic austerity measures prescribed by ECOFIN. The elected government cannot reduce interest rates to stimulate the economy, because it is subject to the interest rate policy of the ECB (which is itself circum-scribed by global capital market conditions). It cannot devalue its currency, because it no longer has one of its own. It cannot increase its budget deficit, because it is already in breach of the Stability Pact and facing financial penalties that it cannot afford. It cannot raise taxes without committing political suicide. Among the few remaining courses of action to this elected government, perhaps the least offensive, is to sell its national assets: its gold, its US dollar reserves, its public buildings, its land, and so on. The circumstances of this country are not dissimilar to those of a nation defeated in battle.

In fact, there are two other courses of action open to this beleaguered government. The first is to resign from the single currency system and to reclaim the reins of national economic policy-making, even if this might also require the creation of a new currency. The second is to repudiate its debts and to suspend the payment of interest. In effect, this would be a declaration of bankruptcy. Long before a sovereign European nation was driven to such humiliation, the bond market would have recognized the risk. Its government bond yield, although denominated in euros, would have built in a risk premium for the possibility of default or secession from the EMU.

A long-standing structural weakness of the EMU is the absence of a federal authority with independent tax-raising powers. In the US system, federal social security and health programmes provide 40 cents of replacement income for every dollar of state income lost. The EU's budget, which is financed by a fixed proportion of value added tax from the member states, is absorbed predominantly by agricultural subsidies, the Brussels bureaucracy and investment grants. There is very little capacity to offer emergency financial aid to a region suffering from natural peril or civil unrest, much less from economic mismanagement. The inadvisability of building monetary union without first achieving full political union strongly suggests that a successful EMU is synonymous with the latter.

Such tensions among EMU countries are a predictable consequence of the policy strictures contained in the Stability and Growth Pact. This pact traces its lineage back to the Maastricht Treaty and to the Treaty of Rome, the latter having set out the original blueprint for economic, monetary and political union in 1957. As discussed in Chapters 9 and 13, Europe's governments have been accumulating debt at a cracking pace since the 1970s, in direct contradiction of the

Figure 14.1 Foreign holdings as a percentage of total privately held US public debt

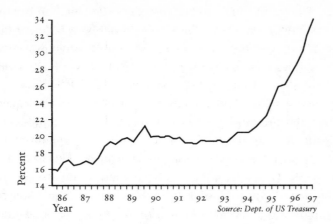

Source: Dept. of US Treasury

code of fiscal stability that they now espouse. The ability and the desire of the EMU countries to abide by new fiscal rules must be seen in the light of past budgetary lapses and heavy net interest burdens.

A BOND MARKET CRISIS IN THE USA

A second candidate capable of triggering a financial breakdown is an abrupt loss of confidence in the US bond market. By a remarkable turn of events, America's perennial budget deficits have established the US Treasury bond market as the largest, most respected and most actively traded financial market in the world. These accumulated deficits, once regarded as an albatross, have been transformed into a source of national prestige and global influence. Foreign ownership of Treasury bonds, a $3.5 trillion market, has increased dramatically in recent years, as shown in Figure 14.1. Adding in government agency debt, private mortgage-backed debt and corporate debt, the size of the US bond market was estimated at more than $9 trillion at the end of 1997. Over the years, the USA's economic fortunes have become more and more intertwined with the progress of its bond market.

Since 1982, a broadly rising trend in US bond prices, accompanied by falling bond yields, has heaped benefits on the real economy and has attracted a huge amount of foreign capital. Personal and corporate borrowers have been able to borrow at progressively lower interest rates and the government has made considerable savings on its debt service bill. The question is: how much lower can US bond yields go? After such a long bull market, the advent of falling bond prices, implying rising bond yields, would have far-reaching consequences.

So far as the Treasury bond market is concerned, the steep increase in foreign ownership since 1993 requires careful interpretation. There are three distinct categories of foreign investor in Treasuries: foreign central banks, US hedge funds based offshore, and the remainder, consisting mainly of overseas investment managers and the treasury operations of trans-national corporations. Since 1980, these three sources of foreign buying have traced divergent paths, except in 1995 when they combined to spectacular effect. Foreign central banks, with Japan and Singapore featuring prominently, bolstered the US Treasury bond market consistently between 1994 and mid-1997 but, in the following year, holdings were reduced slightly. The tax haven countries, including the Netherlands Antilles, the British West Indies and the Bahamas, by contrast, were net sellers of US Treasuries between 1992 and early 1995, but turned aggressive buyers for the next three years. The remaining group of foreign investors built up their holdings during the period of cheap US credit (1991–3), took fright when the bond market slumped in the first half of 1994, and resumed with greater vigour than ever in 1995.

It is clear that foreign purchases, in various guises, have been extremely influential during the mid-1990s, and particularly during the 1995 bond rally. There is every reason to suppose that this influence could be applied equally effectively in the opposite direction. Three scenarios are next explored. The first considers the circumstances in which foreigners could become persistent net sellers of US debt instruments. In the second, the hedge funds become convinced that the USA faces a resurgence of inflation and rush to take up an aggressively bearish stance. Finally, the slow-burning erosion of consumer credit quality suddenly erupts into a domestic financial crisis.

Under what circumstances could foreigners begin to abandon the US bond market? Central banks in Japan, Hong Kong, Singapore, the People's Republic of China and Taiwan have amassed vast foreign exchange reserves of US dollars in their efforts to restrain their currencies from appreciating. For years, these accumulations of reserve dollars have been routinely parked in short- and medium-term US bonds. However, after the appreciation of the yen versus the US dollar reached its climax in the spring of 1995, the yen lost 45 per cent of its value in a little over three years. Downward pressure on the yen was particularly severe after the East Asian banking and currency crisis broke in July 1997, leading to depreciations of between 30 per cent and 70 per cent of the Korean, Thai, Indonesian, Malaysian and Philippine currencies relative to the US dollar. While these Asian currencies were either pegged to the US dollar or were appreciating in value against it, their central banks were natural buyers of US government bonds. In a sustained phase of Asian currency depreciation, which might ultimately encompass China and Hong Kong, foreign central banks would become more likely sellers than buyers of US bonds.

For foreign companies and individuals that have acquired US dollar-denominated wealth through import–export businesses, tourism and many other commercial activities, there is less likelihood that currency movements, by themselves, would persuade them to sell dollar assets. But if the Asian banking crisis leads to the paralysis of the regional economy and the destruction of domestic wealth, then the repatriation of wealth from the USA becomes an eminently plausible scenario.

A second potential source of a shock to the US bond market would be a sudden change of heart by the hedge fund community. Although their combined funds under management would not place them in the top ten of US asset managers, most hedge funds are much more daring in their attitude to risk and asset allocation. The largest five or six funds would probably hesitate to gear up their capital by more than three times, but the smaller funds routinely use gearing ratios of six or even ten times. As a generalization, the hedge funds have been extremely optimistic regarding the progress of the US bond market in the 1990s; some funds expect the 30-year bond yield to fall as low as 4 per cent before the year 2000. It is impossible to know how much money has been committed to this ultra-positive view, but it is a safe bet that these positions are highly leveraged. On the evidence of the 1994 débâcle, a shocking US inflation report or a tiny increase in US interest rates might be all that is necessary to eliminate the profitability of highly leveraged hedge fund positions relating to the US bond market. In their efforts to escape from unprofitable trades, hedge funds can have a very powerful effect on bond prices and yields, stretching out over a period of months.

Third, there is a danger that the credit quality problems described in Chapter 10 could erupt as a full-scale insolvency crisis in the non-bank financial sector, echoing the problems of the Savings and Loan crisis in the 1980s. In Chapter 13, the role of US financial companies in the debt accumulation process was discussed. With bonds as their dominant liability and consumer loans as their dominant asset, the financial sector is especially vulnerable to an increase in non-performing consumer and business loans. The interest received on the loans is used to pay the interest due on the bonds. In theory, the risk of debt delinquency is built into the profit margins on mortgages and other consumer debt. In practice, keen competition in the financial sector and over-optimism concerning the incidence of delinquent loans are a recipe for insolvency. The negative implications for the pricing of government-sponsored mortgage bonds, such as Fannie Mae and her brothers and sisters, would be extremely disturbing for all classes of US government bonds.

Whether the trigger is foreign bond sales, a hedge fund panic or a domestic credit quality crisis, America's confrontation with economic reality will probably originate in its bond market rather than its equity market. Wall Street has derived enormous comfort from the cascade of bond yields; for as long as the bond market embodies the views that consumer price inflation is dead and that global savings are plentiful, not scarce, then it is safe for the equity market to believe them also. Because the bond market is much more finely tuned to macro-economic, political and even meteorological news than the equity market, it is rare for equity markets to turn down without a prior signal from the bond market. When the illusions concerning the foundations of this long bull market – in bonds and equities – are uncovered, it is the bond market that will most likely sound the trumpet. The economic purpose of these higher bond yields, which would inevitably be transmitted from the USA to Europe, will be to restrain consumption and promote saving. Bond yields will need to stay high enough, long enough, for the rebuilding of national saving rates among the western developed nations to occur.

ASIAN FINANCIAL MELTDOWN

In Chapter 1 Japan was described as a case study in credit excesses. The extent of borrowing by individuals, corporations and the 'official' public sector is well documented. However, the true liabilities of Japan's other public financial institutions may never be known. Funded by the postal savings system and state pension funds, the Fiscal and Investment Loan Programme (FILP) has baled out the public finances repeatedly since 1991. The so-called 'second budget' operates rather like a development bank, making non-commercial loans, and is administered by the Trust Fund Bureau of the Ministry of Finance. The Trust Fund Bureau has borrowed from the Postal Savings Bank at pitiful interest rates, linked to the yield on government debt. These funds have been used to finance largely unnecessary and unprofitable public infrastructure projects, such as the construction of bridges between virtually uninhabited islands. The ineffectiveness of the numerous fiscal packages can be attributed, in part, to the heavy dependence on the second budget.

It is fanciful to suppose that credit growth ceased in Japan after the financial bubble burst in January 1990. A rich, developed country with apparently strong public finances, Japan sought to mitigate the impact of the sharp fall in property and equity prices. State-owned banks made new sources of finance available to struggling enterprises. While private sector borrowing stagnated, public sector borrowing expanded at an unspecified but alarming rate. Financial analysts David Asher and Andrew Smithers have argued in a research paper that the public sector's second budget should be consolidated in its official accounts, since the Japanese taxpayer is liable for any losses. On this

Figure 14.2 Bankruptcy liabilities as a percentage of nominal GDP for Japan

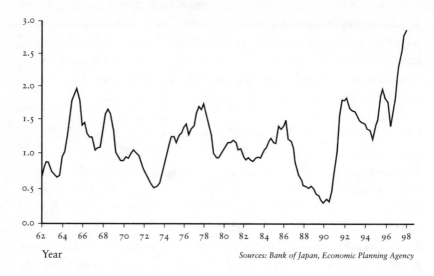

Year   *Sources: Bank of Japan, Economic Planning Agency*

basis, they estimate that the true public sector debt to nominal GDP ratio was about 150 per cent in 1996, larger than that of Italy or Belgium. This would entail a revision to Figure 9.3, placing Japan in the outward and most vulnerable segment of the financial stability cone.

The ongoing expansion of credit, via the FILP, the Housing Loan Corporation, the People's Finance Corporation and the Japan Finance Corporation for Small Businesses, helps to explain why credit quality in Japan did not decline monotonically in the 1990s. Figure 14.2 reveals that the value of the liabilities of bankrupt firms and individuals amounted to just 0.3 per cent of the current value of GDP at the end of 1989, before the crisis broke. The escalation to 1.7 per cent of GDP was extremely rapid in 1990–91, but thereafter the problem seemed to be under control. The return of respectable economic growth in 1996 and a fall in the bankrupt liabilities ratio to 1.4 per cent may have persuaded the Japanese authorities that it was safe to reinstate a higher rate of sales tax in April 1997. However, the effect was to send the economy into its first technical recession since 1974 and to double the impact of bankruptcy to 2.8 per cent of GDP. A bankrupt liabilities ratio of 5 per cent of GDP would be considered highly dangerous by most analysts.

If left to pursue its natural course, the erosion of credit quality in Japan has ample potential to trigger a financial meltdown in the entire Asia Pacific region, with significant repercussions for western financial markets. Japan's domestic banking and credit problems have been exacerbated by heavy involvement in the economic development of East Asia, through bank loans and foreign direct investment. The banking and currency turmoil that enveloped the region in July 1997 has added to the long list of non-performing loans and other under-performing assets owned by Japanese banks and financial institutions. Despite a huge state bail-out of the largest banks using medium-grade debt issues in March 1998, the banks have remained nervous and reluctant to renew lines of credit to domestic customers. Until the true scale of the non-performing loans problem is admitted and addressed, the virtual paralysis of the domestic credit system is unlikely to be resolved.

The catalyst for a confrontation with economic reality could well be the liberalization of Japan's financial system that began to take effect in April 1998. As a result of the first wave of reforms, individual investors and firms are free, in principle, to open higher-yielding bank accounts in foreign currencies and to acquire US-style mutual funds or life assurance contracts, either in Japan or abroad. To assess the significance of these institutional changes, it is important to bear three factors in mind: first, that there is a very powerful incentive for Japanese households to diversify their savings out of yen deposits; second, that the traumas of the 1990s have made these households very conservative and risk averse; and third, that the Ministry of Finance is unlikely to stand by and watch a flood of capital leave Japan.

In comparing the structure of personal sector financial assets in Japan with those of the USA or the UK, the obvious difference is the much greater commitment to liquid assets in Japan. With roughly 60 per cent of assets located in deposit accounts, money market mutual funds and cash, Japanese households are roughly three times more liquid than their American and British counterparts. One-third of Japanese household liquidity is held in the postal savings system, representing Y228 trillion of deposits. As the yen has lurched from a 1995 high of Y80 per US dollar to Y140 per dollar three years later, the dollar value of these deposits has fallen by over 40 per cent. Under normal circumstances, investors demand a high rate of interest as compensation for the loss of currency value, but Japanese households have endured a miserly annual return of around 1 per cent. Japanese savings are crying out for a better deal.

Assuming that the Japanese authorities do not succeed in dissuading large-scale capital outflows, vast sums are expected to migrate from yen deposits to US dollar, sterling or other higher-yielding deposits or money market funds by the close of the year 2000. Once Japanese savers acquire a taste for competitive returns, the capacity of its banking system to disguise the full extent of the non-performing loan problem will also disappear. As households desert the Postal Savings Bank in increasing numbers, its dilemma will become acute. Unless the FILP offers higher returns, enabling the bank to offer more competitive deposit rates, then it must choose between balance sheet contraction and heavy losses. The FILP stands to lose a dependable source of cheap funds (from the Postal System) and the underlying condition of the public finances will be revealed.

If, during the course of 1997, Korea, Indonesia, Malaysia, Thailand and the Philippines had hoped and expected that Japan would rush to their aid, they were disappointed. Japan's preoccupation with its own economic and financial difficulties rendered it unable to provide sought-after leadership and financial support in the Asia Pacific region. Instead, the most affected nations were forced to ask for help from the IMF, and to accept its conditions and policy prescriptions. The depreciation of the yen has compounded the region's economic and financial woes. It appears that financial liberalization arrived in Japan at an inopportune time, when frustration with low returns coincided with a tumbling yen and an economy in recession. Depending on the length of time required to restore and repair Japan's banking and financial infrastructure, the Asia Pacific region could drift further towards a total collapse of its financial system. In this scenario, the sale of US and European financial assets would assume a high priority.

MILLENNIUM BUG AND OTHER
TECHNICAL DISRUPTIONS

The fourth potential trigger of an economic and financial panic in the western world is a technical disruption to the computer systems that pervade virtually every aspect of modern life in the large western economies. The USA is more dependent on computer networks than any other country, with 42 per cent of the world's computing power and 60 per cent of the resources of the Internet, according to a CIA risk assessment carried out in 1997. By contrast, China has only 1 per cent of the world's computing power, and Russia less than 1 per cent. Chapter 6 highlighted the role of technological change as a catalyst for capital market development, especially in relation to the calculation of options prices. However, this is a highly specific application. More generally, integrated circuits are deployed in navigational equipment for aircraft, life support equipment in hospitals, the electronic settlement systems of stock markets, bank payment clearing systems and the payment systems for state benefits, to name but a few. A failure of information technology (IT) systems can result in chaos if back-up systems are unavailable.

There are two basic attitudes to the threat posed by the technology disruptions. One is to regard the disaster scenarios as hype, possibly generated within the IT industry as a ploy to boost its profile and revenues. On this view, a serious IT disruption is no more likely than for the earth to be jolted from its orbit by a meteor. The second reaction is to take a practical interest in the vulnerability of companies, government departments and financial institutions to a technology-related disaster. Most large firms now take disaster recovery strategies very seriously. An examination of the evidence usually leads to a greater degree of concern and awareness of the potential problems that could arise, without falling into the trap of believing that chaos is inevitable.

Next, we consider three types of IT discontinuity. First, there is a possible dislocation to continental payments systems following the introduction of the euro in 1999. Second, we look at the issues surrounding a major systems failure arising from the beginning of a new century on 1 January 2000, also known as the millennium bug and the year 2000 (Y2K) problem. Third, there is the increasing threat of computer terrorism and acts of sabotage.

The implications of operating dual accounting systems in the Eurozone from the start of 1999 may not seem an unduly onerous task, given the advanced capabilities of modern technology. However, for the payments system to work smoothly, every bank, financial institution and most companies of any size must offer their customers the facility to settle bills either in euros or in the national currency. Accounts must be maintained in both currencies and, for cash transactions, notes and coins of both types must be held. While large banks and large corporations will make the transition to dual accounting with relative ease, many smaller enterprises and local banks will probably be thrown into confusion. Even if they insist that their customers continue to make payments in, say, Belgian francs, they will be required to settle many of their own bills in euros. Privately, large banks and financial institutions envisage that many of their smaller rivals will be driven out of business as they fail to update their systems in time, or because they have not been able to afford the IT costs of doing so.

The decision to press ahead with EMU on 1 January 1999 was taken despite the growing unease regarding the burden of reprogramming computers to be compliant in the year 2000. There is an outside chance that the euro payments system will break down due to a lack of preparation and testing by some of Europe's smaller banks. This raises the possibility of some debtors being unable to settle their bills electronically and some creditors being deprived of the amounts due to them. If all goes well, these will be minor hitches and the system will function smoothly within a few weeks.

Clearly, the Y2K problem is of an altogether more serious nature. The inability of millions of mainframe computers to distinguish the year 2000 from the year 1900 dates back to the 1960s and 1970s when computing power and hard disk space were monstrously expensive by today's standards. As an economy measure, instead of coding the year as a four-digit number, only the last two digits were used. Thus, these lines of code will turn over from (19)99 to (19)00 at midnight on New Year's Eve 1999. There have already been instances of credit cards expiring in the year 2000 being rejected as invalid and 103-year-old ladies being invited to attend nursery school.

The upgrading of software is one route to overcoming the problem, but this is feasible only for applications that are sufficiently general to cover thousands of users. Most organizations rely on programs that have been written specifically for them. Replacing lines of code is a tedious and extremely costly affair. Industry estimates range from $1 to $10 per line, including the costs of testing the corrected code. The Gartner Group in the USA has calculated the cost of global Y2K compliance as between $300 billion and $600 billion, but this assumes that there are enough programmers available who can read and understand the 400 different mainframe computer languages in existence. A particular problem is the widespread use of embedded circuits in electrical equipment. In many cases, the calendar might be irrelevant to the proper functioning of the equipment. However, if the circuit includes the date as one of its attributes, then the equipment may become prone to malfunction in the year 2000.

The breadth of concern that this arouses is beyond the scope of this book. The specific relevance of the millennium bug lies in the damage that could be inflicted on the world's money transmission mechanisms and the global capital markets. One of the key issues for payment systems, as for military systems, is synchronization. Assistant US Secretary of Defense, Emmett Paige Jr, testified to a Congress Subcommittee in 1996 as follows: 'With our global economy and vast electronic exchange of information among our systems and databases, the timing of co-ordinated changes in date formats is critical. Much dialogue will need to occur in order to prevent a "fix" in one system from causing another system to "crash". If a system fails to properly process information [sic], the result could be the corruption of other databases, extending perhaps to databases in other government agencies or countries.'

Gary North, in an improbable but chilling private newsletter, describes a scenario in which a failure of bank payment systems provokes a bank run: literally, a scramble by customers to withdraw cash from their accounts. This reaction is so foreign to western post-war experience that it is tempting to dismiss it out of hand. However, fractional banking systems, which were described in Chapter 4, hold only a small percentage of their assets as notes and coin under normal circumstances. It is easy to see how banks could be embarrassed by the public's panic demand for cash if such a crisis occurred.

It is unnecessary to buy in to such a doom-laden scenario to appreciate the potential significance of the Y2K problem for the western financial system and its constituent economies. What is interesting about the 'bank run' scenario is the about-turn in consumer preferences for cash versus financial assets that it implies. The abandonment of low-yielding liquid assets, which was discussed in Chapter 6, is exposed as a critical error of judgement. Neither equities nor bonds would be readily exchangeable into cash in the event of a breakdown in the payments system.

Finally, it is necessary to mention techno-terrorism under this heading. 'Hacking' into other people's computers is a well-understood phenomenon, but the connotations of amateurism and harmless fun are unhelpful in the modern context. The development of the Internet has raised the profile and the potential for computer terrorism very significantly. There is no longer any need for a hacker to worm his way into a system; the Internet cloud can provide connectivity and anonymity. To be connected to one place is to be connected to every place. There is no doubt that military security is a much more obvious target for security attacks. But banks and other financial institutions could also become targets in the years to come.

CONCLUSION

These four groups of circumstances represent pressure points in the financial system, but there may well be others that have been neglected. The kernel of the argument is that the parallel accumulation of debt and financial assets in a low inflation environment cannot continue indefinitely. There are many indications, detailed above, that this departure from economic reality is destined to reach its terminus in the relatively near future. Whether it is EMU that pulls the trigger, or US bonds, or the Japanese credit system, or the millennium bug, is impossible to know in advance; but when it happens, we will all know. How much time do the institutions, companies and citizens of prestigious western nations have to change course? Until the end of 1999? Probably. Until the end of 2001? Possibly. Until the end of 2003? That would take a miracle.

15

Borrowed Time

'Economic distress is leading the people to be more amenable to authority as representing the only hope of salvation from the present state of affairs. Unemployment is taking the gilt off the gingerbread of democracy, while the working classes realise that striking is useless since nothing would be more welcome to employers.'

Joseph Addison, *Letter to Sir Alexander Cadogan*, 1923

'You know how to interpret the appearance of the sky, but you cannot interpret the signs of the times.'

Matthew 16: 3

There is an interval of time between cause and effect which can sometimes be so short as to deem worthless an understanding of the process connecting them. Knowing that the pulling of a trigger precedes the release of a bullet provides scant opportunity to take evasive action. In the case of the consequences of an over-accumulation of debt, the opposite problem presents itself. Sometimes the interval between cause and effect appears to be so long as to separate them by oceans of doubt. Every generation balks at the suggestion that historical precedent holds sway over present circumstances. The argument of this book is that all the conditions sufficient for a repetition of debt-related calamity are in place. These conditions include the complacency of the authorities and the ignorance of the people.

The overwhelming purpose of this book has been to sound a warning. Many arguments have been advanced to convince the reader that the economic and financial achievements of North America and

Western Europe since the mid-1980s rest on shaky foundations. Like a punch-drunk boxer, it is only a matter of time before this unstable structure drops to its knees under the weight of its own absurdity. Chapter 14 investigated four potential triggers of financial collapse, but declined to speculate on the precise timing for such an event. This chapter describes how the delusion may unravel, bearing in mind the close and immediate linkages between national and international financial markets, and considers how significant its impact will be on ordinary life. During the interval, short or long, before the crisis strikes, some suggestions for appropriate action by individuals, businesses and governments are offered. Finally, a brief agenda for financial reform is proposed.

THE ANATOMY OF A FINANCIAL CRISIS: HOW THE DELUSION MAY UNRAVEL

To envisage the impact of financial collapse on ordinary life, it is first necessary to speculate a little on the precise sequence of events leading up to it. Let us suppose that the shock originates in the US bond market and, within a few months, the news breaks that a major financial institution is in trouble, squeezed between a rise in consumer debt delinquency and the cost of debt service. Unable to find emergency credit at an affordable cost, the institution defaults on its bonds by failing to make an interest payment. The Federal Reserve considers a support operation, but Congress is vehemently opposed to the use of public money for a bail-out. While the political wrangling is still going on, US bond yields jump higher still and credit quality spreads widen. Several other mortgage and credit card agencies admit to cash-flow problems and a crisis is born. Meanwhile, the rise in US bond yields is transmitted via the futures markets to Europe.

On Wall Street, shares in US banks and financial companies plummet on account of the credit quality scare and the rise in bond yields. Because financial company shares have a large weight in the S&P index, the whole market turns down. Respected technical analysts, working in the financial markets, examine the chart patterns of the stock market and cast their votes unanimously to the effect that the long bull market in equities is over. The S&P futures index opens limit down one Monday morning and the US equity market falls by 5 per cent during the session, leading European markets sharply lower the following day. When Wall Street opens for its next session, the futures index is limit down again, and shortly afterwards the New York Stock Exchange suspends trading. The news emerges that one of the large US broking firms has suffered a massive hit on derivatives trading and its capital has been wiped out. The crash has happened and it is already too late for individuals to avoid substantial losses on their investments. The futures and options exchanges remain closed and, when the stock markets re-open, the major share indices are 25 per cent lower than previously. Institutional investment firms are forbidden by the central banks to sell any of their equity holdings, but waves of private selling continue to send share prices lower.

Months pass by and, gradually, the wider implications of the crisis become apparent. More financial companies are declared insolvent as it transpires that they were borrowing against the security of unrealized gains on share holdings. Large industrial and commercial companies report sharply lower earnings after discovering that their finance directors had been using stock market-related devices to boost profits. Personal bankruptcies and debt arrears continue to mount as consumer credit companies refuse extensions and renewals of credit facilities. Starved of new sources of credit, both households and businesses begin to sell assets in order to raise cash.

As bonds mature and large tranches of credit fall due for refinancing, now at much higher interest rates, corporate cash flow deteriorates. Each week brings fresh examples of unwise financial behaviour and sporadic instances of deception. Insurance companies suspend discretionary bonuses and warn that the market value of existing policies has fallen. Insurance premiums climb dramatically. Newly minted pensioners notice that their money purchase (defined contribution) schemes entitle them to substantially lower pensions than they had expected.

By now, all the large western economies are suffering the impact of the financial crisis. Employers announce wage and salary freezes as an emergency measure, to help conserve cash. Consumers become fearful for their jobs and scale back demand for goods and services as a precaution. Temporary workers find that contracts are not renewed when they expire, and unemployment rises. Government tax revenues fail to match expectations, inducing some countries to raise tax rates – with disastrous consequences. Central banks congratulate themselves on the achievement of zero inflation. Short-term interest rates are falling, but to no avail; there is no one willing to lend or to borrow.

WHAT WOULD LIFE BE LIKE IN THE EVENT OF A FINANCIAL SLUMP?

It is difficult to grasp the enormity of this question. The sophistication of late-twentieth-century life in the developed western economies takes so much for granted: electricity, medical services, household appliances, a secure payments system, advanced communications and transportation, and so on. Western civilization has a great deal more prosperity to lose from a financial slump than any that has gone before. Such is the confidence of the post-war era that unemployment, infirmity and old age have largely relinquished the stigmas that have attached to them throughout history. The state, as the appointed agent for income redistribution, routinely transfers huge amounts of money from financially viable to non-viable households such that these two groups cannot easily be identified by their living standards.

The human dimension to financial crises has almost been lost from the consciousness of the western world. All that remains of the Wall Street Crash of 1929 is a folklore memory: sepia images of the prohibition era and some wild anecdotes about stockbrokers throwing themselves from tall buildings. While today's media bulletins and magazines keep us in touch with the real terrors and privations of armed conflict and of natural disasters, the idea that a serious financial crisis could recur in a developed western country is regarded as fanciful in the extreme. Surely crises happen in primitive, singular societies, not in financially sophisticated ones? Once again, the faintest familiarity with past financial crises would give the lie to such a complacent attitude. Futures and options contracts relating to the stock of the Dutch East India Company were traded in the first half of the seventeenth century. An edict forbidding short selling (that is, selling stock one does not already own) was issued in the Netherlands as early as 1610, but was widely flouted!

Ask your friends what they know about the effect of tulip mania on the people of Amsterdam in 1636, or the bursting of the South Sea Bubble on the citizens of London in 1720, or the collapse of the Mississippi Scheme on Parisians in the same year. Perhaps this was all too long ago. How about Berlin in the summer of 1923; New York in October 1929, spilling into Europe and Japan in 1931? The purpose of asking these questions is to establish how many people understand what happens to ordinary life in the wake of a financial crisis. The comparative orderliness and financial stability of the western world since the early 1950s is exceptional in the context of the full spectrum of human experience. To lose contact with these desperate moments in history is to assert a false superiority over those who have succumbed to the traps of excess debt and financial speculation over the centuries.

The experiences of recession in 1974–5, 1980–82 and 1990–92 have given uncomfortable reminders of economic hardship, but only a small minority have suffered harshly by them. Unemployment has touched the lives of an increasing proportion of the population of western Europe from one decade to the next, but generous benefits and pensions have often been available. Moreover, throughout these recessions there has been a widely held belief that the onward march of economic progress was merely taking a breather. An avalanche of new products and technological discoveries has embodied an underlying optimism that there will always be a healthy demand for these items. Above all, an increasing incidence of personal, corporate and government debt is evidence of an underlying confidence in future prosperity. Certainly, the eagerness to borrow in younger life has not dampened expectations of high living standards in old age.

At the stock market valuations of mid-1998, Anglo-Saxon households appear to be more prosperous than ever before. The increase in their indebtedness is easily covered by the progressive revaluation of financial assets. Continental Europeans, although slow to join the stampede to own equities and mutual funds, have responded enthusiastically to the bull market that began in 1995. Many commentators and financial strategists believe that the equity markets within the Eurozone will enjoy spectacular capital gains in the years leading up to the completion of EMU in mid-2002. On the assumption that the Eurozone remains a low interest rate zone for most of this time, there is every reason to expect that continental households will switch out of bank deposits and into investments, abandoning liquidity just as the Anglo-Saxons have done.

When the illusion of prosperity fostered by stellar equity market performance and indefinite borrowing facilities is ultimately blown away, a sober reality will dawn. Governments, whether acting individually or in concert, will not be able to throw a few switches to turn the lights back on. A serious failure of the credit and payments system is in prospect, a failure that tears at the fabric of ordinary life and could take many years to mend. The prospect is one of broken dreams, broken promises and broken relationships. On the evidence of previous depressions, the public mood turns quickly from euphoria to anger, frustration and despair. Ironically, the task of restoring confidence in the financial system and the currency will rest ultimately with the central banks, the experts in crisis management.

WHAT CAN HOUSEHOLDS DO TO FORESTALL DISASTER?

It is facile to suppose that a subtle rearrangement of household assets and liabilities can offer fail-safe protection against a complex financial storm. There are no secluded islands or fortified castles to visit until the storm blows over, nor any barricades to hide behind. Because the entire structure of financial arrangements in the western world is threatened, it would be unwise to assume that disaster will strike only at the margins. Many well-regarded and reputable financial institutions could be ensnared, leaving policy-holders and beneficiaries stranded. It is important to distinguish between the solvency and the liquidity of ailing financial institutions in a financial crisis. While very few, if any, may declare themselves insolvent, there could be many which lack sufficient liquid assets to meet the eager demands of the public for encashment. In effect, individuals' entitlements would be frozen. The institutions would doubtless explain to their customers that the consequence of attempting to exchange their investments for cash in depressed financial markets would be counter-productive. The unspoken truth is that such institutions are solvent only in respect of the book value of their assets; at market values, they may not be.

One of the lessons from previous episodes of financial distress is that households fail to look far enough ahead. Even when disaster strikes, many still believe that the shock will be short-lived and refuse to change their lifestyles or spending patterns. This, of course, is perfectly consistent with an addictive pattern of consumer behaviour. A by-product of this myopia is that actions taken to relieve short-term hardship can intensify the problems later on. The classic predicament of an unprepared household in a financial crisis is to have pressing debts and no cash. Naturally, additional credit from existing or new sources is likely to be unobtainable or be exorbitantly expensive. In an effort to raise cash, valuable household assets have to be relinquished at knock-down prices. Aside from the foolishness of poor financial management, this often entails great emotional anguish and resentment towards those to whom they must sell.

The best protection against adversity is to have minimal debt and ample liquidity. It is preferable to have as few creditors as possible as, in general, they treat borrowers of larger sums with more respect than those of small amounts. In contrast, it is advisable to distribute liquidity around six or even a dozen accounts, with at least one in a reputable foreign currency. The justification for this advice is that there is usually an upper limit to the amount of deposit insurance that an individual can obtain with a single bank. In the extreme event that some banks may fail, it is better to spread liquidity around rather than risk losing it all.

For a household with $100,000 of debt and $200,000 of directly owned investments, there is already a powerful economic argument to sell equities and fund units and to use the proceeds to pay off debt. In a rising or gently falling stock market, it is possible to take investment profits; in the aftermath of a crash, it may not be feasible even to realize losses. Where there are persuasive reasons to maintain some debt (for example, to gain tax relief), it is sensible to hold a matching amount in cash or short-term government bonds. In this way, the household retains the option of shedding the debt at a later stage, should interest rates rise or tax relief be withdrawn.

In addition to any liquidity that is matched to debt, households should plan to have sufficient cash and deposits to meet all expenses for at least six months. In stark contrast to an inflationary crisis, in a debt deflation money gains value. While these deposits may attract a very low interest rate, they will carry a positive real return. The watchword is flexibility. A household with ample readily accessible funds need not be forced into making rash decisions, even if its principal earner becomes unemployed. Liquidity acts as a buffer between adversity and calamity.

For the more adventurous, there is a third reason why liquidity is worth accumulating in advance of a crisis. Past experience has yielded repeated examples of valuable physical assets offered for sale at ridiculously low prices. Those who wait patiently for the crisis to work its way through the financial system will then be presented with opportunities for bargain purchases of houses, flats, vehicles, boats and everything else that their distressed owners are compelled to sell. As an aside, there is nothing to be lost by establishing lines of credit (that is, the approval of credit facilities) with major banks and financial institutions before the crisis breaks. While these facilities may lie unused for a long time, and they may in any case be revoked after the crisis begins, they could prove useful in the context of bargain hunting.

WHAT CAN BUSINESSES DO?

Superficially at least, large international businesses appear well equipped to cope with a financial crisis. Out of the Anglo-Saxon recession of the early 1990s, businesses emerged with a much sharper focus on financial performance, whether expressed as profits, cash flow or shareholder value. A steady improvement in aggregate profitability occurred during 1982–97, returning the share of profits in GDP in most western OECD economies to levels unseen since the 1960s. A particular feature of the 1990s has been a ruthless preoccupation with cost control. Employment costs in Anglo-Saxon countries have been controlled in a number of ways. A steady fall in the proportion of workers covered by collective pay bargaining agreements and an extension of part-time and temporary working have produced more flexible, but also more fragmented, labour markets. International businesses have also exercised cost control by drawing attention to the ease with which production can be transferred from one country to another. Moreover, these large corporations have developed their own financial subsidiaries as gateways to the capital markets; they have become less and less dependent on the banking system as a source of finance.

While the corporate sectors of the large western economies appear to be in great shape to withstand a crisis, there are three important qualifications to this assessment. First, the orientation of corporate balance sheets to debt (bonds and loans) rather than to equity exposes them to financial strain in the event of a sudden drop in income or an unavoidable rise in the cost of borrowing. This is particularly relevant to industries where debt-financed mega-take-overs have taken place, such as banking, insurance, pharmaceuticals and utilities. Second, corporate profitability in the 1990s may have been flattered by substantial income derived directly or indirectly from financial transactions and the use of clever accounting devices. Third, in the event of a financial crisis, the capacity of businesses to protect their profitability through cost cutting may be much less than imagined. While companies operating in countries with de-regulated labour markets may be able to terminate contracts and institute wage freezes, the deflationary implications for personal incomes would soon rebound upon them in falling sales revenues. Corporate profitability is typically a significant and early casualty of a debt deflation spiral.

The businesses in best shape to withstand the type of financial crisis outlined above will be those with net cash, that is, liquid assets in excess of debt, high interest cover, good cash flow management and no superfluous assets. As with households, a net cash position grants the luxury of flexibility of response; if creditors begin to make unreasonable demands, then they can be paid off. Similarly, current income should cover debt interest payments by at least four times. A business with strong cash flow management is one that is constantly monitoring the days of credit received from suppliers and granted to customers. Whereas, in prosperous times, the incidence of bad trade debts tends to be very low and the great majority of bills are paid within 60 days, late payment and non-payment of accounts are classic signals of customers' financial distress. The fate of the Indonesian corporate sector in 1998 gives an illustration of the devastation that can occur as a result of acute liquidity problems. Finally, well-prepared firms will shed unwanted business and property assets before the crisis breaks, using the proceeds to repay debt.

It is unlikely that there will be many deathbed conversions to the virtues of equity finance; the opportunity to exchange debt for equity on favourable terms will cease to exist almost immediately after the crisis begins. One of the curiosities of the mid-1990s was the eagerness of so many cash-rich multinational companies to buy back their own shares as a means of boosting their return on equity. At a single stroke, these companies reduced their liquidity and increased their balance sheet gearing, failing to comprehend that debt repayment was a more pressing priority than equity redemption.

WHAT CAN GOVERNMENTS DO?

The prevailing orthodoxy regarding the government's finances in the large western democracies is that of the balanced budget. Since the early 1980s, the US legislature has grappled with the issue of how best to enforce the balanced budget discipline on successive administrations. The Gramm–Rudman–Hollings Act of 1985, formally known as the Balanced Budget and Emergency Deficit Control Act, required the federal budget deficit to be lowered in stages for the following five fiscal years, reaching zero by 1991. This Act was revised in 1987 and 1990, and eventually the notion of a target date for the balancing of the federal budget was abandoned. In a sumptuous irony, the USA achieved the target in 1998, partly as consequence of spectacular increases in tax revenues related to capital gains from the stock market and to the stronger consumer expenditures financed by lower borrowing costs! Attempts to curtail budget deficits in Europe have focused on the less ambitious upper limit of a budget deficit equivalent to 3 per cent of GDP, as discussed in the last chapter.

The attitudes of some politicians, and even government officials, to sporadic successes in attaining fiscal objectives are illuminating. Their reactions are akin to those of a golfer winning his or her first tournament after 25 years as a professional. In the instant that a balanced budget is achieved, 25 years of deficits are forgotten; it is as if they had never existed – and they certainly no longer mattered. Failure is swallowed up in victory. The depth of misunderstanding concerning the consequences of debt accumulation, and even about the workings of compound arithmetic, among elected representatives is stunning.

Whatever merit exists in balancing the government's budget as a medium-term objective, it must be accepted that a balanced budget is no insurance against adversity. Politicians of all hues have a tendency to treat economic rules of thumb like sprigs of lucky heather. An excellent example is Herbert Hoover's letter to the US President-elect, Franklin Roosevelt, in February 1933: 'It would steady the country greatly if there could be prompt assurance that there will be no tampering or inflation of the currency; that the budget will be unquestionably balanced even if further taxation is necessary; that the Government credit will be maintained by refusal to exhaust it in the issue of securities.'

In his classic study of the 1929 crash, John Kenneth Galbraith comments: 'The rejection of both fiscal and monetary policy amounted precisely to a rejection of all affirmative government policy. The economic advisers of the day had both the unanimity and the authority to force the leaders of both parties to disavow all the available steps to check deflation and depression. In its own way this was a marked achievement – a triumph of dogma over thought. The consequences were profound.'

What should governments do to forestall a financial disaster? Forget the budget! If a mile-wide asteroid were on collision course with planet earth, would national leaders be worrying about the climatic effects of the disaster? No! They would be preoccupied with evacuations, radiation risks, floodwater barriers and emergency medical aid. In the same way, western governments should already be preparing for the consequences of an impending financial crisis. What practical information or advice should be offered beforehand to help the population to prepare for and survive the shock? How would the authorities cope with a doubling of the numbers entitled to state support? How would public order be preserved in the aftermath of a crisis? What emergency powers should the government take in order to conserve energy and other strategic resources? In short, what action should be taken to minimize human distress, limit economic damage and preserve the common way of life?

The role of government in a free society is most clearly defined in times of national or international emergency. It is a wonder that the western economies have acquired so much government during the past 50 years when such a state of emergency has seldom arisen. Since the beginning of the 1980s, several Anglo-Saxon countries have begun to dismantle their public sectors for this very reason. However, this tendency to transfer functions and assets into the private sector and to diminish the influence of government could be stopped in its tracks by a real crisis.

Apart from disaster recovery planning, is there anything useful that government can do to protect its citizens? One small suggestion is to clear up any confusion about personal responsibility for losses arising from price movements in financial assets. A modest advertising campaign with hoarding messages such as 'Stock market returns are not guaranteed by the government', 'Lost your home in '89? – Don't lose your shirt in '99' or 'Your decision; your investment; your funeral' might have an appropriately sobering effect.

DEBT FORGIVENESS MECHANISMS

More seriously, there is an important role for government in this interval before the mist clears. In Chapter 2 it was observed that inflation creates winners as well as losers. An important consequence of the crusade against inflation has been to shut down one of the key debt forgiveness mechanisms in developed western economies. Over a period of time, unpaid and unforgiven debt has combined with consistently positive real interest rates to magnify the degree of wealth inequality in many western countries. This increase in the concentration of wealth among the richest 1 per cent or 5 per cent is well documented for the USA and the UK since 1980. At some indeterminate stage, the polarization of wealth in the hands of a relative few and the polarization of debt among a sizeable minority are likely to create unbearable social tension. As far as the internal debt is concerned (that is, debt owed by one citizen or company to another), the point will ultimately be reached when debt is erased through either forgiveness or delinquency.

These are the only two options available to the western world: to reinstate a working mechanism for debt forgiveness or to precipitate an economic and social climate in which debtors throw in the towel. In the first instance, the alternative processes are inflation and compulsory debt cancellation. Inflation allows foolish over-indebtedness to be melted away over time without the two parties ever coming to blows. Alternatively, the creditors could be compelled in law to cancel debts after a certain length of time (e.g. seven years). Voluntary debt forgiveness is extremely rare in commercial circles. In the second instance, the absence of an effective forgiveness mechanism ultimately brings creditors and debtors into conflict, either legally or literally. Creditors attempt to prevent debtors from defaulting on their obligations and threaten them with eviction from their properties and seizure of their possessions. It soon becomes obvious that these debts are no longer worth their face value. If a secondary debt market develops, then a dollar of delinquent debt might trade for 30 cents, representing the likely proportion of the amount that can be recovered, net of the costs of recovery. An interesting example of this phenomenon is the purchase of *yakuza*, or gangster, debt assets in Japan by American bounty-hunters for a tiny fraction of their face values. The entrepreneurs soon appreciated the reason for the cheapness of their purchases when they began to approach the debtors for payment! The second option, of conflict rather than forgiveness, carries with it the risks of violent crime, disorderliness and even totalitarianism. Perhaps, occasionally rapid inflation doesn't seem so bad after all!

A BRIEF AGENDA FOR FINANCIAL REFORM

This agenda has three parts: measures to deter excessive risk-taking behaviour; measures to restore symmetry between the responsibility for taking deposits on one hand and for granting credit on the other; and measures to alleviate the burden of private and public indebtedness.

Under the first heading, it is proposed that companies that do not offer a product or a service for general sale (whether direct to the public, to other companies or to the public sector) should have their limited liability status withdrawn. Financial speculation should remain legal, but firms known to engage in these activities should cease to enjoy the privilege of protection from their creditors in the event of losses being made. It is also proposed that convictions for financial fraud and deception carry the potential for confiscation of all the offender's personal assets, whether in their own name or in their spouse's name. Such funds should be used to compensate the victims of financial fraud and deception.

The derivatives markets are overdue for a regulatory overhaul. The two most pressing reforms appear to be as follows. One, to establish a global capital adequacy regime for all users of derivatives which is based on a standardized Value-at-Risk model. This could be backed up by the requirement of banks and financial institutions to make cash deposits with central banks in proportion to their overall exposure to derivatives. Two, to prohibit government agencies, industrial and commercial companies, pension and insurance funds from entering into derivatives contracts.

In parallel to these reforms, innovations in risk measurement and accounting are required to enable individuals and institutions to compare financial investments on an informed risk-return basis. Even subjective risk measures made by an independent risk assessment unit would be an improvement on nothing at all. Corporate profits that derive from financial activities should be identified separately in their accounts. Finally, the central bank should issue public warnings, as above, to the effect that financial market returns are not guaranteed by the government.

On the second area of reform, the proposal is to tighten up the law relating to the granting of credit facilities. The intention is to bring the burden of responsibility more closely into line with that placed upon deposit-taking institutions. For example, all directors of new credit granting companies should have at least five years' relevant experience, and some must have professional qualifications. A new ethical code for lending to the general public should be established and all credit grantors (domestic and foreign-owned) should be bound

by it. An ombudsman or procurator should have the power to pros-
ecute credit companies if they break the code. Lenders experiencing
more than twice the industry average incidence of non-performing
assets should also be called to appear before the ombudsman.

In a low inflation, or even a deflationary, economic climate, the
private and public debts accumulated during the 1980s and 1990s will
not erode as they have done in the past, and they could actually
increase in real value. One proposal is to establish a state-owned
institution, separate from the central bank, whose sole function is to
redeem government debt with monetary assets on a systematic basis.
The central bank, of course, can create monetary assets at will. Its
effect on bond prices would be neutral or mildly negative, as the
positive impact of bond purchases (redemptions) would be offset by
the market's anticipation of higher inflation rates for goods and
services. The pace of transformation of government debt into money
should be increased, the greater the degree of deflationary danger.
The impact of these monetary injections would be to scale down the
real value of private debt as well as of public debt. All new government
deficits should be financed through the banking system rather than
by new bond issues.

CONCLUSION

**The story of the western financial system since the early 1970s is one
of debt addiction. In the Anglo-Saxon countries, access to affordable
forms of borrowing has risen exponentially, encompassing the young
as well as the old, the feckless as well as the astute. In other developed
countries, conservative attitudes to personal borrowing have been
negated by profligate attitudes to public debt. Even as the agonies of
Japan's debt-induced calamity are being re-expressed in East Asia,
western governments insist that all is well. However, the absence of
serious inflationary problems during the 1990s does not prove that
the debt addiction has been broken. Rather, there is persuasive evidence that the problem has migrated elsewhere. Over-emphasis, to
the point of obsession, on the inflation objective has blinded governments and their central banks to the risk of widespread debt default**

by borrowers. The unpreparedness of the western world can be understood only in terms of ignorance. Most of those under 50 years of age
hold only a small proportion of their assets in the form of cash and
deposits. They do not appreciate how fragile the financial system has
become, nor how easily the investment gains of many years could be
forfeited. One day the mist will clear and the collective delusion of
effortless wealth creation will be shattered. Until that day, we are
living on borrowed time.

The argument of this book is not that governments are powerless,
but that their central banks have let them down. They should have
warned, long ago, of the dangers of relying on bond issuance to finance
persistent government spending excesses. They should have been more
circumspect about financial innovations and their potential effects on
the system. They should have insisted on tighter accounting standards,
reporting procedures and capital requirements for derivatives trading.
They should have co-operated more readily with other financial regulators, stock exchanges and each other for the sake of financial stability.
The credit and capital markets have grown too rapidly, with too little
transparency and accountability. Prepare for an explosion that will
rock the western financial system to its foundations.

Appendices

Appendix 1:
The Quality Theory of Credit and
the Quantity Theory of Money

The Quantity Theory of Money is a very old hypothesis relating the nominal quantity of money in an economy to the volume of goods and services that are available for purchase. The basic idea can be found in the writings of David Hume: 'Lowness of interest is generally ascribed to plenty of money. But . . . augmentation [in the quantity of money] has no other effect than to heighten the price of labour and commodities . . . In the progress toward these changes, the augmentation may have some influence, by exciting industry, but after the prices are settled . . . it has no manner of influence' (*Of interest; Of money*, 1752).

What may be called 'The Quality Theory of Credit' is not a re-statement of the Quantity Theory of Money, but a complement to it. The stock of credit and the stock of money are very different concepts; there need not be any stable relationship between them, much less an identity. The Quantity Theory of Money in the form popularized by Irving Fisher, in *The Purchasing Power of Money* (1911), states that:

$M \times V = P \times T$, where V is taken to be either a constant or a linear relation of time (t).

M represents the stock of money available for transactions,
V represents the transactions velocity of money, or the speed with which money circulates in the economy,
P represents the aggregate price level, and
T represents the quantity or volume of transactions in goods and services. Usually, this is interpreted as total income or output measured at constant prices.

The responsiveness of one variable to another can be formalized using calculus. The first derivative of V with respect to t will be denoted as dV/dt. If V is time-trended, then dV/dt will be a constant, and if V is a constant then dV/dt is zero. It is contended by the theory that dT/dt is determined in the long run by an aggregate production function, combining the inputs of physical capital and labour into an array of marketable goods and services. If the trend growth rate of T can be approximated by a constant, then it follows that, all other things being unchanged, a shock to dM/dt will necessarily be transmitted to dP/dt, the rate of inflation.

The Quality Theory of Credit can be expressed as follows:

$$C \times Q = P \times T$$

C   represents the stock of credit available for transactions use, and
Q   represents the quality of outstanding credit, measured by the proportion of existing debt which is serviced promptly and in full or by the probability that it will be so.

The theory holds that the impact of a shock to C, raising dC/dt, has a positive short-run impact on the rate of growth (dT/dt), but no long-run effect. In the limit a credit shock has no effect on economic growth, even in the short run. The shock to C has a negligible impact on the rate of inflation (dP/dt) in the short run, but a negative long-run effect. The primary long-run impact of a rise in C is a fall in Q.

However, the story doesn't end here, because a fall in Q ultimately leads to a contraction in M (as banks write off bad loans and the counterpart deposits) and therefore has a long-run deflationary effect on P through the Quantity Theory of Money. The real burden of existing debts increases, causing a further deterioration in Q, as debtors struggle to service their debts. This is the phenomenon of debt deflation described by Irving Fisher (1933). Ultimately, the downward spiral ceases as C becomes properly rationed and credit quality (Q) begins to improve.

Conversely, a rise in Q provokes a rational expansion of M (because the creditworthiness of the marginal borrower has improved) and has an inflationary effect on P. This reduces the real burden of existing debts, leading to a further increase in Q. The result is an inflationary spiral as asset prices confer gains in paper wealth across the general population. This wealth is used as collateral for additional credit, some of which is monetized.

A deficiency of modern macroeconomics is the failure to comprehend the significance of large changes in the ratio, C/M. The direct effects of a trend increase in C/M on the pace of economic growth or the rate of inflation are minor, but ultimately there is a deterioration in Q. When this deterioration reaches a critical level, debt delinquencies and write-offs result.

One policy solution is to authorize or facilitate the monetization of part of the stock of existing credit, thus reducing C/M. In equilibrium, of course, this would bring a surge in inflation but, in the context of rapidly deteriorating credit quality, the monetization of debt merely counteracts the deflationary impact of rising debt service costs. Otherwise the ratio will be reduced as the most prone segments of C are deemed irrecoverable and are written off. Since many bond-holders and equity-holders are among the providers of C, these investments would necessarily lose value.

Appendix 2:
Rival measures of equity valuation

The vulnerability of performance measures such as EPS growth, the P/E ratio and the return on capital employed (ROCE), which was mentioned in Chapter 5, to manipulation and abuse became widely recognized in the 1980s. Alfred Rappaport, a professor at Northwestern University, delivered a penetrating critique of prevailing valuation measures in a book entitled *Creating Shareholder Value*. He pointed out that earnings growth can be achieved not only when management is investing at or above the market discount rate (or cost of capital), but also when it is investing below the discount rate and thereby decreasing the value of the common, or ordinary, shares. In 1986, he cited established names such as Coca-Cola, Eli Lilley and Xerox as examples of companies with double-digit percentage growth of EPS over a ten-year period which delivered *negative* rates of return to shareholders. Similarly devastating criticisms were levelled at ROCE, which is a historic accounting measure of return and is quite incompatible with the economic return demanded by investors. Instead, Professor Rappaport proposed a shareholder value approach, recognizing that true value is created by cash flow, not by accounting convention.

His framework begins by defining shareholder value as corporate value (CV) minus debt, where debt includes the market value of debt, unfunded pension liabilities and other contingent claims. CV is calculated as the sum of the discounted present value of three components: cash flow from ongoing operations over the forecast horizon, the residual value of the business at the end of the forecast period, and the current value of marketable securities and cash which is not essential to the operation of the business. The appropriate rate for discounting the company's cash flow is the weighted average of the costs of debt and equity capital. The relevant cost of debt variable is the after-tax long-term rate which reflects the current demands of debt holders. The cost of equity is composed of the risk-free borrowing rate, implied by the current yield on government securities, plus an additional equity risk premium. This premium is normally estimated as the expected return on the equity market minus the risk-free rate, multiplied by an index (beta) of the company's specific exposure to economy-wide risk. The more volatile the company, the greater the risk premium.

This framework embodies all the necessary elements for a careful and sober judgement of corporate performance; it takes account of leverage, it focuses on cash flow rather than earnings and it employs a risk-adjusted forward-looking measure of the cost of capital. The problem is that it involves a lot of hard work, especially where the merits of hundreds or thousands of companies need to be considered. Furthermore, some of the information is disclosed only when the annual accounts are published, leaving long intervals of time when significant changes in shareholder value could escape unnoticed.

While financial newspapers have stuck with P/E ratios as their key valuation barometer, investment analysts have gravitated towards two rival summary measures of company valuation which make some concessions to Rappaport's ideal. These are the ratio of enterprise value (EV) to gross earnings (EBITDA) and the ratio of share price to free cash flow per share (P/CF). EV/EBITDA (hereafter the EV multiple) was designed to facilitate comparisons between large companies based in different countries and using different accounting conventions. EV is defined as a company's total capitalization. It embraces all classes of equity, including preferred stock, and financial debt, less cash. It excludes the value of a minority stake in another company that is not fully consolidated and includes the estimated value of substantial minority shareholdings in fully consolidated businesses. The denominator is defined as earnings (profits) per share before deducting net interest payments, minority interests, other income, taxes, preferred dividends and non-recurring gains or losses and adding back depreciation and other asset write-downs.

The EV multiple is similar in structure to the P/E, indicating the number of years of current income represented by the current market valuation. Using earnings before subtraction of depreciation and amortization brings the definition closer to a cash flow concept. What represents a normal valuation range for the EV multiple? In the case of a company with no debt and no write-offs of goodwill, ROCE is approximately equal to the inverse of the EV multiple. In the simple case where the value of financial capital is identical to the value of the company's fixed assets, then ROCE equates to the rate of return on physical capital. For the past 25 years, the average rates

Figure App. 2.1 EV/EBITDA for the UK stock market

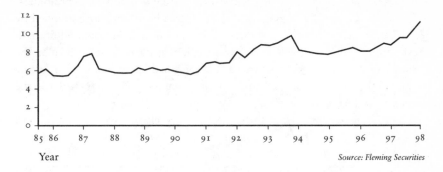

Source: Fleming Securities

of return for the business sectors of the OECD economies have fluctuated between 10 per cent and 20 per cent per annum, implying a normal range for the EV multiple of between five and ten. The UK market ratio, shown in Figure App. 2.1, observed this range between 1985 and 1997, before breaking above it in 1998. However, for individual companies, this simple rule of thumb does not provide a good description of reality. Indeed, the association between ROCE and the EV multiple across samples of large North American and European companies has tended to be positive, not negative, in recent years.

The example, par excellence, of this perverse relationship is Coca-Cola, which combined a racy ROCE of 53 per cent with an EV multiple of 23.4 in 1997! Other consumer companies, such as Colgate-Palmolive (26 per cent and 9.9), McDonald's (21.5 per cent and 9.2), Guinness (16 per cent and 8.4) and Nestlé (13.5 per cent and 7.0), appear to confirm the existence of a positive correlation between ROCE and the EV multiple. This slick transformation is achieved by minimizing the amount of financial capital employed (the denominator of ROCE) while taking every opportunity to bid up the perceived value of company brands. The valuation of proprietary products, including would-be products in the research pipeline, is also evident in the elevated EV multiples of pharmaceutical companies, such as Merck, Johnson & Johnson, Glaxo Wellcome and SmithKline Beecham. Media companies (e.g. Elsevier NV, Reuters), clothing and textile companies (e.g. Tommy Hilfiger and Adidas) and hotel groups (e.g. Four Seasons and Hong Kong & Shanghai Hotels) offer further examples of exaggerated EV multiples in the context of dominant consumer-recognized brands. By mid-1998, literally hundreds of major European and North American companies sported double-digit EV multiples.

Figure App. 2.2 US stock market capitalization as a percentage of nominal GDP

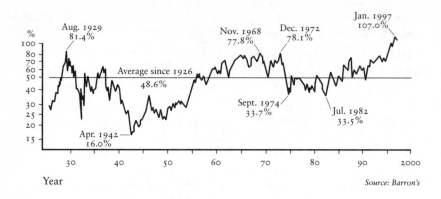

Source: Barron's

Year

Price to asset value comparisons

The striking gains recorded by the US stock market between 1995 and 1998, replicated to a greater or lesser extent around the developed world, have excited strong emotions ranging from euphoria to disbelief. Figure App. 2.2 confirms that the ratio of US market capitalization to GDP reached a 70-year high in 1997. One of the objections raised by the sceptics has been the widening gulf between the market valuation of companies and the net value of their fixed assets. These assets constitute the effective earning power of the corporate sector. Certainly in the industrial sector, the quantity and quality of the plant and equipment is a critical determinant of the capacity of the company to expand its balance sheet and pay dividends.

Accountants and financial analysts tackle this issue by relating the prevailing share price to the book value (P/BV) of the net fixed assets under the company's control. The valuations of fixed assets that appear in the company's balance sheet have the advantage of being readily available, but there is no guarantee that these values represent realistic measures of the economic usefulness of the assets in current use. When the pace of technological change is rapid, commercial pressures may dictate that equipment is replaced long before it wears out. If companies are laggardly in writing down asset values, then book value will tend to overestimate the true capital employed. This has tended to be more of an issue for telecommunications and information technology companies than for industrials and energy utilities.

The expected range of P/BV for industrials and utilities is difficult to determine, but there are practical reasons to expect the ratio to observe a range of between 0.5 and 2.0, approximately. At the lower value, there is likely to be predatory interest in the company, while at the upper value the company ought to contemplate issuing more capital, perhaps to make its own acquisitions. In the European oil and gas sector, the P/BV range ran from 0.7 to 3.0 among the majors (using April 1998 market prices and end-1996 book values as the basis), but some oil exploration companies had much larger readings. In the USA, P/BV multiples have exploded since 1995, with only the Dow Jones Utility Average remaining at a recognizable 1.77. The P/BV for Dow Jones Transports was a lofty 3.93 and for the Dow Jones Industrial Average (DJIA), a stratospheric 6.41. The broader S&P Industrials index topped the lot with a multiple of 7.67, compared to 5.0 only 12 months before. No equity market in living memory has reached such extended multiples of book value, not even pre-crash Japan in 1989.

Glossary of terms

Anglo-Saxon countries Countries either linked by the English language or having a similar financial structure to the UK; for most purposes, this comprises the UK, the USA, Canada, Australia and New Zealand; but in some contexts the argument can be extended to the Netherlands and the Scandinavian countries also.

Arbitrage The purchase and sale (or vice versa) of the same or similar financial instruments with a view to realizing a profit from the difference in prices (e.g. in the foreign exchange or money markets).

Arbitrageurs (Arbs) Individuals or companies that risk their own capital (or borrowed funds) in order to engage in arbitrage.

Asset-backed Securities (ABS) Securities collateralized by assets such as car loans and credit card receivables (but not mortgages).

Bad debts Debts that cannot be recovered or that are assumed to be irrecoverable.

Balance of payments Normally taken to mean the current account balance, which is the difference between the money value of all receipts from abroad and all payments to recipients abroad.

Bancassurance The merging of banking, life assurance and pensions businesses within a single company, with a view to offering synthetic financial products to individuals and businesses.

Bank credit Loans of all types originated by a banking (or monetary) institution and appearing on its balance sheet.

Bank for International Settlements (BIS) An international central banking institution based in Basle, Switzerland, which promotes the co-operation of national central banks and implements capital adequacy directives.

Bank monopoly The sole currency-issuing authority for a particular country or region, typically the central bank.

Bank payments system (or banking system) The payments or clearing system is the arrangement whereby banks honour each other's electronic transfers and paper cheques and settle inter-bank accounts at the close of each business day.

Bank reserves (or reserve assets) Cash and short-term claims (for example, money balances that commercial banks and other deposit-taking institutions are required to hold at the central bank for settlement purposes), call money, Treasury bills and bonds held as backing for the bank's deposit liabilities.

Bank runs Occasions when significant numbers of bank customers are fearful for the security of their deposits and demand immediate repayment in cash.

Bank spreads The difference between the interest rate charged by a bank on a loan and that paid on a deposit. In the context of syndicated loans, the bank's cost of funds is normally assumed to be the local interbank or eurocurrency interest rate.

Banking sector (*see* Monetary sector) Consists of all licensed deposit-taking institutions and some other providers of specialized banking services within the jurisdiction of a national central bank.

Banks' balance sheets The record of banks' total assets (loans, advances, investments and property) and liabilities (mainly deposits).

Banks' capital requirements Formal requirements of commercial banks to hold equity and long-term debt equivalent to a minimum proportion of their risk-weighted assets.

Banks' capital reserves Amounts set aside from profits in company accounts for an unspecified purpose. Reserves are part of retained earnings and belong to the ordinary shareholders of the company.

Banks' off-balance sheet activities Examples of bank assets which do not have to appear on their balance sheet are those acquired by leasing or hire purchase, project finance, letters of credit, financial derivatives and loan assets that have been securitized.

Basis point One-hundredth of 1% (i.e. 0.01%).

Bear market A market in which prices are declining or are expected to decline.

Benchmark or bellwether bond A bond that is usually the most recently issued of good size, the terms of which set standards for the market. The benchmark issue is the most heavily traded of its type.

Bespoke banking Banking services that are tailor-made for the customer and for which premium fees and commissions may be charged.

Blue-chip stocks A generic term for shares of major companies with sound earnings and dividend records and above-average share performance. The description may be still be applied even when an established blue-chip company is in decline.

Bond future A fixed and binding contract for a standard amount of bonds to be bought or sold at a fixed price at a fixed future date. The title to ownership is exchanged freely from hand to hand.

Bond issue A form of interest-bearing security issued by central or local government, companies, banks and other institutions normally with an initial maturity of between 5 and 30 years. Interest is usually payable annually or semi-annually.

Bond market Once issued, bonds are traded electronically using prices posted by securities dealers at the major investment banks.

Book building A method of selling international equities whereby an investment firm seeks bids for a new issue at indicative prices. When the book is complete, the firm prices and sells all the issue in a single day.

Boom-bust cycle An economic or business cycle in which the peaks, characterized by the over-utilization of resources and the appearance of inflation or rapid absorption of imported goods, give way to troughs in which resources are under-employed and expectations are depressed.

Brady bonds Named after US Treasury Secretary Nicholas Brady, who proposed the concept of sovereign bonds backed by US Treasury (zero coupon) bonds but with the actual repayments being made by the sovereign government of a developing country. Brady bonds are a form of debt rescheduling.

Broad money There are a variety of definitions of broad money, but a general definition is the stock of all types of bank deposits plus notes and coin in circulation with the public (*see also* M2, M3 and M4 definitions).

Bull market A market in which prices are rising or are expected to rise.

Capital adequacy requirements Under an accord of 1988, the central banks of the Group of Ten (G10) nations set out convergent capital adequacy standards for the commercial banks they regulate. This was formulated under the auspices of the BIS. The rules determine how much and what type of capital banks can raise in the financial markets and what type of loans they are allowed to make.

Capital flight The expatriation of capital, by legal or illegal means, from a country believed to be in serious economic or financial difficulties, or where there is a material risk of confiscation. These circumstances would normally include a rapid domestic inflation rate and/or severe currency depreciation.

Capital market The market for longer-term loanable funds, as distinct from the money market, which deals primarily in short-term funds. There is no clear-cut division between the two markets. The capital market is increasingly international and embraces the activities of the banking system, the stock exchange, insurance companies and other financial intermediaries.

Capital requirements (*see* **Banks' capital requirements**)

Capital risk The risk that a company's share price, or other form of investment, loses its value or becomes valueless, resulting in a loss of capital. There are several forms of capital risk: business risk, specific risk, liquidity risk, systemic risk, operations risk, political risk, legal risk and taxation risk.

Central bank The major regulatory bank in a national monetary system. Central banks act as lenders of last resort, influence the interest rate structure, accept deposits, make loans to the commercial banks and in most countries supervise the banking system. They also act as the government's own bank, manage the national debt and control the note issue.

Certificate of deposit (CD) These are negotiable money market instruments which certify that a time deposit has been made with a bank at a fixed interest rate for a fixed period. The instrument is quoted on an interest-bearing face value basis rather than at a discount. Interest is paid at maturity.

Collateral (*see* **Loan collateral**)

Collective investment funds Funds such as mutual funds, unit trusts and investment trusts that gather up investment subscriptions from a variety of individuals or businesses with the purpose of investing more efficiently than a single investor acting independently. Collective funds are often very specific in their investment objectives.

Commercial bank A privately owned bank, otherwise referred to as clearing banks (UK), national banks and state banks (USA), joint stock banks and, in Western Europe, credit banks, to distinguish them from investment banks.

Commodity banking Banking services that are mass-marketed to individuals and businesses, such as instant-access bank accounts, unsecured loans and mortgages. Commodity banking is usually very competitive, with many active participants.

Concentration (**or market concentration**) The degree to which the supply of goods or services to a market is dominated by a small number of providers: the smaller the number, the higher the concentration.

Consumption (**or consumers' expenditure**) The purchase and use of goods, services, materials or energy. The part of current income that is not saved.

Contingent liabilities Similar to provisions, except these liabilities are too difficult to estimate for them to be included in banks' accounts. An unresolved lawsuit is one example.

Convertibles A security that carries the right for the holder to exchange it at a fixed price for another form of security.

Corporate sector The collection of all incorporated industrial and commercial businesses in a particular country or region. The act of incorporation carries with it a separate body of law and, in particular, a limitation on the collective liabilities of the owners of the business.

Counterparty risk The risk that, between the time the transaction has been arranged and the time of actual settlement, the counterparty to the transaction (e.g. the buyer of a financial instrument) will fail to make appropriate payment. This is a form of credit risk.

Credit creation The act of granting additional purchasing power to an individual or business, whether initiated by a bank, a finance company, an insurance company or any other intermediary. A credit transaction involves an exchange of claims over resources which are separated in time. Credit is typically granted in connection with a purchase of assets, goods or services.

Credit cycle The recurrence of alternate phases of credit expansion and credit contraction, which may or may not coincide with business or trade cycles. Phases of credit expansion are usually terminated either by an increase in interest rates or by a rise in borrowers' default rates.

Credit expansion An increase in credit market debt, of which the principal categories are government bills, notes and bonds; securities issued by government agencies but without explicit government guarantee; residential and commercial mortgages; corporate and foreign bonds; bank loans; commercial paper; securitized loans and consumer credit instruments.

Credit facilities Permissions to borrow at will from a company or financial institution up to a fixed nominal amount.

Credit instrument (or debt instrument) A medium for raising a loan, usually a short-term loan.

Credit markets Once credit instruments (such as loans and bonds) have been issued, they are frequently traded. Trade in bonds and securitized loans is organized electronically. Trade in loan assets between financial institutions is dominated by the sale and purchase of distinct loan portfolios in one-off transactions.

Credit policies The manipulation of money market interest rates (i.e. the price of credit) by central banks is the most obvious example of credit policy. Other examples of credit policies are credit controls on banks (e.g. the imposition of reserve asset ratios) and hire purchase or instalment loan controls.

Credit quality Loans and bonds can be graded according to the likelihood of default by the borrower. Credit instruments of high quality have low default or credit risk.

Credit risk The risk faced by a lender or creditor due to the possibility that the debtor may fail to honour his or her financial obligation. Credit (or default) risk can be distinguished from market (or capital) risk that results from changes in market conditions such as inflation, interest rates or exchange rates.

Credit spread Credit instruments of differing qualities (for example, investment grade and junk grade bonds) will normally carry yields or interest rates that reflect this discrepancy in credit quality. The wider the quality gap, the greater the expected credit spread. The credit spread is usually measured in basis points.

Credit supply Offers of diverse forms of credit by companies and financial institutions can be considered as part of an aggregate credit supply schedule that varies positively with the risk-adjusted price of credit.

Credit system All transactions in which purchases of assets, goods and services are not settled immediately belong to the credit system. The credit system interconnects all countries' payment systems and all types of economic activity.

Credit-worthiness criteria The criteria used to judge the credit-worthiness of a large borrower, such as a sovereign nation or an international company. Credit rating agencies, for example Standard and Poor's, Moody's and Fitch-IBCA, monitor the speed with which borrowers pay their bills, their financial performance and other specific characteristics that may affect the likelihood that a debt issue will pay principal and interest on time.

Currency devaluation In a regime of fixed exchange rates, a country with severe payments problems may elect to devalue its currency by adjusting its central exchange rate parity. A currency devaluation is a discrete change, as distinct from a gradual currency depreciation.

Currency options A binding contract to buy or sell a currency at a specific price, the date of the transaction being left to the choice of the holder of the contract. First traded on the Philadelphia Stock Exchange in 1982.

Current replacement cost (or replacement value) Asset valuation based on the current cost of replacement rather than its original or historic cost or book value.

Debt deflation The interaction of an excessive accumulation of debt contracts (fixed in nominal value) and a falling price level. In its virulent form, debt deflation is associated with economic depression as debtors' incomes decline and the real burden of their debt service increases.

Debt delinquency A failure to fulfil any of the obligations of a debt contract, including the prompt payment of interest or the repayment of principal.

Debt forgiveness The unconditional release of the borrower from the obligations of an outstanding debt contract by the lender or creditor.

Debt interest Regular interest payments laid down by the terms of the debt contract.

Debt markets (*see* **Credit markets**)

Debt trap A situation in which a debtor is able neither to clear his debts (through the sale of assets) nor to meet the obligations of his debts.

Deflation A situation in which the average price level, commonly measured by the consumer price index, is falling. The inflation rate is therefore negative.

Depreciation The erosion in the market value of a physical asset (e.g. a piece of machinery) due to physical deterioration in use (e.g. wear and tear or damage) or obsolescence (e.g. its displacement by a superior or more cost-effective alternative).

Derivatives markets Markets in derivative financial products such as futures, options and swaps. These products are traded on recognized exchanges and over the counter (OTC).

Developed countries (**or OECD countries**) Countries with economic structures dominated by manufacturing and service industries, rather than agriculture, energy and extractive industries. Countries with high standards of sanitation, public health and literacy. Typically, countries with GDP per capita greater than $15,000 per annum in 1996.

Developing countries Countries lacking some or all of the attributes of developed countries.

Dis-saving Negative saving; over-consumption of current income achieved by borrowing or the depletion of wealth (i.e. past savings).

Dividend yield The return that the annual dividend of a share represents in relation to the current share price. It is calculated by dividing the annual dividend per share by the current market price.

Dynamic hedging (**or delta hedging**) A method used by option writers to hedge the risk exposure of their option book by purchasing and selling the underlying security in the spot market in proportion to the propensity of the option's price to follow that of the underlying security.

Earnings per share (**EPS**) The amount of a company's annual earnings after deduction of tax and interest which is available for distribution to each outstanding ordinary share.

Economic efficiency An efficient economic process is one that generates a given quantity or value of output using the lowest cost of inputs (e.g. labour, capital, materials and energy).

Emerging markets Securities markets in the early stages of development. The host countries vary from less prosperous developed countries (e.g. Portugal) to quite poor developing countries (e.g. Botswana).

Equity index options Options contracts that grant the beneficiary the right to buy or sell a basket of company shares in proportion to their weight in an equity share index such as the (US) Standard & Poors 500 share index or the (UK) Financial Times – Stock Exchange 100 share index.

Equity index volatility The extent to which an index of equity prices fluctuates over a given time-interval, usually measured by hourly percentage changes.

Equity market The market in the ordinary and preference shares of companies. In most cases, the term is used only of shares quoted on recognized stock exchanges, such as the New York Stock Exchange. A few stock exchanges still operate in a physical location, but most are electronically traded.

Equity portfolio An investor's or an investment fund's collection of equity holdings in various companies.

Equity risk premium (or equity premium) The term refers to the difference between the real rate of return on an equity market index and the real rate of return on a riskless asset, which is normally taken to be a benchmark government bond or bond index.

Equity warrants These confer the right to buy company shares over the life of the warrant at a fixed exercise price which usually represents a premium over the current or average share price. It is often attached to a bond but, unlike a convertible issue, the bond itself continues to exist if the investor buys the shares. Because of this inducement, the bond can pay a lower coupon at par.

European Central Bank (ECB) Formed in July 1998, the ECB is responsible for monetary policy and financial management in all the European countries whose governments have agreed to adopt the single European currency, the euro, in place of their local currency.

Financial corporation (*see* **Financial institution**)

Financial credit A term sometimes used to denote loans by non-bank financial intermediaries.

Financial de-regulation The relaxation or removal of regulations relating to the availability of credit, the level of interest rates to be charged or the permissions to undertake specific types of financial activity. These regulatory powers may have been delegated by government to the financial services industry or through official regulatory agencies.

Financial derivatives A generic term for forwards, futures, options and swaps. These are instruments derived from direct dealings in securities, currencies and commodities. By construction, derivatives prices are much more volatile than those of the underlying securities.

Financial engineering The design, development and implementation of innovative financial instruments and processes, and the formulation of creative solutions to problems in finance. In particular, the use of sophisticated instruments to smooth a company's earnings in successive periods or to enhance the appearance of the accounts for a particular purpose.

Financial gearing The use of borrowed funds to gain a proportionately greater interest in some business or financial asset. In the context of a company's capital structure, financial gearing refers to the relative importance of loans versus equity. The higher the gearing, the greater the risk to the equity shareholder.

Financial innovation The purpose of financial innovation is to develop new financial instruments and processes that will enhance shareholder wealth. The factors primarily responsible for financial innovation are: the reallocation of risk or the reduction of yield; taxation anomalies; regulatory or legislative change and the level or volatility of interest rates.

Financial institution or intermediary A company, society or charitable trust whose sole or main purpose is to engage in financial, rather than industrial or commercial, transactions. Financial intermediaries are enterprises in the business of buying and selling financial assets. Examples are banks, building societies, insurance companies, pension funds and credit card companies.

Financial intermediation The process whereby the privately owned wealth of the economy is converted into the specific financial instruments in which its owners hold their accumulated savings (e.g. bank deposits, bonds and equities).

Financial liberalization The removal of controls and restrictions governing the freedom of capital to flow around the financial system or between countries. Also, the abolition of cartels or monopolies in the provision of financial services.

Financial markets An encompassing term for the money, foreign exchange, equity, bond and derivatives markets.

Financial regulation The supervision and control of the activities of private enterprise by government in the interests of efficiency, fairness, health and safety. All stock exchanges and national banking systems are regulated. Regulations may act as a barrier to entry and often inhibit competition.

Financial saving Saving in the form of financial instruments or assets as opposed to physical or tangible assets (such as property, ships or vehicles).

Financial sophistication A tendency towards the use of complex financial instruments in everyday transactions and contracts. For example, options are used to create guaranteed investment products sold to individuals.

Financial speculation Speculation in financial assets, as distinct from tangible assets such as property or land.

Financial stability The condition of a financial system in which the risks of a general collapse are negligible. This is usually associated with careful supervision by its central bank and conservative lending practices among its financial institutions.

Financial supervision This is concerned fundamentally with the protection of depositors and investors, and the financial health and safety of banks and other financial institutions. Supervision entails monitoring the solvency and capital adequacy of financial institutions, imposing penalties and other deterrents on excessive risk-taking behaviour and fostering an environment of public trust and confidence.

Fixed exchange rates A system of predetermined rates of exchange between two or more currency units. In its ideal form, these rates are irrevocably fixed and there are no constraints on the convertibility of one currency into any of the others.

Flexible (or floating) exchange rates A system of variable exchange rates between two or more currency units. The frequency and type of variation differs between an adjustable peg system, in which parity changes are made at frequent, discrete intervals and a freely floating system, in which rates move continuously in response to the forces of demand and supply.

Floating rate finance Debt instruments that pay coupons that are tied to a floating index such as a Treasury bill rate or an inter-bank interest rate. Floating rate mortgages charge interest determined by some market reference rate.

Futures contract A legally binding contract that specifies precisely the quantity and quality of an asset or a commodity to be delivered, as well as the date and location. Futures contracts can be bought and sold on exchanges, which provide guarantees against default risk.

Global capital markets An umbrella term for all financial and property markets, both national and international.

Globalization The process of geographical integration, especially in financial activities. An increasing dominance of international and multinational companies in financial transactions and a progressive standardization of financial products and services.

Government bond A bond issued by central or local government, such as a UK gilt-edged security (a gilt) or a US Treasury bond.

Government budget deficit A shortfall between a government's total income (comprising tax revenues, trading income, rent, proceeds of asset sales and interest) and its total expenditure (consisting of purchases of goods and services, wages, salaries and pensions of government employees, debt interest and international transfers). A budget deficit must be financed by the issue of money, bills, bonds or other instruments.

Government or public sector All agencies of government including central, state and local government and publicly owned corporations.

Government securities All liabilities of the government sector that can be traded. Bonds, notes and bills are the most common categories of government securities.

Great Depressions The protracted recessions of 1873–96 and 1929–39, affecting the countries of North America and Europe to varying extents, are often referred to as Great Depressions.

Gross Domestic Product (GDP) The value of goods and services produced in a country or region during a particular period (e.g. a year or quarter). GDP is usually defined at constant prices (known as real GDP); its annual change is a measure of economic growth. Movements in GDP at current market prices, or nominal GDP, reflect changes in real GDP and the rate of price inflation.

Gross national saving A measure of saving across all the domestic sectors of an economy: the sum of personal, corporate, financial and government saving, inclusive of depreciation.

Hedge funds Leveraged investment funds whose objective is to generate extraordinary rates of return for their investors by whatever (legitimate) means and in whatever markets the proprietors decide. These funds tend to be domiciled in tax haven countries where disclosure requirements are minimal. Hedge funds make full use of financial derivatives, take long or short positions at will and often exit positions abruptly, sometimes affecting price trends and market sentiment.

Hedging strategies Strategies that rely on the complex use of futures and options to maximize potential gains or minimize potential losses on financial transactions.

High-powered money (or monetary base) This refers to the stock of national currency in circulation plus commercial bankers' operational deposits with the central bank. It is the hard core of the monetary system, being under the ultimate control of the central bank.

Historic cost accounting An accounting convention that records actual costs at the time they are incurred. Assets are shown on the balance sheet at the prices paid for them, even though they may now be worth more or cost more to replace.

Hyperinflation Generally, an uncontrolled upward spiral of price inflation which often results in economic collapse. A commonly used definition is a monthly inflation rate of 50% or greater, equivalent to 12,875% per annum or above.

Illiquid investment An investment in financial or property assets that cannot be readily sold at its prevailing market value for cash, either because there is a penalty for early redemption or because the second-hand market for the asset is inefficient or non-existent.

Index matching (or indexing) Constructing a portfolio (of equities) that matches the constituents of a share index such as the Standard and Poor's Composite Index and weights them in the same proportions as the Index.

Inflation uncertainty At any particular level of inflation, the variability of the inflation rate around this level and the consequent difficulty in predicting future inflation rates.

Inflationary expectations Expectations, held by the government, the business sector, the financial markets or by individuals, concerning the future behaviour of price inflation.

Institutional funds (or investment institutions or investment funds) Pension, insurance and other investment funds that aggregate the assets entrusted to them by individuals, companies and governments and manage them collectively.

Inter-bank market The money market in which banks borrow or lend money among themselves, either to accommodate short-term liquidity problems or for the lending on of surplus funds.

Intermediation (*see* **Financial intermediation**)

International financial markets Markets on which the financial instruments of foreign countries are traded as well as domestic ones. For example, the London International Financial Futures Exchange (LIFFE) trades Japanese and German government bond futures contracts.

Investment (in fixed assets) The deployment of current national income in the acquisition of fixed assets that are expected to yield a return over a succession of years, rather than in the current year only. In a country with no foreign trade, gross fixed investment is identical to gross saving.

Investment bank A financial intermediary acting as an underwriter for new issues of equities or bonds and which, as part of a syndicate, redistributes the issue to investors.

Investment management (*see* **Fund management**)

Investment returns (*see* **Rate of return on financial assets**)

Investment risk (*see* **Capital risk**)

Legal risk The risk that a financial transaction with a counterparty will be annulled by a legal judgement, for example, on the grounds that the counterparty did not have the authority to enter into the transaction.

Lender of last resort (LLR) An institution, normally a central bank, that stands ready to lend to the commercial banking system when it has a liquidity shortage. Such shortages arise routinely because of the seasonal fluctuations in customers' cash requirements, but acutely on occasions when individuals lose confidence in a bank.

Leverage (*see* **Financial gearing**)

Liquid assets Assets, such as cash and instant access bank deposits, that are immediately available to settle debts or procure goods, services or other assets.

Liquidity Availability of funds in an acceptable form to meet claims on demand.

Loan arrears Late payments of interest or capital due under a loan contract.

Loan collateral Assets held as security against a loan, for example goods, property, intangibles, bills and bonds.

Loan default Failure to meet the obligations of a debt contract, such that the creditor has the legal right to sue the borrower. Such loans are sometimes reclassified as sub-standard, non-performing or value-impaired.

Loan provisions A charge against a financial institution's profits designed to reflect the risk of a specific loan or a class of loans becoming unrecoverable in the future.

Long positions Of securities or currencies, having an abnormally large holding or exposure, either by design or by accident.

M0 (*see* **High-powered money**)

M1 A definition of the money stock (or money supply) that includes notes and coins in circulation and instant access (or sight) bank deposits.

M2 A definition of the money stock (or money supply) that attempts to identify the transactions balances (the deposits held for purposes of expenditure rather than investment) of the private sector.

M3 A definition of the money stock (or money supply) that includes all the elements of M1 and in addition bank deposits (called time deposits) for which a notice period must be given before withdrawal.

M4 A definition of the money stock (or money supply) that includes most bank deposits and money market instruments (such as CDs). M4 can be separated into its retail component (M2) and its wholesale component (M4-M2).

Margin call A requirement for an immediate increase in the original deposit, or margin, placed on a futures or option contract, when the buyer has increased the size of the position, or when market prices have become heavily adverse. Margin requirements are clearing-house restrictions on the amount that investors can borrow from brokers and dealers for the purpose of buying securities.

Marginal rate of tax The proportion of each additional dollar of income taken in tax.

Market-maker A broker-dealer who is prepared to buy and sell specified securities at all times that a market is open for business, and thus makes a market in them. Market-makers act in a dual capacity, dealing for their clients and on their own account.

Market risk A form of capital risk related to a general fall in the market value of a group of securities or a securities index.

Market transparency The degree to which it is possible to identify the major buyers and sellers in a financial market, and thereby interpret the evolution of the market price in terms of the responses of these agents to specific events.

Market turnover Measured either by the volume of shares, bonds, currencies or derivative contracts traded per day, or by their market value. Market turnover is an indication of active interest in the market.

Minimum capital requirements (*see* **Banks' capital requirements**)

Mobilization The awareness of investors of the returns on competing investments, coupled with the motivation to move funds from lower-yielding to higher-yielding instruments. The opposite of inertia.

Monetary base (*see* **High-powered money**)

Monetary policy Actions taken by central banks (but possibly under instructions from the Treasury) designed to affect monetary and other financial conditions in pursuit of the broader objectives of sustainable growth of real output, high employment and price stability. The objective of price stability, usually defined as inflation rates of 0% to 2%, is dominant.

Monetary sector In a particular country, the monetary sector is defined by the list of banking institutions licensed and supervised by the central bank.

Monetization The financing of a budget deficit through the sale of short-term government debt to the banking system and similarly to banking sector purchasers in other countries. The purchase of Treasury bills by banks adds to their reserves and thus to their capacity to create money.

Money creation Synonymous with an increase in the liabilities of the monetary sector

Money demand The notional quantity of money balances (bank deposits) desired by the private sector, conditional on their aggregate nominal income and wealth and on the level and structure of interest rates.

Money market The market in short-term (normally up to one year) financial claims, e.g. bills of exchange, Treasury bills, inter-bank money and eurocurrency deposits. The market is wholesale, traded not by individuals but by banks and other financial intermediaries.

Money supply (money stock) A measure of the stock of liquid assets circulating in the domestic economy and denominated exclusively in domestic currency. A wide variety of definitions exists, including M0, M1, M2, M3 and M4.

Moral hazard An unintended and undesired consequence of government policy or corporate decisions. For example, a rise in unemployment claimants following an improvement in the generosity of unemployment benefits.

Multinational company (or trans-national corporation) A company having production and other facilities in a number of countries outside the nation of origin. Typically, at least 30% of its assets and workforce will be located in foreign countries.

Mutual fund A pooled system of group investment, similar to a unit trust, which was first developed in the USA in the 1930s. The funds are invested chiefly in stocks (equities), corporate and government bonds, and some funds specialize in money market instruments.

MZM Literally, money of zero maturity. A definition of the money stock (or money supply) used in the USA that corrects for the distorting effects of money market mutual funds on M2.

National income For most purposes, this is equivalent to GDP, measured at current market prices. The only difference is an accounting adjustment to reflect net property income from abroad.

Negative equity Where the market value of an asset is less than the value of the financial claims (i.e. debts) attached to it, then its owner is said to have negative equity in the asset.

Net worth (of the personal sector) The market value of all personal sector tangible, intangible and financial assets, less the value of all its outstanding liabilities.

New paradigm A trendy term used to summarize the belief that an information-based economy can grow more rapidly than the conventional economic structures of the 1960s and 1970s, before generating a given rise in price inflation.

Non-bank Any financial intermediary outside the commercial banking system.

Non-performing assets or loans Income-earning assets for which the income stream has been interrupted, usually due to a deterioration in the economic or political circumstances of the borrower.

Notional principal amount The notional value of the underlying securities traded in the context of financial derivatives.

Off-balance sheet finance (*see* **Banks' off-balance sheet activities**)

Oligopoly A situation where a few large firms, typically between 3 and 8, collectively dominate the supply of goods or services to a market.

Open market operations Dealings in the money market by a central bank, with the object of influencing short-term interest rates, in pursuit of monetary control. These operations are distinct from other policy measures such as reserve asset requirements, bond sales and direct lending.

Operations risk A form of capital risk in which financial losses arise from operational failure. Examples are the failure of equipment and operator error.

Options contract A contract giving its beneficiary the right to buy or sell a financial instrument or commodity, including gold, at a specified price within a specified period. The option can be freely exercised or disregarded, there being no obligation to complete the transaction.

Overseas sector Every individual country trades with the rest of the world, otherwise known as its overseas sector. In a country with a deficit on the current account of its balance of payments, the overseas sector is in surplus: it has acquired more domestic assets than liabilities.

Over-the-counter (OTC) markets Any securities trading activity carried on outside stock exchanges, and therefore without their guarantees against default risk. OTC options are those written by a single seller for a single buyer under a private and confidential arrangement, as distinct from traded options.

Over-trading (of assets) The over-commitment of the capital assets of a financial intermediary. This can arise when management controls over trading activity are slack or inconsistent. The risk is that the firm's capital can be wiped out by an event that triggers simultaneous trading losses in diverse instruments.

Personal sector Households, unincorporated businesses and non-profit making bodies (e.g. charities and trusts).

Portfolio balancing or portfolio management Fund management using a conventional, mean-variance approach to portfolio choice. This approach seeks to maximize returns for a given amount of risk or to minimize the risk associated with a given rate of return.

Portfolio hedging instruments Future and options attached to baskets of securities, for example the Standard & Poors 500 future or the UK FTSE 100 future.

Portfolio insurance Hedging strategies which are designed to protect portfolios of assets against losses. An example is the use of offsetting transactions in the futures market to compensate for price changes in the spot (or underlying) securities or commodities market.

Portfolio theory Economic analysis of the means by which investors can minimize risk and maximize returns. Portfolio theory maintains that risk can be reduced by diversifying holdings of assets, while returns are a function of expected risk.

Price-earnings ratio (P/E ratio) The quoted price of an ordinary share (or equity) divided by the most recent year's earnings per share, also known as the multiple.

Prime age cohort The age range 40 to 59 inclusive.

Privatization The sale of government-owned equity in nationalized industry or other commercial enterprises to private investors. In some cases, government may retain a 'golden share', which is intended to give it the power of veto over an unwelcome take-over bid.

Property loan foreclosure The action in law of depriving the borrower of the right of redemption on the mortgaged property. Once a loan is foreclosed, the right to the property passes to the lender.

Property speculation Speculation in property assets, such as houses, flats, shops or offices.

Proprietary trading Trading with one's own interests at heart and one's own capital at stake.

Purchasing power The claim over real resources, such as food, housing, energy or manufactured goods. As the general index of prices rises, so the purchasing power of money falls.

Pyramid investment scheme (also Ponzi scheme) A fraudulent scheme whereby a proportion of each member's subscriptions are returned as profits or dividends to earlier subscribers. For as long as new subscribers can be attracted, the pyramid grows. When the supply of new subscribers is exhausted (usually as a result of a loss of public confidence), the scheme collapses.

Rate of return on physical capital employed A measure of the profitability of fixed investment in productive use, expressed as a percentage per annum. A broad definition is the division of annual profits after deduction of depreciation and income tax by the current replacement cost of the stock of fixed capital.

Rate of return on financial capital employed (ROCE) A financial ratio showing profit as a percentage of total financial assets or capital employed. Profits are normally defined after deduction of tax, interest charges and depreciation. Assets are usually valued on a historic cost basis.

Redemption value The repayment value of a loan, bond or other security at its par value when the loan term expires or the security matures.

Redemption yield A measure of the return from a fixed-interest security, including income and any capital gain on redemption. The redemption yield takes into account the purchase price, the interest payments, the redemption value and the time remaining to maturity.

Real bond yield Bond yields, usually redemption yields, after stripping out the influence of price inflation.

Real interest rate An interest rate, of any maturity, defined after taking account of the effect of price inflation. In simple terms, the subtraction of an inflation rate from an interest rate.

Recession An absolute decline in the level of economic activity, normally measured by real GDP. Since temporary one-period falls in GDP can occur for a variety of reasons (e.g. abnormal weather patterns or labour strikes), the standard definition of recession is a drop in GDP lasting 2 or more quarter-years.

Refinancing The exchanging of one loan for another, either on the expiry of the original arrangement or to take advantage of an alternative loan on better terms.

Reflation The act of stimulating economic activity so as to increase the growth rate of nominal GDP. The antidote to deflation.

Regulatory costs (*see* **Financial regulation**) Fees and other costs paid by member firms of a stock exchange or other organized exchange in return for the privileges of membership, such as insurance against the default of a counterparty, the smooth administration of trades and the guarantee of prompt settlement.

Replacement cycle Fixed assets, such as plant, machinery, vehicles and aircraft, and consumer durables, such as washing machines and televisions, have finite working lives. At the point where repair ceases to be economically viable, replacement is required. The bunching of replacement demand observed at various times is a feature of the replacement cycle.

Replacement value (of derivatives) A measure of the commitment of financial capital to a derivatives position, as estimated by the amount that would need to be paid to a third party to persuade them to take over an existing derivatives position.

Repo markets (sale and repurchase) Transactions in sale and repurchase arrangements, usually between a central bank and the money market. The nature of these transactions is that funds are borrowed by the central bank (for the government) through the sale of short-term securities (e.g. one week to one month) on the condition that the instruments are repurchased (by the central bank) at a given date.

Reservation price The minimum price at which the owner of an asset is prepared to sell.

Reserve currency Reserve currencies are those that are accepted internationally and held by foreign central banks in order to facilitate international transactions and to protect the value of their own currencies in times of crisis. Most countries' foreign exchange reserves are dominated by balances in the currencies of other countries, principally the US dollar, the German mark and the Japanese yen.

Reverse yield gap The dividend yield on the equity market minus the redemption yield on long-term government bonds (of the same country).

Risk arbitrage The purchase and sale (or vice-versa) of financial instruments with differing risk characteristics, with a view to realizing a profit from the alleged mis-pricing of risk in the market.

Risk premium The risk premium associated with a risky financial asset is defined to be the difference between the expected return on the asset, conditional on all available information, and the return on a riskless asset (e.g. a government bond of relevant maturity).

Savings deposits (or savings accounts in Europe) Deposits of sums, large and small, paying competitive rates of interest but requiring prior notice of withdrawal. Commercial banks and savings banks (such as building societies and savings and loan associations) offer these accounts.

Savings supply The net new flow of private saving into the capital markets.

Securities markets The markets in bills, bonds, equities and derivatives.

Securitization The substitution of securities for bank loans. For example, a bank may purchase or accept a bill of exchange, a note or other security instead of lending to a customer. Securitization relieves banks of reliance on traditional interest rate spreads and also enables them to avoid balance sheet expansion when desired.

Share options Arrangements for granting employees a share in the profits of the company for which they work. Specifically, schemes that give employees the option to buy shares at a fixed price that may, after a time, be substantially less than the prevailing market price.

Short selling A strategy of selling before buying, typically by committing to supply at a future date, securities or commodities that are not currently owned. In a bear market, short selling will enable the securities to be purchased at a lower price than the agreed selling price, thus yielding a profit.

Sovereign loans or sovereign debt Bank loans to a government, usually of a developing country.

Speculation The act of taking a long or short position in the market in anticipation of a favourable price movement, which should result in a gain when the position is converted to cash, but may possibly result in a loss.

Stock lending The lending of (e.g. fixed-interest) securities by long-term holders, such as pension funds, when these securities are in short supply. Often the borrower will use the stock as an underlying instrument in a derivatives strategy.

Stock market A market, whether or not there is a physical exchange, in which securities are bought and sold. The term is used synonymously with the equity market in common parlance.

Stock market crash A precipitate fall in stock market values, usually occurring within one week. Falls in excess of 20% in one week, or in excess of 5% in one session, are often referred to as crashes.

Stock market valuation The notion that the stock market in a particular country represents good or bad value rests on some external point of reference. Price to earnings (P/E ratio), price to sales, price to book value and the reverse yield gap are examples of valuation frameworks.

Stock of physical capital The aggregated value of fixed capital assets (including land, buildings, equipment and transport assets) belonging to a company or located in a country.

Stop–go cycle Alternating phases of speeding up and slowing down of economic activity, especially in the context of fixed exchange rates. The stop refers to a necessary tightening of policy to correct a balance of payments deficit; the go, to the relaxation of constraints on expansion such as credit controls.

Stop loss order A limit order to buy or sell which operates only when a given price is reached. Such an order is normally intended to cut the losses on an existing position.

Swap A transaction whereby securities of the same value are exchanged with the purpose of obtaining an improvement, in the eyes of either of the parties, in the quality of the security or to anticipate a change in yield or exchange rate, e.g. an interest rate swap.

Systemic risk The risk associated with a change in the overall financial system, such that a bankruptcy or a failure in one part will spread to the whole system, causing widespread damage.

Tobin's Q A popular and intuitive definition is the ratio of the value of the firm, as evaluated in financial markets, to the after-tax replacement cost of the firm's existing capital.

Tokkin fund Literally, 'special investment fund'. A privileged type of investment fund, created in the 1980s, to accommodate Japanese companies with excess liquidity that they wished to invest in the stock market. The attraction of the tokkin funds was that companies were enabled to place additional funds in the market without incurring fresh liabilities to capital gains tax.

Trade deficit A shortfall in the value of traded merchandise, i.e. import values exceeding export values.

Unmatched swaps Swap transactions in which a financial intermediary (usually a bank) accommodates a request from a client to exchange financial assets of differing maturities. The bank is not obliged to take on this trade, but does so if it believes that profits can be made.

Yield convergence The compression of yield differentials (such as credit spreads) between two bonds or classes of bonds.

Yield curve A curve that can be derived by plotting the yield on benchmark securities of all maturities ranging from, say, 1 week to 30 years. The normal tendency of this curve is for yields to rise as the maturity of the security rises. When the opposite occurs, this is described as an inverted yield curve.

Yield divergence The widening of yield differentials (such as credit spreads) between two bonds or classes of bonds.

Yield gap (*see* **Reverse yield gap**)

Yield ratio The ratio between the redemption yield on long-term government bonds and the dividend yield on a comprehensive equity market index (for the same country).

Bibliography

The primary reference source used throughout was:

Peter Newman, Murray Milgate and John Eatwell (editors), *The New Palgrave Dictionary of Money & Finance* (London: Macmillan, 1992)

The Bible quotations are taken from the *New International Version* (London: Hodder and Stoughton, 1984)

Chapter One

John Authers, 'Bears are consigned to outer darkness', *Financial Times*, 4 July 1998

Ulrich Baumgartner and Guy Meredith (editors), 'Saving Behaviour and the Asset Price "Bubble" in Japan', IMF Occasional Paper 124, April 1995

Larry Burkett, *The Coming Economic Earthquake* (Chicago: Moody Press, 1991)

James Dale Davidson and William Rees-Mogg, *The Great Reckoning: How the World Will Change in the Depression of the 1990s* (London: Sidgwick & Jackson, 1992)

E. Philip Davis, 'The Role of Institutional Investors in the Evolution of Financial Structure and Behaviour', LSE Financial Markets Group Special Paper no. 89, November 1996

Harry E. Figgie, Jr with Gerald J. Swanson, *Bankruptcy 1995: The Coming Collapse of America and How to Stop It* (Boston: Little, Brown, 1992)

The Brothers Grimm, *Popular Folk Tales* (London: Victor Gollancz, 1978)

David Smith, 'Has Britain Blown Itself a Money Bubble: and is it about to Burst?', *Sunday Times*, 8 February 1998

Richard Thomson, *Apocalypse Roulette: The Lethal World of Derivatives* (London: Macmillan, 1998)

Peter Warburton, 'Private Sector Recession: Business Cycle or Credit Cycle?', Flemings Research bulletin, 21 February 1992

Peter Warburton, 'US Interest Rates: The Myth of Policy Control', Flemings Research bulletin, 2 May 1995

J. Brian Waterhouse, 'Banks, Bankruptcies and Bad Debts', James Capel Pacific Ltd, 14 October 1991

Richard Werner, 'The Quantity of Credit and Japanese Capital Outflows', Institute of Economics and Statistics, University of Oxford, April 1993

Chapter Two

Robert J. Barro, 'Inflation and Economic Growth', *Bank of England Quarterly Bulletin* vol. 35, no. 2, May 1995

Viscount D'Abernon, *An Ambassador of Peace, the diary of Viscount D'Abernon* (London: Hodder & Stoughton, 1929) in 3 vols, covering his service in Berlin 1920–26, quoted in Adam Ferguson, *When Money Dies* (London: Kimber & Co. Ltd, 1975)

Charles P. Kindleberger, *A Financial History of Western Europe* (London: George Allen and Unwin, 1984)

Mervyn A. King, 'Monetary Stability; Rhyme or Reason?', The Economic and Social Research Council Seventh Annual Lecture, 17 October 1996

Helen MacFarlane and Paul Mortimer-Lee, 'Inflation over 300 years', *Bank of England Quarterly Bulletin* vol. 34, no. 2, May 1994

Gail E. Makinen, 'Hyperinflation: experience', in *The New Palgrave Dictionary of Money and Finance* (London: Macmillan, 1992)

B. R. Mitchell, *European Historical Statistics 1750–1970* (London: Macmillan, 1975)

E. Henry Phelps-Brown and Sheila V. Hopkins, 'Seven Centuries of the Price of Consumables, Compared with Builders' Wage-Rates', *Economica* vol. 23, November 1956

Michael Sarel, 'Non-linear Effects of Inflation on Economic Growth', in *IMF Staff Papers*, vol. 43, no. 1 (Washington, DC: IMF, 1996)

Gary A. Shilling, *Deflation* (New Jersey: Lakeview Publishing, 1998)

Chapter Three

Bank for International Settlements, 'The Evolution of Central Banking', in BIS Annual Report, 1997

Robert Browning, *The Pied Piper of Hamelin* (London: Orchard Books, 1993)

Central Banking, 'How Central Banks are seen from the Outside', in *Central Banking*, vol. 2, no. 4, Spring 1992

Roald Dahl, *The BFG* (London: Puffin Books, 1984)

Charles A. E. Goodhart, *The Evolution of Central Banks* (London: London School of Economics, 1985)

Grant's Interest Rate Observer, 'Exit, central banks', 3 June 1994

Alan Greenspan, 'Gold and Economic Freedom', *The Objectivist*, July 1966

Alan Greenspan, Monetary Policy Testimony and Report to the Congress, Board of Governors of the Federal Reserve System, 26 February 1997

Rosa Maria Lastra, *Central Banking and Banking Regulation* (London: LSE Financial Markets Group, 1996)

John Stuart Mill, 'Review of books by Thomas Tooke and R. Torrens', *Westminster Review* vol. 41, June 1844

Robert Pringle and Ashraf Mahate, *The Central Banking Directory* (London: Central Banking Publications, 1993)

Kurt Richebächer, 'The Fed Abdicates', The Richebächer Letter, no. 264, April 1995

Kurt Schuler, *Should Developing Countries Have Central Banks?* (London: Institute of Economic Affairs, 1996)

Vera C. Smith, *The Rationale of Central Banking and the Free Banking Alternative* (Westminster: P. S. King and Son; Indianapolis: Liberty Press, 1990)

Paul A. Volcker, Foreword to Marjorie Deane and Robert Pringle *The Central Banks* (New York: Viking, 1995)

Chapter Four

Bank for International Settlements, 'Core Principles for Effective Banking Supervision', Basle Committee on Banking Supervision, September 1997

Roger Bootle, *The Death of Inflation* (London: Nicholas Brealey, 1996)

Milton Friedman and Anna Schwartz, *A Monetary History of the United States 1867–1960* (Princeton: Princeton University Press, for the National Bureau of Economic Research, 1963)

Milton Friedman and Anna Schwartz, *Monetary Trends in the United States and the United Kingdom: Their Relation to Income, Prices and Interest Rates, 1867–1975* (Chicago: University of Chicago Press, 1982)

John Maynard Keynes, *The Consequences to the Banks of the Collapse of Money Values* (1931), reprinted in *The Collected Writings of John Maynard Keynes*, vol. 9 (London: Macmillan, for the Royal Economic Society, 1973)

Charles P. Kindleberger, *Manias, Panics and Crashes* (New York: Basic Books, 1978)

David T. Llewellyn, 'Secular Pressures in Banking in Developed Financial Systems: Is Traditional Banking an Industry in Secular Decline?', in *Economia, Societa' e Istituzoni*, no. IV, 1992

David T. Llewellyn, 'Scandinavian Banking: The Crisis and the Lessons', in *Banking World*, October 1992

Gordon Pepper, *Money, Credit and Inflation* (London: Institute of Economic Affairs, 1990)

John Presley and Paul Mills, *Islamic Banking: Theory and Practice* (London: Macmillan, forthcoming)

Frederick C. Schadrack and Leon Korobow (editors), *The Basic Elements of Bank Supervision* (New York: Federal Reserve Bank of New York, July 1994)

Albert M. Wojnilower, 'Some Principles of Financial Regulation: Lessons from the United States', First Boston Asset Management, 1991

Chapter Five

Andrew Crockett, 'Monetary policy implications of increased capital flows', *Bank of England Quarterly Bulletin*, November 1993

Charles A. E. Goodhart, 'Financial Globalisation, Derivatives, Volatility and the Challenge for the Policies of Central Banks', LSE Financial Markets Group Special Paper no. 74, October 1995

David D. Hale, 'The Economic Consequences of Global Capital Market Integration', in *University of Pennsylvania Journal of International Business Law* vol. 12, no. 4, Fall/Winter 1991

IMF, *International Capital Markets: Developments, Prospects and Policy Issues* (Washington, DC: IMF, August 1995)

IMF Staff Studies for the *World Economic Outlook*, September 1995 (covering saving behaviour in industrial and developing countries and the measurement of the global real interest rate)

Richard O'Brien, *Global Financial Integration: The End of Geography* (London: The Royal Institute of International Affairs, and Pinter Publishers, 1992)

OECD, *The New Financial Landscape: Forces Shaping the Revolution in Banking, Risk Management and Capital Markets* (Paris: OECD, 1995)

Office for National Statistics, *United Kingdom National Accounts Blue Book* (London: The Stationery Office, 1997 edition)

Gordon Pepper, *Money, Credit and Asset Prices* (London: Macmillan, 1994)

Harold Rose, 'The Changing World of Finance and its Problems', London

Business School Institute of Finance and Accounting Working Paper 167–93, October 1992

Joseph de la Vega, *Confusión de Confusiones* (1688), reprinted in *Extraordinary Popular Delusions and the Madness of Crowds & Confusión de Confusiones* (New York: Wiley, 1996)

Albert M. Wojnilower, 'Business Cycles in a Financially Deregulated America', The Clipper Group, September 1997

Chapter Six

Board of Governors of the Federal Reserve System, 'Flow of Funds Accounts of the United States', various quarterly issues, 1994–8 and historical supplement

E. Philip Davis, 'The Role of Institutional Investors in the Evolution of Financial Structure and Behaviour', LSE Financial Markets Group Special Paper no. 89, November 1996

The Economist, 'Welcome to bull country', 18 July 1998

Marc Faber, 'New Eras, Manias and Bubbles', *The Gloom, Boom and Doom Report*, 3 June 1996

Adam Ferguson, *When Money Dies* (London: Kimber & Co. Ltd, 1975)

John Kenneth Galbraith, *The Great Crash, 1929* (New York: Penguin Books, 1954)

David Miles, 'Financial Markets, Ageing and Social Welfare', in *Fiscal Studies*, vol. 18, no. 2 (Aberdeen: BPC-AUP Aberdeen, 1997)

Chapter Seven

Bank for International Settlements, *International Banking and Financial Market Developments* (Basle: BIS, various issues between February 1994 and May 1998)

Bank for International Settlements, *Proposals for Improving Global Derivatives Market Statistics* (Basle: BIS, July 1996)

Bank for International Settlements, 'Survey of Disclosures about Trading and Derivatives Activities of Banks and Securities Firms', Basle Committee on Banking Supervision and the Technical Committee of the International Organisation of Securities Commissions, November 1996

Jane W. D'Arista and Tom Schlesinger, 'The Parallel Banking System', in *International Economic Insights*, vol. 5, no. 3, May/June 1994

Deutsche Bundesbank, 'Off-balance sheet operations of German banks', Special Statistical Publication no. 13, December 1997

Franklin R. Edwards and Frederic S. Mishkin, 'The Decline of Traditional Banking: Implications for Financial Stability and Regulatory Policy', in *Federal Reserve Bank of New York Economic Policy Review*, vol. 1, no. 2, July 1995

General Accounting Office, *Financial Derivatives: Actions Needed to Protect the Financial System* (Washington, DC: GAO, May 1994)

General Accounting Office, *Financial Derivatives: Actions Taken or Proposed Since May 1994* (Washington, DC: GAO, November 1996)

Grant's Interest Rate Observer, 'John Succo doesn't work here anymore', 8 May 1998

Alan Greenspan, Evidence to US Congressional Committee on Energy and Commerce, 25 May 1994

Alan Greenspan, Remarks at the Annual Meeting and Conference of the Conference of State Bank Supervisors, San Diego, California, 3 May 1997

Patricia Jackson, David J. Maude and William Perraudin, 'Bank Capital and Value at Risk', Bank of England working paper no. 79, May 1998

Stephen Lewis, 'Global Speculation – Threat to Economy', *The Fifth Column*, no. 248, 22 June 1994

D. P. O' Brien (editor), *The Correspondence of Lord Overstone* (Cambridge: Cambridge University Press, 1971), vol. 1, p. 368

Anthony Robinson, 'Financial Derivatives', Fastnet Associates, 1994

Securities and Futures Authority (UK), 'Derivatives Risk Warning Notice', 1997

John Succo, 'Derivative Risk in the System', transcript of Grant's Spring Investment Conference, St Regis Roof, Manhattan, 28 April 1998

Richard Thomson, *Apocalypse Roulette: The Lethal World of Derivatives* (London: Macmillan, 1998)

Chapter Eight

Business Week, 'The Market's Revenge', 18 April 1994

Financial Times, 'Trillion-dollar imports barely noticed', 20 February 1998

Group of Ten, 'Saving, Investment, and Real Interest Rates', October 1995

IMF World Economic Outlook, May 1995 (Special Topic: Global Saving)

OECD Economic Outlook, June 1998

Barry Riley, 'The Saver's Paradox', *Financial Times*, 21 February 1998

Peter Warburton, 'Low National Saving Rate Leaves UK Economy and Gilts at Risk', Flemings Research bulletin, 16 May 1994

Chapter Nine

Rosario Benavides, 'How Big is the World Bond Market?', Salomon Brothers International Bond Market Analysis, August 1996

Tim Congdon, *The Debt Threat* (Oxford: Basil Blackwell, 1988)

E. Philip Davis, *Debt, Financial Fragility and Systemic Risk* (Oxford: Clarendon Press, 1992)

David Miles, 'Financial Markets, Ageing and Social Welfare', in *Fiscal Studies*, vol. 18, no. 2 (Aberdeen: BPC-AUP, Aberdeen, 1997)

OECD Economic Outlook, various issues, June 1987 to June 1998

Peter Warburton, 'The 1994–95 World Trade Boom: Made on Wall Street', Flemings Research bulletin, 22 March 1995

Chapter Ten

Samuel L. Clemens [Mark Twain] and Charles Dudley Warner, *The Gilded Age: A Tale of Today* (New York: Harper & Brothers, 1873)

E. Philip Davis, 'Financial Fragility in the early 1990s: What can be learnt from International Experience?', LSE Financial Markets Group Special Paper no. 76, November 1995

The Economist, 'When firms go bust', 1 August 1992

Gene Epstein, 'Bankrupt Theory', in *Barron's*, 3 February 1997.

Grant's Interest Rate Observer, 'Canadian yield grope', 6 June 1997

Jonathan McCarthy, 'Debt, Delinquencies and Consumer Spending', *Federal Reserve Bank of New York Current Issues in Economics and Finance*, vol. 3, no. 3, February 1997

Donald P. Morgan and Ian Toll, 'Bad Debt Rising', *Federal Reserve Bank of New York Current Issues in Economics and Finance*, vol. 3, no. 4, March 1997

Adrian Orr, Malcolm Edey and Michael Kennedy, 'The Determinants of Real Long-Term Interest Rates: 17 Country Pooled-Time-Series Evidence', OECD Economics Department working paper no. 155, 1995

US Federal Reserve Board, 'Survey of Consumer Finances', 1983–1995

Peter Warburton, 'The return of high real interest rates: the bright side and the dark side', Fleming Securities UK Economic Comment, 4 August 1995

Peter Warburton, 'Bond yields, inflation and the misunderstanding of business risk', Fleming Securities UK Economic Comment, 29 February 1996

Chapter Eleven

Business Week, 'The Top Companies of the S&P 500', 30 March 1998

E. Philip Davis, 'Institutional Investors, Unstable Financial Markets and Monetary Policy', LSE Financial Markets Group Special Paper no. 75, November 1995

The Economist, 'Capitals of capital', 9 May 1998

Charles Mackay, extracts from *Memoirs of Extraordinary Popular Delusions* (1841), reprinted in *Extraordinary Popular Delusions and the Madness of Crowds & Confusión de Confusiones* (New York: Wiley, 1996)

McKinsey & Company, *The Global Capital Market: Supply, Demand, Pricing and Allocation* (Washington, DC: McKinsey Global Institute, November 1994)

Stephen A. O'Connell and Stephen P. Zeldes, 'Ponzi games', in *The New Palgrave Dictionary of Money and Finance* (London: Macmillan, 1992)

Peter Warburton, 'Global capital scarcity: the case for the prosecution', Flemings Research bulletin, 26 July 1994

Chapter Twelve

Wayne Angell, 'Understanding 1929', in *Wall Street Journal*, 10 March 1997

The Bank Credit Analyst, 'US Corporate Profits: Less Than Meets The Eye', September 1996

Robert Browning, *The Pied Piper of Hamelin* (London: Orchard Books, 1993)

Kevin Cole, Jean Helwege and David Laster, 'Stock Market Valuation Indicators: Is This Time Different?', *Financial Analysts Journal*, May/June 1996

Tony Dye, 'Equities may not be Good for Your Wealth', *Daily Telegraph*, 25 August 1997

Benjamin Fulford, 'Deft Accounting Hides Finance Sector's Ills', in *Nikkei Weekly*, 14 October 1996

David D. Hale, 'Has America's Equity Market Boom Just Begun *or* How the Rise of Pension Funds will Change the Global Economy in the 21st Century', Zurich Financial, March 1998

Richard F. Hokenson and Michael S. Rome, 'Deflation, Demand and Demographics', Donaldson, Lufkin & Jenrette Securities Corporation, 26 December 1995

John Maynard Keynes, *The General Theory of Employment, Interest, and Money* (1936) reprinted in *The Collected Writings of John Maynard*

Keynes, vol. 7 (London: Macmillan for the Royal Economic Society, 1973)

Charles P. Kindleberger, *Manias, Panics and Crashes* (New York: Basic Books, 1978)

Richard Lambert, 'A fabulous fifteen years', *Financial Times*, 12 August 1997

Sandy Nairn, 'Historic Bull & Bear Markets 1954–1997: A Study of their Magnitude & Duration', Templeton Global Equity Research, 1997

Terry Smith, *Accounting for Growth: Stripping the Camouflage from Company Accounts* (London: Century Business, 1992)

James Tobin, 'Clinton's Bull Market', *Wall Street Journal*, 30 November 1993

Frank A. J. Veneroso, 'US Economy: The Stock Market . . . Are Corporate Profits Overstated?', Veneroso Associates, 18 June 1997

Chapter Thirteen

Bank of Japan, 'Debt-Deflation in Japan', paper presented by Kagehide Kaku, Director of the Research and Statistics Department, to the Debt Deflation conference in London on 14–15 April 1994

Paul W. Boltz, T. Rowe Price Associates, *Credit Market Comments*, 9 February 1998

Paul Krugman, *The Age of Diminished Expectations* (Cambridge, Mass.: MIT Press, 1994). This book was first published in 1990 by the Washington Post Company

James Medoff and Andrew Harless, *The Indebted Society: Anatomy of an Ongoing Disaster* (Boston: Little, Brown, 1996)

Hyman P. Minsky, 'The Financial-Instability Hypothesis: Capitalist Processes and the Behaviour of the Economy', in C. P. Kindleberger and J.-P. Laffargue (editors), *Financial Crises: Theory, History and Policy* (Cambridge: Cambridge University Press, 1982)

John Presley and Paul Mills, *Islamic Banking: Theory and Practice* (London: Macmillan, forthcoming)

William Shakespeare, *Hamlet, Prince of Denmark*, reprinted in *The Complete Works* (London: Spring Books, 1958)

Gabriel Stein, 'Mounting Debts: the Coming European Pension Crisis', Politeia Policy Paper no. 4, 1997

Paul Van den Noord and Richard Herd, 'Pension Liabilities in the Seven Major Economies', OECD Economics Department working paper no. 142, 1993

Michael M. White, 'The United States and The World: The US Credit Economy', 1 November 1997

Martin Wolf, 'The Deflation Nightmare', *Financial Times*, 24 February 1998

Robert Zielinski, 'Banks: Avoid being robbed', Flemings Global Emerging Markets Research, May 1997

Chapter Fourteen

John Arrowsmith (editor), *Thinking the unthinkable about EMU: Coping with turbulence between 1998 and 2002* (London: National Institute of Economic and Social Research, 1998)

Tim Congdon, 'The single currency project and European political union', *Lombard Street Research Monthly Economic Review*, no. 107, May 1998

Walter Eltis, *The Creation and Destruction of EMU* (London: Centre for Policy Studies, 1997)

Walter Eltis, *Further Considerations on EMU* (London: Centre for Policy Studies, 1998)

Martin Feldstein, 'EMU and International Conflict', in *Foreign Affairs*, vol. 76, no. 6, November/December 1997

Eddie George, 'Monetary Policy in Britain and Europe', the sixteenth Mais Lecture in *Bank of England Quarterly Bulletin* vol. 37, no. 3, August 1997

Intelligence International, 'Computer Terrorism: a CIA risk assessment' (Gloucester: Intelligence International Ltd, November 1997)

Intelligence International, 'Hacking into the Pentagon' in *Terrorism & Security Monitor*, March 1998

David Lascelles, 'The Crash of 2003: An EMU Fairy Tale', Centre for the Study of Financial Innovation paper no. 25, December 1996

Gary North, 'The Mother of All Bank Runs Has Been Programmed', *Remnant Review*, June 1998

John Plender, 'Can Japan reflate?', *Financial Times*, 11 June 1998

Kurt Richebächer, 'Contagion Watch', *The Richebächer Letter*, no. 298, February 1998

Department of the US Treasury, Office of Market Finance, 'Foreign Ownership of Treasury Securities', 28 April 1997

Chapter Fifteen

Joseph Addison, letter to Alexander Cadogan (1923), quoted in Adam Ferguson, *When Money Dies* (London: Kimber & Co. Ltd, 1975)

John Kenneth Galbraith, *The Great Crash, 1929* (New York: Penguin Books, 1954)

Grant's Interest Rate Observer, 'The big fix', 10 April 1998

Herbert Hoover, letter to President-elect Frankin Roosevelt, February 1933, quoted in John Kenneth Galbraith, *The Great Crash, 1929* (New York: Penguin Books, 1954)

Will Hutton, 'Good Housekeeping: How to Manage Credit and Debt', Institute for Public Policy Research Economic Study no. 9, 1991

Appendix 1

Irving Fisher, *The Purchasing Power of Money* (1911), reprinted (New York: Kelley, 1963)

Irving Fisher,'The Debt Deflation Theory of Great Depressions' *Econometrica* vol. 1, 1933

David Hume, 'Of interest: Of money" in *Essays, Moral, Political and Literary* (1752), vol. 1 of *Essays and Treaties* (Edinburgh: Bell and Bradfute, Cadell and Davies, 1804)

Appendix 2

Alfred Rappaport, *Creating Shareholder Value: The New Standard for Business Performance* (New York: The Free Press, 1986)

Kurt Richebächer, 'Shareholder Value – The Great Fake', *The Richebächer Letter*, no. 302, June 1998

Glossary

Graham Bannock and William Manser, *The Penguin International Dictionary of Finance* (London: Penguin Books, 2nd edition, 1995)

Reuters Glossary of International Financial & Economic Terms (Harlow: Longman, 3rd edition, 1994)

Donald Rutherford, *Dictionary of Economics* (London: Routledge, 1992)

Index

Latin America 29, 130
Lawson, Nigel (Lord) 63
Leach, Jim 116
Lear Corporation 170
Lehman Brothers 120
'lender of last resort' (LLR)
    function 16–17, 38–9, 42, 50
liberalization
  of credit 12
  of financial systems 41–2, 56, 97,
    239
  see also regulation and de-
    regulation
limited liability status 259
lines of credit 253
liquidation of assets 223–4
liquidity 54–5
  as distinct from solvency 251
  distribution of 252
  measures of 93–4
  of personal sector's assets 89–90,
    105, 189, 239, 252–3
  true meaning of 90–93
London 110, 205
Long Term Credit Management
    (LTCM) 17
losses
  aversion to 92
  concealment of 118
low income households, debts of
    173
Luxembourg 132

M2 94
M3 150
Maastricht Treaty and criteria 137,
    149, 222, 229–30, 232
McDonald's 266
Malaysia 235
managed funds 75

'marking to market' 86, 120
media companies 266
Merck Corporation 266
Mercury Asset Management 80,
    185
mergers of financial institutions 56,
    60, 68, 103, 184, 188
Merrill Lynch 80, 184–5
Metallgesellschaft 108, 112
Mexico 128
  currency crisis (1994) 16, 135–6,
    166
Microsoft 192
military expenditure 22–3, 155
millennium bug 240–44
Mills, Paul 55, 224
miners' strike (UK, 1984) 63
Minsky, Nyman 224–5
mis-selling of financial products 83
Mishkin, Frederic 118
Mississippi Scheme (1720) 250
monetary policy 23, 38, 41
monetization of borrowing 13, 264
money, demand for 66–7
'money magic' 49
money markets 9, 16, 143, 149–51
  glossary of 4
money supply 13, 15, 23, 150
  control of 44–6, 65–9
  definition of 64, 68
  impact on inflation 62–7
  see also broad money; M2, M3
Moody's 156
Moore Capital (hedge fund) 153
moral hazard 17
Morgan Stanley 184
  equity price index 101
mortgage associations 180
mortgage bonds 181, 236
mortgage pools 215

multinational companies 255
MZM (money of zero maturity) 94

Nasdaq Composite index 209
national debt 143, 148; *see also*
    government borrowing
NatWest Markets 111
Nestlé 266
net worth 75, 201
Netherlands 15, 26, 58, 78, 90, 98,
    147, 165, 217, 222
'New Paradigm', the 20, 205, 207–8
New York 109–10, 205
New Zealand 8, 27, 218
Nicaragua 29
nominal value outstanding (on
    bonds) 144
nominee accounts 190
non-performing assets and loans
    11–12, 60, 93, 236, 260
    in Japan 239–40
North, Gary 243
Norway 15, 57, 218

O'Connell, Stephen 176
off-balance sheet activities 56, 69,
    114, 124, 157
Office of Fair Trading, UK 46
offshore markets 124, 181–2, 234
oil companies 268
oil price shocks 15, 23, 25, 146, 155,
    165, 169
older people, savings of 129
ombudsman for credit companies 260
open market operations 39
optimism
    of consumers 252
    of financial markets 140
options trading 86, 109
Orange County 16, 108, 112, 118

Organization for Economic Co-
    operation and Development
    (OECD) 180
OTC (over-the-counter) trade 106,
    110–17 *passim*, 124
over-funding 155
over-indebtedness 223–4

Paige, Emmett 243
parallel financial systems and
    markets 30, 83
Paris 205
payment systems, breakdown of
    242–4, 251
pension funds 80–82, 101, 127,
    147–8, 178
pensioners 27–8
pensions time bomb 128
Pepper, Gordon 64
personal sector, ultimate ownership
    by 75, 147–8;
    see also liquidity; savings
Peru 29, 128
pharmaceutical companies 266
Phelps-Brown, Henry 21
Philippines, the 235
physical capital 75–8, 201
planning, economic 26
Plender, John 228
Poland 29
polarization of wealth and of debt
    257
political independence of countries
    230
political instability 155
Ponzi, Charles 176
portfolio balancing 84
portfolio insurance 122–3
portfolio theory 100, 103, 204
Portugal 222, 229–30